U.S. Power and the Social St

The book analyzes the elite-led efforts to transform the Brazilian legal order in the period between 1930–1975 and how U.S. Power played a major role in such a process. Besides the global circulation of ideas, the book discusses the Brazilian institutional development in the period.

A profound "Crisis of Civilization" marked the first decades of the century: the references of space and time vanished with the vertiginous expansion of cities and industries, while a myriad of immigrants and former slaves were alleged to be threatening the country's traditions. Brazilian elites blamed liberalism for such a "Crisis." Based on a decade of research, this book centralizes Brazilian history in liberalism and offers a genealogy of the jurisprudential and institutional struggles to correct the culture of laissez-faire. Using archival sources, it shows the direct U.S. influence on Brazilian thought and development. Recasting the history of legal ideas in the 20th century and providing novel interpretations on major political processes, it offers a rigorous and fresh look at the development of liberalism in the country.

Covering five decades of history and offering a transnational approach involving the U.S. hegemonic role in Brazil, this book will be of interest to scholars and students of law, U.S. foreign policy, area studies, and international relations.

Júlio Cattai is an historian of political ideas with interests in liberalism, law, Latin America, and Contemporary History. He also has an interest in Lacanian psychoanalysis. He is a member of the Cold War Studies Research Group (University of Sao Paulo, Brazil) and the Centre for Contemporary Culture Studies (Research Institute, Brazil). He is the author of *Guerra Fria e Propaganda: a U.S. Information Agency no Brasil* (2019) and is currently researching the birth of neoliberalism in Brazil.

Routledge Studies in US Foreign Policy

Series Editors: Inderjeet Parmar, *City University*, and John Dumbrell, *University of Durham*

This new series sets out to publish high-quality works by leading and emerging scholars critically engaging with United States Foreign Policy. The series welcomes a variety of approaches to the subject and draws on scholarship from international relations, security studies, international political economy, foreign policy analysis and contemporary international history.

Subjects covered include the role of administrations and institutions, the media, think tanks, ideologues and intellectuals, elites, transnational corporations, public opinion, and pressure groups in shaping foreign policy, U.S. relations with individual nations, with global regions and global institutions and America's evolving strategic and military policies.

The series aims to provide a range of books – from individual research monographs and edited collections to textbooks and supplemental reading for scholars, researchers, policy analysts and students.

Public Choice Theory and the Illusion of American Grand Strategy
How Generals, Weapons Manufacturers, and Foreign Governments Shape American Foreign Policy
Richard Hanania

U.S. Power and the Social State in Brazil
Legal Modernization in the Global South
Júlio Cattai

The United States and Greek-Turkish Relations
The Guardian's Dilemma
Spyros Katsoulas

Rhetoric, Media, and the Narratives of US Foreign Policy
Making Enemies
Adam Lusk

For more information about this series, please visit: www.routledge.com/series/RSUSFP

U.S. Power and the Social State in Brazil

Legal Modernization in the Global South

Júlio Cattai

Routledge
Taylor & Francis Group
LONDON AND NEW YORK

First published 2022
by Routledge
2 Park Square, Milton Park, Abingdon, Oxon OX14 4RN

and by Routledge
605 Third Avenue, New York, NY 10158

Routledge is an imprint of the Taylor & Francis Group, an informa business

British Library Cataloguing-in-Publication Data
A catalogue record for this book is available from the British Library

Library of Congress Cataloging-in-Publication Data
Names: Cattai, Júlio, author.
Title: U.S. power and the social state in Brazil: legal modernization in the global South / Júlio Cattai.
Other titles: United States power and the social state in Brazil
Description: Abingdon, Oxon; New York, NY: Routledge, 2022. |
Series: Routledge studies in US foreign policy |
Includes bibliographical references and index.
Identifiers: LCCN 2021032971 (print) | LCCN 2021032972 (ebook) |
ISBN 9780367643164 (hardback) | ISBN 9780367643188 (paperback) |
ISBN 9781003123941 (ebook)
Subjects: LCSH: Law–Brazil–History–20th century. |
Constitutional history–Brazil–20th century. |
Liberalism–Brazil–History–20th century. |
Brazil–Politics and government–20th century. |
Law–Brazil–American influences–History–20th century.
Classification: LCC KHD292 .C38 2022 (print) |
LCC KHD292 (ebook) | DDC 342.8102/9–dc23
LC record available at https://lccn.loc.gov/2021032971
LC ebook record available at https://lccn.loc.gov/2021032972

ISBN: 978-0-367-64316-4 (hbk)
ISBN: 978-0-367-64318-8 (pbk)
ISBN: 978-1-003-12394-1 (ebk)

DOI: 10.4324/9781003123941

Typeset in Times New Roman
by Newgen Publishing UK

For Alice
In memory of my grandparents

Contents

Tables

Acknowledgments

This book was only possible because of some people and institutions that I would hereby like to thank.

First of all, I would like to thank Prof. Inderjeet Parmar, who invited me to write a book proposal for evaluation. In addition to his brilliant acumen as a researcher and analyst of the international order, Parmar has a rare professional generosity. I wish also to thank Robert Sorsby and Claire Maloney at Routledge for their support. I am finally very grateful to Marco Alexandre de Oliveira for editing the manuscript, and to Felipe Colla de Amorim, who generously reviewed it.

At the University of São Paulo, I had fundamental institutional support to carry out this project. I am particularly grateful to my Ph.D. advisor, Professor Elizabeth Cancelli, a provocative intellectual who has always encouraged me on the paths of historical research. My colleagues in the Cold War Studies Group are an integral part of this book. They have generously discussed ideas and read draft chapters. Thank you all so much. I owe a special thanks to Aruã Lima, Diego Penholato, Felipe Colla de Amorim, Natália Mello, Thiago Amado, and Wanderson Chaves. They heard about my intentions and were always supportive. With them, I have also had the pleasure of sharing friendships, which makes it possible to bear the horrible times in Brazil.

I am very grateful to the Brazilian National Council for Scientific and Technological Development (CNPq) for the grant that enabled me to develop a part of this research. I am also grateful to the Rockefeller Archive Center for the research stipend that made possible to consult RAC's collections. I am indebted to the archivists and librarians with whom I came across over these years and who kindly provided the documents and materials I needed. I am particularly thankful to Bethany J. Anthos at the Rockefeller Archive Center, who diligently assisted me during my time there. I also note my gratitude, with special affection, to Tom Rosenbaum, who was always engaged and interested in helping with the intricacies of my research project.

My family was always supportive throughout the research and writing process. Without their encouragement, this book would not have come to life. I conclude with a special thanks to my mother, who spoke of the many wonders, and to my daughter, Alice, the irreverence that faces the inclement phantom who habits my existence.

Abbreviations

The following abbreviations recur throughout the book. Abbreviations that appear infrequently are defined as they appear.

ABA	American Bar Association
AI	Institutional Acts
CCF	Congress for Cultural Freedom
CEPED	Center for Studies and Research in the Teaching of Law
CIA	Central Intelligence Agency
DASP	Administration Department of the Public Service
FGV	Getúlio Vargas Foundation
IAB	Institute of Brazilian Lawyers
IADL	International Association of Democratic Lawyers
ICA	International Cooperation Administration
ICJ	International Commission of Jurists
IDPCP	Institute of Public Law and Political Science
IPES	Institute for Research and Social Studies
OAB	Brazilian Bar Association
PAEG	Government Economic Action Program
PUC	Pontifical Catholic University
STF	Federal Supreme Court
UN	United Nations
USAID	United States Agency for International Development
USIA	United States Information Agency
USP	University of São Paulo
WCC	World Council of Churches

Introduction

The decline of laissez-faire, U.S. power, and the rise of the Social State

> *Gentlemen, the greatest event of our century is not the worldwide conflagration, it is Einstein's general theory of relativity. We are at the gates of a new world. A general review of values is being undertaken. It is necessary to rebuild everything. Are the most common postulates not already denied? Eça de Queiroz once argued, when he was in a good mood, that the shortest path from one point to another would be not a straight line, but a delirious and lazy curve. Einstein has just confirmed the writer's irony, stating that if the planets describe curves, and not straight lines, it is because in the universe they are in, the shortest distance is the curve, not the straight line. The earth, the stars, the immensity, the ether, light, time, space, everything is being re-created and explained again in their foundations.*
>
> *For the new age, we must build a new spirit* [...] *Onward with the new spirit! Young and old, we march, because to stop is to get lost, to disappear under the avalanche of those who move forward and to be extinguished in the night of the ideas of the old age...*[1]
>
> Nuno Pinheiro (1923, p. 142–143)

By the beginning of the 20th century, social life was unraveling. The references of space and time vanished with the expansion of cities and industries and the "acceleration of the pace of history" (Koselleck, 2018; Rosa, 2010). One noted, with amazement and discomfort, the emergence of a new ritual of time, with a rapid pace and shortened distances, producing the vertigo of a constant and overlapping array of changes: a social time characterized by constant transformation. The thrill of the new technologies of mechanical acceleration was transported to bodies and minds through physical, civic, and mythical celebrations in the streets, bodies and minds of the "masses" – immigrants, the poor, and former slaves – whose discourse was, to Brazilian elites, absent of virtue and exotic to the country's traditional identity. After the Spanish Flu pandemic, the World War I, and the major worker strikes of 1917 and 1918, one could feel in São Paulo – the city which was undergoing an urbanization boom that would transform it into the most modern metropolis in South America – the imperative of a brilliant future. Under revolutionary tensions, expressions all around of modern art, and the jazz frenzy, there was

DOI: 10.4324/9781003123941-1

this growing population in search of a utopian identity (Sevcenko, 1992, p. 24). To the Brazilian elites, the urban life of the masses and the break – presented by the perception of crisis, catastrophe, and danger – with the conventional expectation of time as a linear progression should lead to a new and organic political awareness: a nation.

Gradually, during the Brazilian First Republic (1889–1930), legal thought diagnosed this process as a general crisis, connected with a broader crisis of Western societies.[2] Such a diagnosis was based on the assumption that the evolution in Western societies, since the 17th century, of the liberalism of John Locke and Montesquieu had produced a culture of excesses and self-absorbedness: an individual enterprise detached from any collective interest. At the foundation of the Republic's institutions, liberalism was blamed for the social misery that was raging everywhere throughout Brazil. Moreover, the legal order, in particular the foresight in the 1891 Constitution that the state should not be involved with economic and social issues, prevented the existence of an institutional structure to deal with the social issue.

Historicizing the structure of discourse, there is this insistent reproduction, by the elites, of such an understanding of liberalism. This was an intensely transnational process. The antagonism to laissez-faire liberalism gave rise to experiments, during the 1920s and 1930s, such as the Fascism in Italy, social welfare in Weimar Germany, New Deal in the United States and collective planning in Soviet world. *Modernization* – through reform or revolution – became the corollary of the solution to the crises, defining the horizons of political accomplishment. That was the claim by Nuno Pinheiro, in the early 1920s. Indeed, the political and intellectual elites were committed to disputing – between reformism and authoritarianism – the meaning of and the pathways to a modern Brazil. In any case, it involved rethinking the legal forms of liberalism, which had given the political and institutional contours of the Republic in the country since its first constitution in 1891. Therefore, to modernize meant a doctrinal effort to remake the country's institutional structure, favoring a profound modification of its very legal foundation: the defense of individual freedoms and the primacy of individual rights over state authority. In sum, it involved changing the relationship between state and society.

I argue that elite-led efforts to transform the Brazilian legal order in the period (1930–1975) were influenced by a global circulation of ideas and institutions, particularly of those coming from the United States. Indeed, Brazilian lawyers, jurists, and political figures profoundly relied on European and U.S. intellectuals to legitimize and favor their jurisprudential positions regarding a new model of state intervention and modernization, a process deepened after World War II by the direct influence of U.S. power in the country. This book presents how legal thinking's critique of liberalism in the turn of the century lay the groundwork for a modern national state (the Social State) in Brazil entrusted with a transformation from the individual as the *raison d'être* of political systems toward a new understanding of common good – a concept of social justice based on the correlation of individual interest with broader social, collective interest. Following the development in the 1940s and 1950s of the idea of totalitarianism in the United States and its direct influence in the correlation of forces between conservative and liberal elites in Brazil, the 1964 civil-military coup represented to these elites – and to the U.S. establishment – a way of securing political stability for such a profound political and juridical transformation.

A brief history of the Brazilian Republic

Since the proclamation of the Republic, the Brazilian constitutional typology had, as its mainstay, a certain abstention on the part of the public authority to intervene in social life. In a general sense, legal thought throughout the Western world, from the French Revolution until the first decades of the 20th century, referred to the constitutional structure of a Liberal State or Police State dedicated exclusively to safeguarding public tranquility and health along with private property. Such a state was not charged with questioning or much less interfering in the social order (Bobbio, 2005, chapter 4). World War I (1914–1918) and the rise of war economies in the nation states marked, however, the attempts to establish a new arrangement for these legal forms. Increasingly, public authority developed the role of intervening in public life, organizing the economic and social order to achieve "social justice": a new political sensibility concerning the uprising of the masses as a political phenomenon and the need to integrate them into the Western societies' traditions (Bresciani, 1992). Such a modernization effort would give rise to a Social State or Modern State, which primarily involved the renewal of constitutional texts. After World War I, the first attempts at legal modernization took place with the 1917 Constitution of Mexico and, especially, the 1919 Constitution of Weimar.

In Brazil, despite the constitutional reform of 1926, based on the attempt to change the country's constitutional order, only in October 1930, the date of the coup d'etat led by Getúlio Vargas that put an end to a historical period in Brazil, did the criticisms of liberalism find a systematic response. In sum, the new regime could offer a poilitical arrangement among Brazilian elites after a rapid and disruptive process of urbanization and industrial development in the first decades of the 21st century. Vocalizing a "revolutionary" effort the regime consolidated a view of the modern that was in dispute in the country since the 1870s (Hardman, 1993): it intended to recover the national identity and to establish an organic society, pushing the country away from the cultural forms of liberalism. Indeed, to a great extent, Brazilian elites saw in the liberal precepts an exotic idea in relation to national values and the cause of the country's ethnic and economic fragmentation and political disorder. Vargas regime (1930–1945), thus, established an anti-liberal agenda, expanding the instruments and functions of the public administration to cover different sectors of social life, particularly in the economic domain. To do so, Vargas centralized power in the Federal Government, which occurred to the detriment of the federated entities – states and municipalities. To effectively centralize power, it also became necessary to circumvent the instituitional instruments of control that limited the executive branch. The system that envisioned separation of powers, checks, and balances, and a strong federalism to counteract the Union – all of Montesquieu's premises of the rule of law designed to protect individual fundamental rights against state power and that had greatly influenced the country's legal order – came under attack by Vargas regime. Indeed, a few months after the October coup, Vargas both "retired" and raised the number of Federal Supreme Court ministers, changing the highest tribunal's jurisprudence in order to avoid control of the executive by the judiciary branch. By the same token, the Chief Executive instituted the decree-law instrument, which gave him normative powers, and closed Congress on more than one occasion.

Nevertheless, the Vargas regime (and the modernization intended by it) did not constitute a period of political consensus. By the early 1940s, opposition to the Vargas dictatorship started to gain expression. Based on liberal values, such opposition criticized the distortion of the purposes of the 1930 "Revolution" after the so-called 1937 coup – which reinforced the dictatorial aspects of the regime – and the Vargas' paternalistic intentions concerning the masses (Dutra, 2014, p. 454; Wald, 1965). This growing opposition paved the way for the fall of Getúlio Vargas and the formulation of a new constitutional order. Shortly after the end of World War II, in 1946, the Brazilian Congress approved a new Constitution. It restored the premises of the rule of law and the defense of individual rights with regard to state power – the strict separation of powers and legal instruments such as *habeas corpus* and *mandado de segurança*[3] for appreciation by the Federal Supreme Court. The new charter, however, maintained the public administration's structure and the public authority's constitutional responsibilities created under Vargas concerning the social interest. In other words, despite the opposition to Vargas, the emphasis on the Federal Government was maintained since it would be the only actor capable of carrying out a modernization process and integrating the masses into Brazilian society. Indeed, in the immediate aftermath of World War II, the disputes over modernization agendas resumed, however, maintaining the two interrelated issues that structured legal thought in the period: the masses and the "acceleration of the pace of history."

At that time, totalitarianism gained political prominence. To ensure modernization and lead the masses to a democratic political regime and an urban, industrial capitalist life, Brazilian elites engaged in discussions of how to avoid the risks of falling into totalitarianism. As legal intellectuals saw it at the time, an unlimited expansion of public administration, as the means to promote modernization, could lead to a Soviet-inspired totalitarian regime in which the individual was no longer a founding dimension of political life. The correlation between Vargas' dictatorship and totalitarianism became, indeed, a key argument among juridical elites in Brazil. In a further step, those elites started advocating economic development as a precondition for saving the masses from their own "absence" of virtue, once such economic growth would lead to the establishment of social parameters that did not include collectivist, authoritarian, or totalitarian political orders. More precisely, economic development would have a direct consequence in raising the material conditions of the poor and, thus, improving the democratic standards of political behavior and institutional life.

In all these new arrangements, the political and intellectual elite's in Brazil would find in the Global North a systematic knowledge devoted to offering intellectual and material guidance. Modernization theories and theorists, generated mainly by U.S.-based sociologists, considered that industrial development would lead to democracy. Referring to the countries of Latin America and those of the post-colonial world (the so-called Third World), theorists such as Talcott Parson and other social scientists at the Massachusetts Institute of Technology's Center for International Studies, for instance, indicated that the process of economic and social modernization would allow the transition from "traditional," "rural," and thus "retrograde" societies to the parameters of socio-economic development in "mature," "complex," and, "industrialist" societies. The U.S.–Brazil academic networks established in the 1930s would have, indeed, an impressive impulse after World War II, in particular under the auspices of the Ford Foundation (Parmar, 2012; Chaves, 2018). During the Cold War, as I argue, many Brazilian intellectuals and political figures, such as the political scientist Gláucio Ary Soares (1960), started advocating that economic development would lead to an urban middle-class society. According to these elites, the "social nature" of this middle-class would incline the country toward political moderation and reformist strategies of social change. In a few words, it would oppose totalitarianism.

Nonetheless, and this is a central point in my argument, the critical diagnosis of laissez-faire liberalism continued after World War II and in the Cold War era, not only in Brazil but also in the United States. Even considering the substantial changes between the 1930s and the second half of the 1940s, which are well documented in the literature, this book suggests the permanency in the political thought of the following two assumptions: the disruptiveness of laissez-faire liberalism and the necessity of some degree of state intervention. Indeed, the flaws of laissez-faire capitalism and the role the state should play in compensating the problems of the industrial era were still a common concern to political elites in the United States (Brinkley, 1995; Kornhauser, 2015). The very development of the U.S. National Security State in the interwar period and its reinvigoration after 1945 as an even more complex and organic *consortium* of state institutions devoted to assuring a safe place for the *American way* in an era of crisis, anxiety, and uncertainty may indicate the centrality of such a concern (Bessner, 2018, p. 128; Wertheim, 2020). In any case, a very similar process occurred in Brazil concerning the elites' continued views of the social problems and political instability produced by laissez-faire capitalism and the role state authority should play to solve it.

A fundamental basis for U.S. interventions in the Cold War era, modernization theories proposed that direct involvement by the state in development should be settled by nation-states abroad through counteracting the "excesses" of liberalism but promoting a state governmentality capable of producing a rationale between the collective interest and the fundamental rights of the individual. In this effort, as we shall see, international organizations such as the CIA-financed International Commission of Jurists, the first international organization devoted to human rights, played a major role. In Brazilian legal thinking, this political rationale, the common ground of political engagement, was named the *Estado Social*, or *Social State*.

This rationale, self-imagined as a neutral model for development throughout the world, was nonetheless unclear. Indeed, its parochial character, centered on the Global North and condescending of the parameters of modernization theories, demonstrates the reductionist capacities of these theories regarding Latin America and Third World realities (Gilman, 2003). Such difficulties were developed in Brazil as an intellectual problem. The expansion of the Federal Government would have a "totalitarian vocation," as one of the most important Brazilian commercial law experts, Arnold Wald (1967, p. 423), illustrated. Yet, not putting forward a state-led intervention program would also mean a totalitarian threat, once there would not be any political instrument capable of avoiding the "rebel" character of the masses (Ortega y Gasset, 1994). In both cases, uncertainty of modern times and the "seductive" character of communism and to its strategies of social change favored a sentiment of permanent menace. Therefore, legal thinking reproduced a *malaise*: a "phobia" of the tentacular presence of state powers in social life (Foucault, 2008, p. 75–76) and of falling into collective or totalitarian regimes. Thus, during the Cold War, the commitment in Brazil to "modern constitutionalism," was also based on an ethical and moral anchorage concerned with a transnational *anti-totalitarian* struggle. Legal thought in the country came to be structured as part of an international debate by intellectuals, particularly from the United States and Western Europe. Such elite knowledge networks operated mainly with ideas of "totalitarianism," "modernization," "social justice," and "democracy," directly constituting modern Brazil and the political and intellectual imagination about what constitutes this continental portion of land and the people who inhabit it.

In Brazil, these ideas were largely catalyzed by the 1946 Constitution, which, as has been said, was based on a liberal assumption: the strict separation of state powers, the decentralized exercise of public administration (federalism), and an increased possibility of petitioning for *habeas corpus* and *mandado de segurança* before the Federal Supreme Court. Indeed, the charter would have meant a straightjacket for the modernization effort, since it prevented the expansion of the executive branch and thus the means to achieve the social justice. Fundamentally, the constitutional text prohibited the delegation of legislative powers at the federal, state, and municipal levels to the executive branches, impeding them from producing social normativity and thus from becoming the primary agent for national development. Among elites, these difficulties also became a central concern because the perceived "acceleration of the pace of history" was imposing a dysfunctionality on the normative production. In other words, the time the National Congress was taking to produce and approve legal norms was not following the rapid evolution of the social phenomena under urban and industrial life.

The "Crisis of Parliaments," an expression used by jurists in Brazil and continental Europe to designate the normative "inadequacy" of legislative branches on both sides of the Atlantic, was, in turn, echoing in the period. This could be seen, for instance, in Gaston Morin's *La révolte du droit contre le Code*, later published as a book (1945), or in Fábio Konder Comparato's "divorce between law and the social reality" (1965, p. 14). In other words, law, as a discipline of the social, was no longer able to produce rules capable of accompanying the evolution of social phenomena. It was, then, a crisis of positive law: the written law of the codes, the norms, whose procedure of production (the time it took to be approved) by the legislative branch could no longer follow the "acceleration of social change." Elites diagnosed that since the 1930s, the Brazilian Congress would not have evolved at the same pace as the executive branch, making it unable to offer a legislative policy consistent with efforts for industrial development and the demands for constant transformation in modernity.

Such difficulties were furthermore affecting the Federal Supreme Court. The progressive overcrowding of the Court with trials and cases concerning individual rights and public intervention led to proposals for reforming the Supreme Court and the Brazilian legal system in order to ease the pressure on such a system. The "Supreme Court crisis" also became part of the criticism of liberalism, of an exacerbated individualism that was responsible, as asserted by Alfred Buzaid (1960), future Minister of Justice of the dictatorship, for a culture in which individuals were exclusively attached to their private interests and therefore did not involve private enterprise in the broader designs of the whole society.

These efforts to establish the Social State in Brazil, mark a modification in the origins of law. Previously centered, almost exclusively, on the individual dimension of social life and thus on the limitation of public authority in its interventionist capacities, the sources of law became increasingly positioned toward the expansion of public authority. The Brazilian civil law tradition had been rivaled by public law, thus indicating the transition from private to public legal forms. Such a transformation also marks the discussion on the modernization of teaching in law schools. Some Brazilian jurists saw the teaching style in the country as excessively expository, formal, and supposedly erudite. In sum, a method detached from the social reality. A curricular reorganization became necessary. In other words, modifying the minimum curriculum or basic requirements of law schools became a pressing issue, since it would guarantee adequate legal training to a state power that increasingly was requested to interfere in the economic and social domains. Moreover, it was a reform intended to include law schools in a new understanding of higher education. Occupied by the behavioralism of the applied social sciences, as predicted by the modernization theories, universities in Brazil became the main place to train technical, intellectual, and political elites with modern knowledge about institutions, political behavior, and economic development. These elites would then seek, within a framework of political moderation, to constantly improve the structure of public administration in the country.

During the two decades that followed the end of the World War II, Brazilian history entered a period known as the "democratic experience" (1946–1964). Centralizing Brazilian history in liberalism, I argue that this period is marked by the elites' search for new arrangements for the state-individual binomial relation. This would become, however, a difficult task: they could not find a common ground between state intervention and individual freedom. In the Cold War political and juridical parlance, such an "irresolution" represented the permanent menace of totalitarianism: flanked by the seductive character of the communist agenda of social change (state intervention and a collective response to social justice) and the inherent risks in the precarious material conditions of the country's population, which would permit the uprising of the masses – a hypothesis defended, for instance, by historian Arthur M. Schlesinger Jr. (1949). To a great extent, Brazilian elites absorbed the U.S. Cold War hegemonic agenda, a framework for state intervention: the *anti-totalitarian* struggle. This struggle was indeed at the basis of the United States National Security State and was developed, in a sophisticated way, by the State Department's psychological warfare apparatus on transnational fronts, such as the Congress for Cultural Freedom, the U.S. Information Agency, and the international aid agenda (Saunders, 1999, p. 149; Dezalay and Garth, 2002, p. 6).

By the early 1960s, especially after the failure of the 1962 parliamentary experience, legal and political ideas in Brazil joined forces in a broader formulation of the totalitarian threat. Brazilian elites developed these ideas along with the rise of a politically conservative view deeply connected with a U.S. elite's understanding of the country. In particular, the arguments proposed, since the late 1950s, by the political scientist Samuel Huntington on the risks of political upheaval in countries, such as Brazil, that were going through accelerated processes of social change. Such a threat would be posed by the so-called heirs of Getúlio Vargas, led by the left-wing presidency of João Goulart (1961–1964), who was "allowing" communist-union penetration into the state structure and, like Vargas, "seducing" the masses with paternalistic promises. In this view, the 1964 civil-military coup responded, thus, to this threat, ensuring security for the modernization process in the country (Cancelli, 2017).

The dictatorship was structured on two fronts: security, restricting individual liberties and eliminating political opposition; and modernization, for which the executive branch was empowered to develop a profound renewal of the country's institutional life. In both cases, this represented a new appreciation of the state-individual binomial (the relationship between state and society), favoring the former. Institutional Acts, as I argue, were the legal instrument *par excellence* of this governance. Authoritarian rule was justified, by the actors involved directly and indirectly in the coup and the dictatorship, as a "lesser evil" with regard to totalitarianism, considering the necessity of correcting the culture, the "overly individualistic" character of liberalism in the country. Furthermore, the regime was constituted as a means to a modern Brazil. In other words, the authoritarian legitimacy, founded in an alliance among liberals and conservatives, was based on the assumption that the dictatorship would be an instrument of political transition, from "archaism" to the standards of "modern societies" in the Global North.[4] In such an effort, Brazilian elites could count on the political, military, and intellectual support of the United States.

Here is a brief note on the organization of the chapters. Chapters 1 to 4 have a circular organization around the executive branch and the moral and institutional foundations of the Social State, from the 1930s to the mid-1970s. Chapter 1 discusses the "revolt of facts against the law" as a modular organization of legal discourse: the disruptive effects of the "acceleration of the pace of history" on the process of social discipline via law. It further highlights the disputes over the modernization of Brazilian positive law and how such efforts were devoted to overcoming the laissez-faire culture. Chapter 2 discusses the modernization of public administration, an institutional complex capable of structuring the disruptive character of the masses and the acceleration of the pace of history into a new governance. It explores the evolution of this modernization, especially with regard to the totalitarian threat of the post-World War II era. The controls by the judiciary branch over the expansion of the Federal Government came to play a major role as limit to anti-totalitarianism. Chapter 3 discusses the executive branch and the normative function in Brazil, particularly concerning the "crisis of parliaments." To face the challenge imposed by the "incapacity" of parliaments to develop a normative effort consentaneous with the modernization process, Brazilian elites disputed whether (and under what conditions) the executive branch should be able to create laws. Chapter 4 discusses how these changes in the Brazilian legal order defied the legal traditions of the country, demanding a new, modern training in law. Lawyers in such a changing society should abandon European and especially Portuguese traditions and approach what was termed the social reality, thus becoming a fundamental part of Brazilian modernization. U.S. power, particularly through the Ford Foundation and the U.S. International Aid Agency, played a major role in this modernization effort.

Chapters 1 to 4 conclude after the 1964 Civil-Military coup, at the end of that decade, when the elite-led efforts to develop the Social State had come to an end. Under authoritarian rule, a coalition of liberals and conservatives "solved" the disputes over the aforementioned issues, distancing the totalitarian threat to the country while substantiating the "correction" of the laissez-faire culture. Chapter 5 connects the dots indicated by the end of each chapter and presents how the foundations of the Social State entered a period of moral decline in the mid-1960s. Legal elites began to criticize the state, gradually relating authoritarianism with state intervention. They started echoing the promotion of the individual as a moral dimension to a post-Social State global order. Throughout the period, U.S. power played a major role, directly and indirectly influencing the foundations of the Social State in Brazil, and afterward, its transition to neoliberalism.

Indeed, in a complex way, the 1960s were marked by a gradual undoing of the moral parameter of modernization theories, which involved U.S. support for dictatorships throughout the world in the 1950s and the 1960s. Moreover, the premise of the also known social liberalism started to face growing fiscal and legitimacy crises, fracturing ideas on public interest and the common good (Forrester, 2019). May 1968 was possibly the fundamental face of this process of exhaustion, which found its expressions in the New Left, the counterculture, and the politics of defying the authority of the U.S. political establishment. This led to the renewal of Cold War policies (Ehrman, 1993; Borstelmann, 2012): from the late 1960s throughout the 1970s, Western elites began to look at the moral foundations of political life. The effort involved attempts, particularly from the United States, to recover the moral standards of the institutions that shaped the governance structure in the hemisphere, such as the Church, state institutions, philanthropic foundations, non-governmental organizations, and the United Nations.

Such a process had an important consequence for the governmental legitimacy of the Brazilian dictatorship, which concerned a debate on the political transition (or on what Samuel Huntington would call "political decompression").[5] The negotiated transition to democracy from within was a way to secure the recomposition of the alliance among liberals and conservatives in Brazil and lead the country to a renewed political order. "The most enlightened segments of the ruling elite" (Guilhot, 2005, p. 129; Cancelli, 2017, p. 125) should once again play a major role in the process by removing extremist political proposals from the debate on the transition. Legal thinking in Brazil, coming to the core of the debate, began to promote a necessary recovery of a political humanism that the technocratic rationale of the Social State had put aside. In other words, the technical or supposedly "value-free" approach to social issues had reduced humankind to statistics, to the formulas of economics and management. In this path, Brazilian jurists, lawyers, and political figures would find in a renewed human rights and rule of law discourse, a political and moral language capable of securing an orderly political transition and paving the way to a new, global connected modernity.

In a sense, the Brazilian transition from authoritarian to democratic rule was a reinstatement of the debate that ran through the Brazilian Republic in the 20th century, from the coup of October 1930 until the mid-1970s. Such a renewal involved an understanding that the Social State had fulfilled its role of reforming the culture of laissez-faire liberalism and individualistic political behavior, making it possible to re-establish individual enterprise detached from state tutelage. Additionally, the transition discourse established positions against the centralizing and planning assumptions of the Social State, identifying them as corrupt, incompetent, and paternalistic in their broad relationship with the social (Offner, 2019). In this sense, the human rights and the promotion of individual enterprise paved the way for the institutional foundation for the post-Social State world (Whyte, 2019, p. 27–28; Horn and Moriwski, 2009, p. 160–161). However, not as a laissez-faire revival but as a "project focused on designing institutions" (Slobodian 2018, p. 2) capable of promoting secure boundaries to a competitive, neoliberal order.

Notes

1 All quotes from texts originally published in Portuguese have been translated by the author unless otherwise indicated.
2 During the period covered by this book, Brazilian elites used "Western societies" to refer to the Americas and Europe. In this sense, they consider Brazil and Latin America as part of the same political tradition.
3 There is no adequate translation for the term. Roughly speaking, it could be translated as "writ of mandamus," but this translation can lead to important inaccuracies. In short, for the purposes of this work, the *mandado de segurança* is filed in the following cases: action or omission by the public power, illegality or abuse of power injury or threat of injury to a certain and liquid right, right not protected by *habeas corpus* nor *habeas data*.
4 This book uses Global North to refer to the United States and Europe, and Global South to refer to the regions of Africa, Asia, and Latin America. As historical actors did, it uses Third World to refer only to Africa and Asia.
5 Samuel Huntington. (1973). "Approaches to Political Decompression." Arquivo Paulo Nogueira Batista, Fundo Herbert José de Souza. Rio de Janeiro. CPDOC-FGV.

Bibliography

Bessner, D. (2018). *Democracy in Exile: Hans Speier and the Rise of the Defense Intellectual*. Ithaca and London: Cornell University Press.

Bobbio, N. (2005). *Liberalism and Democracy*. Translated by Martin Ryle and Kate Soper. London, New York: Verso.

Borstelmann, T. (2012). *The 1970s: A New Global History from Civil Rights to Economic Inequality*. New Jersey: Princeton University Press.

Bresciani, M. S. (1992). *Londres e Paris no Século XIX: o espetáculo da pobreza*. São Paulo: Brasiliense.

Brinkley, A. (1995). *The End of Reform: New Deal Liberalism in Recession and War*. New York: Alfred Knopf.

Buzaid, A. (1960). "A crise do Supremo Tribunal Federal," *Revista da Faculdade de Direito*. São Paulo: Universidade de São Paulo. Vol. LV.

Cancelli, E. (2017). *O Brasil em Guerra Fria Cultural: o pós-guerra em releitura*. São Paulo: Intermeios.
Chaves, W. (2018). *A questão negra: a Fundação Ford e a Guerra Fria (1950–1970)*. Curitiba: Prismas.
Comparato, F. K. (1965). "O indispensável direito econômico," *Revista dos Tribunais*, São Paulo, Ano 54, Vol. 353, Março.
Dezalay, Y. and Garth, B. G. (2002). *The Internationalization of Palace Wars: Lawyers, Economists, and the Contest to Transform Latin American States*. Chicago, IL: University of Chicago.
Dutra, P. (2014). *San Tiago Dantas: a razão vencida*. (O ideólogo) Vol. I (1911–1945). São Paulo: Editora Singular.
Ehrman, J. (1993). "Liberals, Neoconservatives, and Foreign Policy: 1945–1985." PhD diss., George Washington University.
Forrester, K. (2019). *In the Shadow of Justice: Post-war Liberalism and the Remaking of Political Philosophy*. New Jersey: Princeton University Press.
Foucault, M. (2008). *The Birth of Biopolitics*. Lectures at the College de France, 1978–79. Translated by G. Burchell. New York: Palgrave Macmillan.
Gilman, N. (2003). *Mandarins of the Future: Modernization Theory in Cold War America*. Baltimore: Johns Hopkins University Press.
Guilhot, N. (2005). *The Democracy Makers: Human Rights and the Politics of Global Order*. New York: Columbia University Press.
Hardman, F. F. (1993). "Memórias, ruinas e imaginação utópica: sobre algumas raízes românticas da modernidade no Brasil," *Anos 90* (UFRGS), Porto Alegre, Vol. 1, No. 1, pp. 145–159. https://doi.org/10.22456/1983-201X.6121
Horn, R. V. and Morowski, P. (2009). "The Rise of the Chicago School of Economics and the Birth of Neoliberalism." In Morowski, P. and Plehwe, D. (Eds). *The Road from Mont Pèlegrin: the making of the Neoliberal Thought Collective*. Cambridge, Massachusetts; London, England: Harvard University Press.
Kornhauser, A. M. (2015). *Debating the American State: Liberal Anxieties and the New Leviathan, 1930–1970*. Philadelphia: University of Pennsylvania Press.
Koselleck, R. (2018). *Sediments of Time: On Possible Histories*. Translated and Edited by Stefan-Ludwig and Sean Franzel. Stanford, California: Stanford University Press.
Morin, G. (1945). *La Révolte du droit contre le Code: la révision nécessaire des concepts juridiques, contract, responsibility, propriété*. Paris: Librairie du Recueil Sirey (Saint-Amand-Montrond, Cher: Impr. by R. Bussière).
Offner, A. C. (2019). *Sorting Out the Mixed Economy: The Rise and Fall of Welfare and Developmental States in the Americas*. New Jersey: Princeton University Press.
Ortega y Gasset, J. (1994). *The Revolt of the Masses*. New York: W. W. Norton & Company.
Parmar, I. (2012). *Foundations of the American Century: The Ford, Carnegie, and Rockefeller Foundations* in the Rise of American Power. New York: Columbia University Press.
Pinheiro, N. (1923). "Bibliographia" (discurso, de 26 de janeiro de 1922, em comemoração à publicação da obra "Systema de Sciencia Positiva do Direito," de Pontes de Miranda, de 1922), *Revista de Direito Público e de Administração Federal, Estadual e Municipal*, Rio de Janeiro, Anno III, Vol., No. 1.
Rosa, H. (2010). *Accélération: une critique sociale du temps*. Paris: La Découverte.

Samuel Huntington. (1973). "Approaches to Political Decompression." *Arquivo Paulo Nogueira Batista, Fundo Herbert José de Souza*. Rio de Janeiro. CPDOC-FGV.

Saunders, F. S. (1999). *The Cultural Cold War: the CIA and the World of Arts and Letters*. NY: The New Press.

Schlesinger Jr., A. M. (1949). *The Vital Center: The Politics of Freedom*. Boston: H. Mifflin Company.

Slobodian, Q. (2018). *Globalists: The End of Empire and the Birth of Neoliberalism*. Cambridge, Massachusetts: Harvard University Press.

Soares, G. A. D. (1960). "Participação eleitoral e Separação de Poderes," *Revista do Inst. De Direito Púb. e Ciência Política*, Rio de Janeiro – FGV, Vol. 3, No. 2, pp. 36–66.

Sevcenko, N. (1992). *Orfeu Extático na Metrópole: São Paulo, sociedade e cultura nos frementes anos 20.* São Paulo: Companhia das Letras.

Wald, A. (1965). "A função do advogado no processo revolucionário brasileiro," *Revista dos Tribunais*, São Paulo, Ano 54, Vol. 356, junho.

______ (1967). "The Law of Development," *Revista Forense*, Rio de Janeiro, Ano 63, Out-Nov-Dez.

Wertheim, S. (2020). *Tomorrow, the World: The Birth of U.S. Global Supremacy*. Cambridge, Massachusetts: The Belknap Press of Harvard University Press.

Whyte, J. (2019). *The Morals of the Market: Human Rights and the Rise of Neoliberalism*. London. New York: Verso.

1 The executive and Modernity

The "revolt of facts against the law"

In the evolution of modernity, particularly since the 18th century, the expansionism of industrial technique and economics found its corollary in the liberal philosophy, in opposition to the ancien régime, that touted the primacy of the individual over state power. The Baron of Montesquieu's *Spirit of Laws* advocated precisely this primacy. The separation of powers among the legislative, executive, and judiciary branches – each one possessing, through the system of checks and balances,[1] the function of supervising the others – aimed to assure the complete exercise of individual freedoms. Gradually, legal thought, especially by German public law experts such as Georg Jellinek (1959),[2] established that any action by the executive, the principal repository of the powers of princes, was tied to the principle of law, institutionally and normatively delimiting it. Based on this assumption, jurists established the recognition of the state as a legal entity. Therefore, it constituted a legal state of law, the state "ruled by law."

> In fact, it is not necessary to resort to fiction to find the means that the state uses to form and express its will, since the state organs are made up of individuals. It is not difficult to see that when individuals act as organs of the state, they express a will that can only be imputed to it and that is not to be confused with individual wills [….] It is through the notion of the state as a legal person, existing in the legal order and seeking to act according to the law, that effective legal limits to the state's action in its relationship with citizens are established.
>
> (Dallari, 1973, p. 108–109)

Legal forms thus required the public authority to abstain from disciplining the private sector, a policy that otherwise performed a *negative* function, for instance, in the Law of Things: guaranteeing protection and security to the complete satisfaction, by the individual, of the functions and uses of property.[3] It encompassed, therefore, the economic liberalism of the physiocrats and Adam Smith, for whom intervention would be inappropriate for the interests of all. Smith, in his 1776 *The Wealth of Nations*, while considering the regime

DOI: 10.4324/9781003123941-2

of "natural freedom," affirms that the state has only three duties: first, that of protecting society from violence and invasion by other nations; second, that of protecting each member of that society from injustice and oppression by another member; and third, that of building and maintaining public works and monuments in favor of the sentiments and the interests of the nation, which would never be in the interest of any individual (Smith, 1977). It was in this sense that, in the Law of Things, European doctrine defined a property by the right of its owner to exercise or even impose, in all of its aspects, his will. Property was thus described in its double aspect: *internal* (economic – the link between the owner and the property that belongs to him) and *external* (legal – the owner's right to exclude third parties from any action relating to the property). By the early 19th century, the functions of the public authority were, therefore, reasonably delimited and separated from private activities, particularly in the economic order: its abstention in such a domain, if it does not constitute a direct causal relationship, at least influenced the technical revolution and industrial capitalism.

The public authority also considered all individuals linearly, not having a systematic intervention program to reduce social inequality. Indeed, as discussed by Michel Foucault (2009, chapter 4), the period is constituted by an era of governmentality – the science of government – focused on a police rationale of isolating and managing the population, which would be the central and defining problem of the art of government. In this rationale, acquiescence with security and disciplinary provisions was essential. Included in the 19th century's legal dogmatism, the Brazilian Republic was organized with the Constitution of 1891: legal norms as protection-coercion devices, whereby, according to the jurist Washington Luiz da Trindade (1976, p. 99), "[...] man may be coerced by man for certain abstentions or certain reparations, so that it could be said, with Tobias Barreto, that law is 'the force that has overcome the violence'."

The abstention of the state came to be supported, as one of its instruments, in the formalization of the law, the written norm, *constitutionalism* – an effort by jurists and parliamentarians, especially throughout the 19th century, to collect and systematize Codes and Constitutions precisely in the name of "preserving the freedom and peculiarities of each people, without prejudice to the values of security, certainty, order, and universality" (Reale, 1961, p. 34). Constitutionalism, then, according to Afonso Arino de Melo Fransco (1957, p. 224), expressed the very political-legal doctrine of liberalism, insofar as it defined, normatively, the motives of public power concerning the individual.

In this sense, against the abuses of power by public authority, the *natural law* of the ancien régime was abandoned, that is, a transcendent, a priori, ahistorical, and self-evident law, the divine right of kings, an ideal, correct, just, true order. To contain such abuses, legal forms were transformed into a sense of immanence, imperfection, from the possible to the City of Men, a *means* to an *end*, defined for a precise territory and time, an order guided by legal principles that, conditioned by political life, translated the political destinies to be pursued. In sum, to contain abuses of power, legal thinking was organizing the law of the codes (Nader, 2003; Medeiros, 1969, p. 377).

It is this positive law, a product of a civil (private) tradition in the Brazilian legal structure, that finds itself in a growing process of deterioration during the first decades of the 20th century. Indeed, under such a tradition, public authority was limited to a power of coercion, to ensure, as Adam Smith said, public health and safety. The tradition was embedded in the most important of Brazilian codes: the Civil Code of 1916, written by Clóvis Beviláquia, which established legal principles such as the *autonomy* of the individual will and the freedom of contract and association (Reale, 1976; Tácito, 1971a). At the time, this codification would come to be interpreted as the mainstay of a "liberal orthodoxy" founded in the name of the defense of individual freedoms. This orthodoxy, furthermore, was imposing significant limitations to a renewal of the law with regard to the need to keep up with the changing social dynamics under industrialism and urbanization. In other words, the organization of *positive law* was based on the individual's revolt against state power. In order to expand state activities, it was necessary to modify the very foundation of the Brazilian legal law tradition.

The crisis of positive law was, thus, part of a broader malaise of modernization. One could consider such a malaise to be the "revolt of facts against the law" – against the formulas and solutions that, crystallized in the codes, were born "aspiring to eternity," according to the Brazilian commercial law expert Alfredo Lamy Filho (1976, p.7). However, since the early decades of the 20th century, attempts have been made to change the organization of this legal system. In Europe, the First World War, specifically the actions of the state authority to discipline the economy in favor of the war effort, catalyzed this change, insofar as it imposed a change to the state's position of abstention in the economic order. During the conflict, public authority subjected the decisions of private agents of the economy to the demands of the war, which marks a doctrinal inflection and the birth of a public economic law related to state intervention in the economy. Such an interventionist process ended up not being circumscribed, as part of the European doctrine believed, to the period of world conflict. Instead, this economic law or law of the economy became a corollary of a "post-liberal" order: the Social State (Kennedy, 2006).

The permanence of the state's propositional or programmatic role was sustained, precisely, in the criticism of liberalism, whose prominence showed not only signs of exhaustion in the economic field, but also was held responsible for exclusionist forms of governance. The rise, in urban life, of the "miserable" and "ignorant" masses was representative enough of such political decay – what Ortega y Gasset (1994), a prominent Spanish jurist had called, in the late 1920s, "the revolt of the masses." The diagnosis, which persisted until the mid-1960s (Piettre, 1964, p. 100–101), was that the liberal regime would require an honest morality on the part of the individual and should be structured according to principles of equality and balanced competition. Such an organization did not take place under laissez-faire liberalism. The end of World War I and later, the crisis of 1929, indeed initiated among the political and legal elites throughout the West, including Brazil, a renewed constitutional effort aimed at a program to solve the social issue.

In opposition to the liberal orthodoxy, the instrumentalization of public authority, in particular the executive branch, with legal and institutional mechanisms of intervention, would make it possible to arrange a cohesive program for industrial development and the achievement of "social justice." Such an instrumentalization had been inaugurated with the Mexican Constitution, in 1917, and the Weimar Constitution, in 1919. Legal thought was moving from a "Police State," in its abstentionist basis, to a programmatic "Social State."

Reflecting on the moral dimension of this changing pattern of legal practice, some elite groups in Brazil concerned themselves, for instance, with J. J. Rousseau's *Social Contract.* Brazilian jurists and political figures, such as Milton Campos (1972, p. 87), managed to find in Rousseau's thinking the formula for arguing that the social order constituted "a sacred right" that was the basis of all other rights. Despite considering that some European authors, such as Cabral de Moncada, Laubadère, Georges Vedel, Zbigniew Brzeziński, and Carl Friedrich, indicated that in Rousseau it was possible to find the origin or at least the inspiration for authoritarian state institutions (Friedrich and Brzeziński, 1965, p. 100; Campos, 1972), those jurists and political figures would rely on the statement made by the French public law expert René Capitant, that Rousseau was the true founder of modern democracy. Milton Campos, echoing Capitant's formula, argued that:

> [...] the general will is the law, under the double condition of being voted by all and applying to all. This definition characterizes a democracy, giving it its modern meaning [....] Certainly, this double generality of the law ensures, as is essential in modern democracies, the double foundation of the popular origin of political power and the equality of all before the law [...] [with the] suppression of privileges [. ...].
>
> (Campos, 1972, p. 91)

In summary, legal thinking was investigating the *Social Contract* in search of routes to renew the moral dimension of Brazilian political-legal doctrine, one that could overcome the culture of laissez-faire without incurring totalitarianism. Campos, as well as Themistocles Cavalcanti, Djacir Menezes, Paulo Bonavides (1962), and other members of the Getúlio Vargas Foundation's Institute of Public Law and Political Science (IDPCP) were concerned with Rousseau because his so-called theoretical ambiguity – the defense of the individual against the authority of the monarch and the primacy of the social over the individual – catalyzed the malaise of those times, particularly after the rise of the "totalitarian threat." Or rather, by scrutinizing Rousseau's thinking on morality (despite a "romanticism" attributed to the philosopher, particularly, the defense of the exercise of popular authority without the mediation of a representative), these jurists sought to clarify the postulates of his democratic doctrine: the foundations of human reasoning, ethical life, and sociability. As put by one of them, "the dream [...] of an egalitarian society, the end of the political alienation of man chained to the iron of oppression. Rousseau [...] a hundred years before Marx, throws the incendiary bomb of popular sovereignty and universal suffrage on the irretrievable liberalism of bourgeois society" (Menezes, 1962, p. 150).

As previously mentioned, by facing the structural crisis of Western civilization, legal elites found their *noblesse oblige*: the challenge of renewing the meanings of the legal order, their source,[4] creative force, and objectives. With that intention, those elites underscored a necessary effort of transforming the absolute primacy of the individual, whose contours and scope went back to the 1789 *Declaration of the Rights of Man and of the Citizen* and the 1776 U.S. *Declaration of Independence*: "freedom consists in doing everything that is not harmful to others."[5] In sum, legal elites started to reorganize the *foundations* of the post-French Revolution legal order, particularly regarding property rights, the separation of powers, and the assumptions of an individual that was morally and ethically, prior and superior to state authority.

In this sense, the early 20th century constituted a "challenge to civilization," according to the British historian Arnold Toynbee (1946); a "decline of the West," according to the German historian and philosopher Oswald Spengler (2016); an "acceleration of history," according to the French historian Daniel Havély (1949). Such ideas – the threat posed by this wide "crisis of culture" (Cox, 2001; Lamy Filho, 1976; Wald, 1965) – informed the legal debate in Brazil). As observed in the mid-1950s by a Brazilian jurist, echoing Toynbee's arguments, it constituted a moment when culture would exhaust "its creative possibilities and should be replaced by another, under the risk of petrifying itself" (Gusmão, 1956, p. 39). The theses articulated by European legal intellectuals, such as Gaston Morin, Silvio Trentin, Giuseppe Capograssi, Georges Rippert, Piero Calamandrei, Francesco Carnelutti, and René Savatier, concerning the "revolt," "ambiguity," "crisis," "decline," and "death" of law, represented a vivid image in Brazilian legal thought. In other words, legal thinking in Brazil had a common approach with foreign intellectuals to what would have become the imperative of not losing the equation of time, by renewing legal forms and thus directing them to the modern world.[6]

Indeed, that was precisely the idea of a "divorce between Law and social reality" advocated by Fábio Konder Comparato (1965, p. 14), one of the most respected jurists in Brazil and a staunch defender of state intervention in the economic order. This was also the reference that Francisco Clementino de San Tiago Dantas (1955) used in his diagnosis of the legal field in the early 1940s, describing the legal practice in the country as a mainstay of conservation, or the barriers and thus the impediment of developmentalism and modernization, producing the chaos in which the legal system, and consequently, the national political organization would find itself at the time. For this reason, Dantas argued for an urgent need to reform law:

> Around us there is a vast and great reform of the legislative system; in Brazil, as in the rest of the world, the system developed based on another positive law does not leave room for innovations. Remaking the doctrine, readjusting legal science to its immutable object, which is the law, is the task to which our efforts must be devoted [....] Labor laws, tax laws, laws that express the transition from the free to the directed economy, the new public law, this world in gestation that is administrative law, everything overwhelms and asks the jurists, who is in the world today as the geographer must have been at the time of the discoveries.[7]

Along this path between the Getúlio Vargas regime and the political transition under the dictatorship in the mid-1970s, there was a common ground on what would be the negative effects of liberalism – a hybrid foreignness to the nation, responsible for the miserable masses and the threat of disruption of national political cohesion, of traditional Brazilian plasticity (Faria, 2006; Bresciani, 2005). However, there is an important inflection in this understanding with the end of Getúlio's regime in 1945. Indeed, in October 1930, elites joined Vargas and his anti-liberal program. To some degree, the post-World War II legal debate maintained its critical stance against liberalism, however understanding that the 1937 coup and the establishment of the Estado Novo (New State) by Vargas had "corrupted" such a program with "populism," "paternalism," and authoritarianism.[8] In the post-World War II era, on the contrary, the primacy of individual freedom as a central value for the definition of political agendas was recovered, actually as an effort by the victors of the international conflict (Judt, 2008). Safeguarding world populations from arbitrariness and totalitarianism, those agendas were based on the assumption of *human nature*, under the aegis of the principles of *natural human rights* as a precondition to political forms, or more specifically, as a principle of authority in the face of the "de-Christianization" of life.

In the Cold War, such a movement to recover the primacy of individual liberties against state authority found its fundamental protection in human rights during two successive moments. First, in the immediate post-World War II period, this movement took place through the affirmation of a renewed morality, arising specifically from a "Christian realism" as opposed to the secularization of life, to the political responses to the phenomenon of the "masses" through a materialist approach and based on liberal optimism with regard to human morality. This new morality appeared, then, as a return to the "sacredness of the human personality," as interpreted in the (realistic and Augustinian) doctrine of original sin,[9] of a human nature founded on the desire for preservation, greed, and the will to power (Craig, 2003). Thus, the assertion of human rights (as a natural law, before material and political life) was due to its ability to bring earthly reality to the Kingdom of God, whose failure would have led to the violence of war, and finally, to Nazism. Only afterward, in the early 1950s and with the threat posed by the nuclear revolution on the horizon, were human rights structured, by the recovery of the memory of the holocaust, as a safeguard against totalitarian or collectivist proposals of rupture of the Western Christian order (Moyn, 2011). In other words, human rights were based on the irreducibility of the individual and bound to the transcendent, but in the framework of a certain position on public life: the Cold War consensus based on modernization theories and their assumptions that value-free scientific knowledge would constitute safeguard for social life (Gilman, 2003; Latham, 2000). Throughout such an arrangement, there was a response to state intervention in public life that bypassed the threat of collectivization or totalitarianism.

As such, legal ideas came to be managed not in the denial of the aforementioned principle based on the individual, but in a *correction* of the legal sense of the post-French Revolution idea: an individual enterprise structured, from the outset, by a broader social interest. According to the Belgian public law expert Fritz Gygi (1962), and to a formula repeated to exhaustion by legal intellectuals in Brazil, the Cold War challenge had become to reconcile social justice and individual freedom. The debate had invested in redefining, in a privileged way – as I argue in Chapter 2 –, the rule of law concept in order to bypass the laissez-faire schemes of strict separation of state power and thus favor an institutional organicity that was both structurally and ethically opposed to ruptures, to collectivist and totalitarian forms of political organization. Legal ideas in Brazil accompanied a broader Cold War debate, in which the rule of law was voiced, particularly from the sophisticated political agenda of the U.S. Department of State, as a universal legal structure for the world. It was aimed, above all, at this "changing world" staged by the nascent "Third World" and the "underdeveloped" countries of Latin America (Dezalay and Garth, 2011, Introduction).

It is this Cold War premise against arbitrary anti-totalitarianism that guides, during the first two decades after the Second World War, the outlines of the Brazilian legal order, and that also marks a fundamental difference to the Vargas period (1930–1945). This premise presided over the spirit of the 1946 Constitution, which, according to the jurist Hermes Lima, was identified with the 1934 Charter, already imbued with the spirit of the post-1918 European constitutional renewal – even though Vargas was able, to a large extent, to suspend it (Cancelli, 1994, chapter 4). The Constitutions of 1934 and 1946, Hermes Lima stated, "were assemblies concerned mainly with preventing an overwhelming Executive, with discretionary tendencies, from dominating the public scene" (1954, p. 14). In defense of Fritz Gygi and following the line of reasoning of Lima, Miguel Seabra Fagundes (1963, p. 7 and 11), one of the main Brazilian public law experts, recalled that the Constitution of 1946, in

Article 145, which opens with the title "On the Economic and Social Order," stipulated:

> [...] that this objective [social justice] must be achieved by reconciling free enterprise with the appreciation of human labor. Free enterprise appears, therefore, alongside the idea of valuing human labor, as one of the pillars on which the country's economic development will be based.

As he later emphasized:

> In the reconciliation between intervening measures and the fundamental rights enshrined in the Constitution of the Republic, there is the most delicate and practical aspect of the intervention process, especially due to the apparent incompatibility of interventionist action, which allows the state to meddle in areas of activity reserved for individuals, with the preservation of the sphere of interests of each individual.

This "delicate and practical aspect of the intervention process" became a focal issue for legal ideas. This common good, the social justice that was sought as a horizon for political achievement, could not be described and translated into objective institutions, except as a political interpretation and will, since it is a disputed value (the *good of all*). It is in this sense that the Brazilian legal debate turned to define the ideas and the appropriate legal institutions for this collective interest. The ideas in the country thus found fundamental support for such a definition in the renewal of the rule of law concept, which was carried out, as a Cold War policy, by the foreign policy establishment of the United States and which was structured by *theories of modernization*. In effect, the search for the common good started to focus on the defense of the individual against abuses of authority, while trying to redefine the classic formula of strict separation of state power – the basis of the classic concept of the rule of law – in favor of a widening interpretation of the rule of law. As a support for this effort, the ideas will be decisively linked to the language and to the technical and scientific knowledge of the applied social sciences, in particular, which was developed in universities and whose "objectivity" would allow for action beyond ideology (Cancelli, 2012, p. 124).

In a complementary way, this definition of the common good – or, more specifically, the means by which it could be realized – could also be supported by Christian morality in the country. In fact, in Brazil, since the end of the 19th century, the search for the common good was supported by the Papal Encyclicals, which translated this morality, particularly after the 1891 *Rerum Novarum*, the cornerstone of the Roman Church's social policy. At the time of the proclamation of the Brazilian Republic, this morality aided the Church's struggle against the secular reason of the liberals, and thus against the theological neutrality of the state on which they were based (Romano, 1979, p. 102–104). In the evolution of this process, a new impulse of Catholic thought takes place throughout Latin America under the influence of the philosopher Jacques Maritain, who would become an important precursor for the Universal Declaration of Human Rights, published in December 1948.

Such an influence can be perceived in the 1st Congress of Christian Democracy, held in April 1947, in the city of Montevideo. Jurists and politicians such as Alceu Amoroso Lima, Sobral Pinto, and André Franco Montoro abandoned the belief in the effectiveness of corporatism, Vargas' authoritarian approach, as a solution to the Brazilian "crisis," to the process of "de-Christianization" of life under socialism or under liberal capitalism. This opposition began to defend the anti-totalitarian struggle and Maritain's "integral humanism" (*Humanisme intégral*, 1936), advocating for a decisive opening of Catholicism to political action. Indeed, the Church's Social Doctrine inspired a "Third Way" – Christian Democracy – as an alternative Cold War solution to laissez-faire liberalism and communist collectivism (Busetto, 2002, p. 15). Such an understanding would not be limited to the Roman Catholic Church and Brazil. One year later, in Amsterdam, the World Council of Churches (WCC) was established, an international organization composed of approximately 140 churches under an ecumenical position by which "the Christian churches should reject the ideologies of communism and *laissez-faire* capitalism." Otherwise, they "should seek to draw men away from the false assumptions that these extremes are the only alternatives" (Christian, Kott, and Matějka, 2017, p. 41).

The Christian principle of authority and the renewal of the rule of law based on a scientific rationale were, thus, an integral part of Brazilian legal thinking in the Cold War period. Exemplarily, it was in these terms that one of the main Brazilian civil law specialists, Nicolau Nazo (1958, p. 29), described the "common good" in 1958:

> To the wise lessons of the Encyclical "Rerum Novarum" – a close collaboration between the various social classes, respect for private enterprise when directed towards the common good, a truly social function of private property, and the due elevation and understanding of the worker as a human person – power-driven dictators preferred class struggle, economic dirigisme, large-scale demagogy.[10]

The condition for this redefinition lied in a new form of governability, giving sense and organicity to the intervention of public administration in the social and economic order. However, almost immediately after the country's democratization in 1945, with the end of the Vargas dictatorship, the legal debate came to realize that the 1946 Constitution, fundamentally based on the premises of formalism[11] in the rule of law, restored the functions and powers of the legislative and judiciary branches, which structurally would not have developed, since 1930, at the same pace as that of the executive. Under such a formalism, the new legal order had become a "straitjacket" for the public authority's ability to carry out this modernizing agenda. In other words, the constituting legislator – despite expanding, as argued by Miguel Seabra Fagundes (1963), the role to be played by public authority on the social and economic domain – prevented the adjustment of the separation of powers. Reestablishing the idea of the primacy of the individual over state authority, the new charter vetoed the projection of the executive branch in its new role of *planning* the national effort toward modernization.

This was, in a general sense, a problematic and urgent matter for Brazilian political life. To some jurists, the threat of a rupture in the order was primarily represented not so much by visible groups of "international communism" in the country,[12] but rather by the prominence, in the poor regions of the world, of the seductive character of authoritarianism. Such an *irresolution* of the political debate, in Brazil, concerning the *equilibrium* between individual freedoms and state power, was postponing the social problem indefinitely into the future and thus permitting the eruption of extremist proposals for social change. It was the conduction of Brazilian political life by the elites that was at risk – the Proclamation of the Republic and the subsequent expansion of educational opportunities was gathering the masses under an elite-led guardianship process organized through state governance. In a sense, however, this process could not avoid the growing weight of these masses in the electoral processes and the normative "inclinations" of the legislatures, in sum, in the country's "future" (Fagundes, 1956; Britto, 1966).

Consequently, a concern with the electoral dynamics, with the meanings of democratic representation, became an important question. The inheritance of a centralized power structure, organized after the 1930 coup, combined with conceptions of anti-partisanship in important political groups, which had been active since the 1930s and which came to preside over the re-democratization process in 1945, significantly limited the appearance of "associative political parties." In sum, there were no party associations sustained by broader social aspirations; on the contrary, they were directly dependent on the state and its bureaucratic machinery (Lamounier and Meneguello, 1986; Souza, 1990). Therefore, there was an "excess of political parties" and a "peculiar" presidential system, in which the president and the vice president were chosen in majority elections, while members of the Chamber were elected proportionally. This generated a fundamental contradiction: the elected legislators did not have the same public agenda or commitment as the presidents, who saw themselves obliged to collaborate, to form a government coalition at times against the agendas for which they had been elected (Spektor, 2018).

During the two decades that followed the end of the Vargas Regime and the Second World War, political life in the country found no terms or consensus for the Brazilian political system. As occurred in other areas of national life, the issue came to be "solved", after the 1964 coup, in an authoritarian way. One of the first measures of the H. A. Castello Branco administration (1964–1967) was to enact an electoral reform in the form of two projects, the National Party Statute, and a new Electoral Code. Such a reform appeared justified, as asserted in 1965 by the current Minister of the Federal Supreme Court, Cândido da Mota Filho, because it would give a new discipline to the "representative regime," making it possible to overcome a state of affairs that had dragged on since the promulgation of the Republic. In sum, the reform intended to revitalize political parties in order to allow greater contact with the people and to improve the governance of a democratic state. Such a representative regime would furthermore prevent the political regime from becoming "absorbing and totalitarian" (1965, p. 48–49).

As an urgent political exercise, legal elites tried to relate public life to the new dynamics of industrialism and urban life, looking to the standards of modern societies in the Global North. To overcome liberal "extremism," without incurring a "revenge against the Old Regime," it was necessary to produce a "new order" through which individual enterprise would be morally and ethically bound to the collective interest (Porto, 1959; Nazo, 1958; Nonato, 1958). In the conservative Miguel Reale's terms (1976), there should be a complementarity of values in which subjectivity was linked to the social and the social encountered in subjectivity the foundational root of its manifestations. It was thus under the rubric of the "revolt of facts against the law," of the insufficiency of positive law to discipline public life and to give organicity to economic development, that the "totalitarian threat" was delineated on the horizon. U.S. power, however, would offer support to Brazilian legal thinking.

Legal ideas in Brazil and the U.S. Cold War debate

At the end of the 1940s, Joseph Willits, then Director of the Social Sciences Division of the Rockefeller Foundation, contemplated the structuring by Rockefeller of a program in *Moral, Ethics, and the Law*. Willits discussed the program with members of the U.S. legal elite, including James William Hurst and Max Rabin, both from the University of California, Berkeley, and John Foster Dulles, a corporate attorney at Sullivan & Cromwell who would come to be Secretary of State in the Dwight D. Eisenhower administration (1953–1961) (Kinzer, 2013, p. 58). The Director of the Social Sciences Division felt that the challenges posed to government leadership in the post-World War II era were not being adequately addressed by the training offered by law schools in the United States. The crisis of the legal field could be noticed, for these jurists, in the gradual process of replacement of lawyers with economists and administrators in U.S. policymaking. Besides the preoccupation with the legal practice's moral foundation, they began to indicate a necessary approximation of law to social reality. In a few words, law – the production of social discipline through a normative effort – should move away from *formalism*, proper to liberal orthodoxy, in favor of detailed empirical work. To them, the technical-scientific tools of the social sciences were the way for legal practice to regain relevance (Garth, 2000).

Such a concern was in line with the new arrangement of power relations at the international level since the early 1940s and principally after 1945. In the United States, this new arrangement became clear with the ideological challenge imposed by the Soviet Bloc, leading to a new definition of the country's foreign policy structure. The immediate post-war years mark, accordingly, the organization and systematization of an entire administrative complex capable of defending and protecting the values of American life. The National Security State involved the entire apparatus of the country's foreign policy, imposing such an institutional order that delimited the political agendas during the Cold War period (Bessner, 2018, p. 128; Wertheim, 2020). The legal structure of this redefinition was largely determined by the National Security Act of 1947, signed by President Harry S. Truman in July. The legislation led to the creation of the Central Intelligence Agency (CIA), which was devoted to centralizing efforts to produce intelligence and counterintelligence, and the National Security Council (NSC), "an institution like no other in government," formed by advisers to the presidency and responsible for defining and monitoring the country's foreign policy guidelines (Gans, 2019, p. 5). Furthermore, it structured the general strategies concerning "psychological warfare," in particular, a tactic of accommodating anti-Stalinist artistic and intellectual elites around the world in the Congress for Cultural Freedom (CCF) (Saunders, 1999; Gremion, 1995; Cancelli, 2012; Iber, 2015), and an international propaganda approach ("Public Diplomacy")[13] which culminated, in 1953, with the creation of the United States Information Agency (USIA) (Cull, 2008; Cattai, 2019). The country's international activism was born on the assumption that it was necessary to defend National Security and thus preserve the American way of life. This has involved, since the early 1940s, the country's primacy, the global supremacy of the United States in world affairs (Wertheim, 2020).

The moral foundation of this state reason could be found in a new articulation of the concept of *totalitarianism*. From a political phenomenon that explained, critically, the tendencies of rupture of the liberal order in modernity, as staged in particular by German Nazism, the concept started to be expressed as an apology to its contrary: the defense of democracy, freedom, and the principle of authority recognized in Christian transcendence (Cancelli, 2012, p. 122). Indeed, after 1945, alongside the threats posed by the Soviet Union, the fragile comprehension of democracy and the economic misery in the post-colonial and "underdeveloped" worlds would also represent a risk of political disruption. The prolongation and irresolution of social justice could lead to a totalitarian rupture.

The political establishment in the United States considered the necessity of a program, to be devised by the nations of these regions, that was aimed at economic, political, and social change and development. This premise began to function as a guide for the formation of alliances with certain elites groups in these regions, directly informing the international aid strategy of the United

States (Chaves and Cattai, 2019, pp. 208–209; Simpson, 1998, p. 39). On April 4, 1948, the *New York Times Magazine* published an enlightening manifesto on the subject. The Harvard University historian and former member of the Office of Strategic Service (OSS), Arthur M. Schlesinger Jr., argued that, contrary to Karl Marx's predictions, communist seduction would appear prominently in the poor regions of the world, in countries where the "social issue" would make the emergence of conflicts and the inclination of social and political groups toward radical political forms (dictatorial and totalitarian) imminent. The title of Arthur Schlesinger's article was *Not Left, Not Right, but a Vital Center*. Reflecting a discussion in Europe and the United States, he called on moderate political forces, on the left and the right, to develop a common agenda based on anti-totalitarianism and the democratizing effort: "a coalition of all those [...] who believe in political freedom and the democratic control of economic life – a coalition affirming a rigorous faith in constitutional and democratic methods against any form of terror or dictatorship" (1948, p. 1).

The "democratic control of economic life" was a hot topic in the post-war era and was not detached, as asserted by Schlesinger's article, from this broader view of political life. Indeed, it came to be systematized by the social sciences, particularly in the main universities in the United States, such as the Massachusetts Institute of Technology (MIT) and Harvard University. Theoretically, Talcott Parsons' sociology of functionalism offered the conceptual framework – an approach to the "social system" – through which modernization theorists would create the conditions for a competent and limited state intervention in social life. It was assumed that modern societies should converge to the same corporate pattern, formalizing a political and social ideal common to the different regions of the world. Incorporating such a conceptual framework, the sociology of development in Brazil sought to scrutinize what would be the obstacles to change, the so-called traditional and archaic characteristics of the country's political culture that would be delaying the development of modern society (Moreira, 1970, p. 33 and 40). These *modernization theories* would explain how the establishment of democracy was linked to the minimization of class differences, an objective that could be achieved through economic growth and state provisions for the benefit of the most vulnerable social groups. "A large middle class," U.S. sociologist Seymour M. Lipset argued, "plays a mitigation role in moderating conflict since it is able to reward moderate and democratic parties and penalize extremist groups" (1959, p. 71). The cornerstone of such a systematization was to propose a program of social change that could avoid authoritarian and totalitarian risks (Gilman, 2003; Latham, 2000).

Modernization theories were, in this sense, based on Keynesian theories of planning and investment of private and state capital, which would make it possible to guarantee, as its ulterior aspect, new levels of political participation and citizenship (Hamby, 1972, p. 663). However, in contrast to the interwar period, with the expansion of the administrative state as a new governance structure, the anti-totalitarian struggle of the Cold War was a signal of the liberal suspicion with such governance. Accordingly, despite the Keynesian consensus of the 1950s, state intervention was organized in a fundamental task of political *stabilization*, favoring, in particular, the protection of individual freedoms (Kornhauser, 2015; Brinkley, 1995). This was due to the discovery of a new dimension of experience – of anxiety, guilt, and corruption, which liberals, such as Arthur Schlesinger (1949), were developing in face of the totalitarian phenomena.

Training technical and political elites became a fundamental part of such an effort. These elites should be capable of producing information, diagnoses, and intervention strategies, favoring a competent interference in the public sphere through direct and indirect public administration "autarchies" as well as mixed and publicly owned companies. They also should favor a legal discipline concerning individual enterprises and freedoms, especially through *police power*, the legal instrument responsible for the balance between the state-individual binomial, as well as equip the executive branch with normative powers and modernize the legislative branch's functions and routine (which are the themes of Chapters 2 and 3). In Brazil, to a certain extent, modernization theories strengthened the tendencies of the interwar constitutional revision by maintaining the directive role of the Federal Government, thus remaking the federative pact stipulated by the 1946 Constitution, under the form of *municipalism*. In the Law of Things, specifically the ends of property, the central institute of industrial capitalism, this renewed use of property has become an exemplary issue in Brazilian legal order. While, in the 1891 Constitution, the individual's will could shape the real content of property, the doctrinal evolution since 1930 was devoted to transforming it into "an appropriate instrument at the service of man, his development, and his integration into society."

> Exacerbated individualism made man a slave to property, considered as an end and not as a means. The democratization of property, which means its proletarianization and humanization, intends to invert the data of materialism and make property a means of liberation and complete fulfillment of man. True individualism is that which does not sacrifice society in the interests of the person or group, but which makes society and goods the means to attend to the full development of the human person, on the material and spiritual plane. The evolution of property and its new dimensions are elements that present an important contribution to achieving this desideratum, which is an imposition for the safeguarding of our western and Christian culture, in whose spirit our law has lived and will always live.
>
> (Wald, 1966, p. 13–14)

In the post-World War II era, the expansion of the state's capabilities and roles corresponded to the Cold War framework of modernization theories, therefore, due to their assumptions of rationalism and scientific and technical expertise as safeguards for a democratic foundation (Gilman, 2003). Moreover, as previously mentioned, this rationale ended up leading to a crisis in the legal profession, since it could not follow the same steps of modern development in Brazil as in the United States (Garth, 2000; Dezalay and Garth, 2002). This was consistent with the shift from the normative function – the action of disciplining social life – from the legislative to the executive branch. Indeed, the executive branch expanded its domain through the administrative field, modernizing its foundations due to the administrative and economic technocracy and the trained elites who mastered such competencies, and who then began to operationalize the legislative function in decrees, regulations, ordinances, resolutions, and shortly after the 1964 coup, decree-laws, thus being able to dispense with the normative role of the Brazilian National Congress. In other words, the law had become an instrument of this state technocracy, especially linked to the executive branch; law and lawyers served Brazilian modernization only in its technical dimension (Gomes, 1974).

The empowerment of the executive branch could also, according to these ideas, respond to the inability of the normative effort by Congress to discipline social life. Legal elites interpreted that the legislative performance of the executive branch could overcome the "slow" and "laborious" process of liberal democracy, in particular concerning the work of the legislative branch. Here, once again, the issue of time in modernity came to play a fundamental role. Since the Federal Government was the major actor in the organization of the economic order, it could embrace the time between the measurement of a new social dynamic and the action of disciplining it. Delegating the normative responsibilities could then shorten the many processes between the formulation of a legal discipline and its approval by Congress, furthermore favoring political legitimacy.

However, as previously observed, the moral parameter to guide this modernization of the state – subjected to duties and rights and to the law, as well as separated into harmonious and independent powers – imposed limits to this expansion of the executive branch and its administrative functions. The modernization of legal orders in the Cold War, particularly based on a sophisticated and hegemonic U.S. strategy, sought to balance the concept of the rule of law between social justice, on the one hand, and the safeguards and rights of the individual, on the other; in other words, between an expanded and efficient action on the part of public authority and the maintenance of political order against authoritarianism. As Orozimbo Nonato, then Minister of the Federal Supreme Court, argued:

> What is now up to him [the jurist] is to give solidity to the "rule of law" – liberal, yes, but not so much that it exacerbates the evil of deep inequalities but rather establishes the balance between political equality and social equality.
>
> (1958, p. 8)

Rule of law and socialist legality

In Latin America and the so-called Third World, the normative function advocated for the executive branch involved a new definition of the rule of law concept. In this new definition, legal elites around the world could find in the International Commission of Jurists (ICJ) a fundamental *locus* of intellectual articulation. The commission's sophisticated work paved the way for an accommodation of the demands of modernization in the post-colonial world and the "underdeveloped" nations of Latin America. Indeed, the international legal elites gathered around the ICJ (its Congresses, meetings, publications) spread the premises of the rule of law to encompass different forms of law throughout the world (Tolley, 1994).

The legal order to be adopted in these countries and especially in the "Third World," which was more broadly aimed at defining "state-building" (Bu, 1999; 2003; Guilhot, 2005, p. 104), had quickly become one of the major fields of the Cold War dispute. In October 1946, in Paris, jurists and lawyers from 24 countries gathered to form, under the leadership of jurists connected to the French resistance, the Mouvement National Judiciare around an anti-fascist and anti-racist agenda. Moreover, such elites welcomed the self-determination aspirations of countries in Africa and Asia that were emerging from the colonial yoke, which posed difficulties to the United States (Pruden, 1998; Moyn, 2018, p. 110). The International Association of Democratic Lawyers (IADL) was thus received with enthusiasm by an international legal community, which established a network of national offices around the world, including in Brazil.[14] Attorneys Joe Nordmann and Martin Popper were elected to the General Secretariat and René Cassin, then vice-president of the Conseil d'Etat, was chosen to chair the association. They led the association's work in tandem with the United Nations (UN) mission to restore, defend, and develop democratic freedoms, as well as to remove all traces of fascism from the legal field. Such support gave the organization the status of a UN *consultative body*, which not only legitimized its work but also made it a participant in the planning of international law by the UN (Tolley, 1994; Van Dal, 1955, p. 1).

The conformity of the IADL to the United Nations mission was based on the denunciation of the problem posed, to international peace and stability, by the White House's foreign policy with the Marshall Plan and the Truman Doctrine, as well as with McCarthyism. These would be expressions of a fascism which, according to IADL's formulations, was being developed in the United States. In this sense, the IADL positioned itself on the following international fronts: (1) suppression of human and civil rights in the United States (persecution of the Communist Party, anti-labor legislation, fascist political life); (2) aggressive war preparations, based on the atomic monopoly; and (3) support for neo-Nazi elements by occupational authorities in Germany. Although not initially known, the association's positions were informed by Comintern's criticisms of U.S. political life, which underpinned a broader agenda of cultural programs organized by the Kremlin, such as World Peace Congresses (Van Dal, 1955, p. 80; Staar, 1991; Koch, 2004).

At the same time, the International Association approached the "colonized and dependent peoples" of Asia, Africa, and Latin America, advocating that their state of oppression and struggle was a challenge to world peace. Therefore, the association appealed for support to "democratic lawyers" around the world. The agenda and appeal to such countries, which included a "racial" debate,[15] became permanent with the creation of a Vice President seat for a representative of these regions, filled in 1952 by Henrique Fialho, a judge at the Court of Justice of the Federal District of Brazil. The country would thereby have one of the most active branches of the International Association of Democratic Lawyers (Van Dal, 1955, p. 24).

Accordingly, the organization offered the premises of *socialist legality*, a legal technique for the realization of socialism that was opposed to the rule of law. Commenting on Soviet jurists, San Tiago Dantas (1958, p. 15) reflected that:

> What characterizes socialist legality, and makes it possible to differentiate it from democratic legality, is that it subjects individuals and administrative bodies of the state to the supremacy of law, but not the government, represented, in the Soviet Union, by the Councils of the Soviets, by their "Presidium" or permanent commission, and by the Council of Ministers. There is nothing inexplicable in this independence of the socialist government from the law. In this conception, the law is nothing more than a technique for the realization of socialism, and the dynamic process of this realization has its organ in the Party and in the government, which interpret and execute the class dictatorship. To suppose that the government can abdicate some decision or measure, when it seems justified as a promotion of the common good, that is, of socialism because there exists, on the contrary, a previous legal norm would be to make a law not a means, but an end, and to deny the government agency the ability to enunciate, in an absolute manner, the interest of society. In such a case, it is up to the government to reform the law and already apply the new solution to the specific case, which it intends to regulate. [....] This is the radical difference between socialist law, conceptualized as a simple instrument of political action by a government, the absolute interpreter of the common good, and democratic law, conceptualized as an instrument of the common good and therefore placed above governments, which considers its interpreters fallible and occasional.

The activism of the International Association of Democratic Lawyers, however, was calling the attention of the U.S. foreign policy establishment. A select group of lawyers in the American Bar Association (ABA) – including John J. McCloy, the "Chairman," a Harvard-trained lawyer and High Commissioner for Occupied Germany (Bird, 1992), and Allen Dulles, a lawyer who graduated from George Washington University, chairman of the Council on Foreign Relations, and the second in command of the CIA (Kinzer, 2013) – organized a reaction.

An International Congress of Jurists held in West Berlin in 1952, under the leadership of anti-communist Theo Friedenau, sparked this reaction spearheaded by McCloy himself and the U.S. delegation present at the event, secretly funded by the CIA (Tolley, 1994, p. 34). At the meeting, legal elites from around the world proceeded to conduct what would be a trial, based on the criminal principles established by the International Court of Nuremberg, of the "system of injustice" enacted by Soviet communism. Eleven jurists exiled from the Eastern Bloc, representing the delegations of Eastern European countries, fulfilled the function of testifying and thus "factually" attesting the horrors of communism, so as not only to revive the trials of the war crimes courts but also bring Nazi-fascism and communism together in the same explanatory anchor: totalitarianism (ICJ, 1952). In a sense, it was the same strategy as Arthur Koestler's 1949 book *The God that Failed*, a collection of essays testifying the failure of the Soviet system and its totalitarian implications – a strategy U.S. intelligence was developing mostly through the Congress for Cultural Freedom (Saunders, 1999, p. 63).

At the end of the following year, the U.S. delegation, with the support of the CIA, reorganized this effort into a new organization, the International Commission of Jurists. Replacing the old leadership structure established for the meeting in Germany and the openly anti-communist approach it engendered, particularly by Friedenau, the ICJ started to gather international legal elites into a noblesse oblige, in the name of a "democratic and peaceful" international order. The structuring effort of the commission, in line with the apparatus of modernization theories, was to conceive an expanded rule of law concept, thus removing "Third World" and "underdeveloped" countries from the risk of totalitarianism. Indeed, in some African countries, the national sections of the ICJ exercised the function of a Bar Association, a starting point for the structuring of the judiciary branches in these countries (Tolley, 1994).

This expansion of the rule of law concept took place, throughout the 1950s and part of the 1960s, in the main publications and the international congresses that the commission organized in defense of the control of the executive by the judiciary branch, stipulating the strict independence of the latter and the protection of defense lawyers (ICJ, 1954). It also stipulated the structure of a system of administration of justice for "proper treatment" to protect the dignity of the individual against authoritarian governments (Marsh, 1957; 1958); the coordination between civil, political, and social rights, embracing material demands, especially from the "Third World" (Lalive, 1959; Rodríguez-Garavito, 2011, p. 58); and, finally, the equalization of the rule of law concept with the Universal Declaration of Human Rights (Lalive, 1960; ICJ, 1961) and the *naturalization* of both as an unequivocal destiny of Western society (Cassin, 1963). In a summoning tone and based on optimism in humanity's capacity for realization, jurist René Cassin, a member of the French Council of State and one of the main articulators of the Universal Declaration of Human Rights (Sluga, 2011), stated:

> To proclaim a great common purpose – repression of the instinct to violence and the elimination of all arbitrary action within different social groups, including States, and in their relations with one another, under the aegis of rules of law to which proper respect is paid, under the protection of a social order conducive both to the dignity and security of man and at the same time to social advance; this is the broad foundation on which jurists, sociologists and practicing lawyers from the old and the new nations, with their diversity of political and social institutions, can bring their ideas into closer accord and map out converging lines of action ... If however indignation and enthusiasm are needed to fire the hearts of those who mean to help build a better world for mankind, the apostles of the Rule of Law must not hesitate to gird themselves with the triple bronze of which the poet sang, to face with lucidity each of the arduous obstacles barring the way to the full realization of law. The miner delves painfully in the dark galleries of the earth for coal to warm mankind. And it is in climbing the rugged escarpments that the pioneer blazes the path to the sunlit heights.
>
> (Cassin, 1963, p. 224 and 242)

The International Commission of Jurists embodied the modernization of legal systems in the Cold War, offering a response to industrialization and urbanization as well as the crisis of positive law. A sophisticated contrast, based on the liberal tradition of the rule of law, was developed against socialist legality. As the generating principle in socialist legality, the government's normative and disciplinary action was given primacy and, thus, a secure direction for the challenge of the rapid processes of economic and social transformation in the 20th century.

This moral, anti-totalitarian mark is present in Brazilian legal thought. Indeed, since the beginning of the ICJ's activities, important figures took part in the commission's work, such as Antonio Ferreira Cesarino Júnior and José Thomaz Nabuco, who, in 1952, was the Vice-President of the ICJ. The creation of the Brazilian headquarters in Rio de Janeiro, in 1957, after a visit by the ICJ's general-secretary at the time, A. J. M. Van Dal, was another important movement in this sense.[16] José Thomaz Nabuco was appointed general secretary of the Rio headquarters, and Levy Carneiro president.[17] In addition, new members included Raul Fernandes, João Neves da Fontoura, Hildebrando Accioli, Prudente de Moraes Neto, San Tiago Dantas, Plínio F. Guimarães, Chermont de Brito, Geraldo Silva, and Afonso Arino de Melo Franco. The renewal of the positive order was supported by the International Commission of Jurists and was intended to present a more appropriate harmonization between the disciplinary action of the law and the evolution of social phenomena under modernity.

Despite such an apparatus, which we are going to analyze further, the irresolution of the precise formula of this renewed conceptualization of the rule of law would remain until 1964. Indeed, a significant part of the jurists involved with the ICJ would support the coup in 1964. The legitimacy of the coup, I argue, could rely on another U.S. front regarding Brazilian modernization. The Civil-Military coup was "justified" as not representing a rupture of democracy in Brazil, but rather an anti-totalitarian political action capable of carrying out this profound cultural redefinition of the country, despite *compressing* individual guarantees. Van Dal, on his visit to Brazil in 1956, questioned by a journalist about the ICJ's work in the fight against totalitarianism, made a curious appropriation of the concept, advancing the premise on which the dictatorship would be articulated in the country: in certain cases, the *compression* of fundamental rights was justified in the name of *secure modernization* – without ruptures of the order:

> In general, yes [the ICJ intervened against all totalitarianism, be they fascists, Nazis, or communists]. We aim to bring together all the free jurists in the world against violations of law and freedom. But certain types of non-permanent totalitarianisms are sometimes necessary [....][18]

The modernization of positive law and *legislative inflation*: from the technocratic coup to the human dimension

In early 1976, the journal *Arquivos*, linked to the Ministry of Justice, published the article *Considerações gerais sobre o projeto de Código Civil*, written by Miguel Reale. The author discussed Bill No. 634, proposed by a commission of lawyers led by Reale himself, and completed in the previous year, to renew the Civil Code, the country's most important written law, developed 60 years earlier by Clóvis Beviláqua. Stimulated by the Ernesto Geisel administration (1974–1979), the bill was an ambitious attempt to entirely restructure private relations in the country. To support the justification of the new project, Miguel Reale recalled that Beviláqua's Code had been produced in the twilight of civilization and a markedly "individualistic" culture, influenced by a "patriarchal" mentality, typical of the "pre-industrial" phase that would characterize the country at the beginning of the 20th century. Thus, the jurist indicated the fundamental aspect of the project: overcoming "extreme" liberalism and "patriarchalism."[19] Completing his defense of the new code, Reale was also responding to a question naturalized as inescapable to legal thinking of that time: in the face of dramatic advances in electronics and the automation of "societies in constant transmutation," was it "a propitious time for codification?"[20]

Miguel Reale proceeded to explain that the concept of code should not be linked to the idea of a law destined to last for centuries, as lawyers such as Alfredo Lamy Filho, for example, denounced. For Lamy Filho, one of the major Brazilian commercial law experts, it was actually unthinkable, in those transition times, for so much energy to be available for discussing the reformulation of the codes, as had been occurring since the end of World War II, particularly after the 1964 coup. The "acceleration of the pace of history" would otherwise require the existence of a permanent study group, responsible for the task "of clearing the legal paths of development" (Lamy Filho, 1970, p. 12; 1976). Reale indicated, in his response to positions such as that of Lamy, that the question of renewing the codes was different, although it was the same concept of time that made sense to him: codifying meant enlacing a consciousness of the present in accordance with the foreseeable future, relating the most living traditions of national law to what should be, over time, the product of labor. The jurist was following a path that he had developed more than a decade earlier. In line with Hegel's idealistic philosophy, the jurist had stated, at a conference on August 11, 1960, at the University of São Paulo Law School, that:

> [...] the difficult, the serious in law is not only to ensure what has already been achieved, but also, without prejudice to what has been achieved, to guarantee the constitutive freedom of the spirit in its projections for unforeseen historical attacks. Law will always be a bidirectional entity: a look towards the past, in defense of what has become a positive asset in history; another look unveiling the future to protect the endless possibilities of the human person.
>
> (Reale, 1961, p. 34)

In other words, the development of a code was based, for Reale, on the need to produce a meaning, in a large sense and for a determined, transitory period, for the country's development. This did not mean impeding the changes that the country would suffer but establishing the national order under secure and stable support. The project, therefore, was offering discipline to the dramatic changes of the social order under this new temporal regime and a correction to the exacerbated liberalism that would have been historically founded in Brazil. For this reason, as Reale stated, the question of the new Civil Code was to produce a new order for the "protection of the values of subjectivity [...] placing people's values at the foundation of the legal system." Nevertheless, these values should not be intrinsic to it. Otherwise, the value of the person had to be linked to the collective interest. Jurists should not be interested in an isolated individual, pure abstraction, but rather one situated, integrated into its circumstances (Reale, 1976, p. 3, 4, 9, and 12).[21]

Reale's bill was in keeping with post-World War II legal thinking. Such an understanding can be exemplarily found in another jurist, Haroldo Valladão, who argued in defense of the transformation of the "lack of public spirit" – the "love" for the public sphere – in Brazilian political life. This diagnosis would find its terms precisely in the "individualist mentality" of liberalism. The transformation of political behavior should then be sought in the foundation of a national culture based on "social" democracy, but keeping the centrality of Christian morality (Valladão, 1962). That was the meaning to the Brazilian elites of the 1964 "Revolution," which would assume, according to Arnold Wald, the motives of 1930 "Revolution," which were lost in the "demagogy" and the "paternalism" of Vargas' Estado Novo:[22] the fight against electoral fraud, institutional failures, the disintegration of a system of values and norms caused, according to Francisco Campos, by the increase in "social substance" but "without the volume and complexity of the government growing in proportion" (1941, p. 175). To those elites, the 1964 "Revolution," therefore, intended to put an end to this long process of political adaptation by establishing the Social State through authoritarian rule, or, in other words, by putting into effect an institutional complex capable of creating and applying various techniques to control the physical and social environment while guaranteeing the adequacy of the norms to the social phenomena (Wald, 1965, p. 567).

Therefore, the Civil Code Project presented in the mid-1970s was the result of a broader debate that had been established, since at least the second half of the 1950s, on what had become the "urgent" and "unavoidable" task of reformulating and updating Brazilian positive law. As expressed in the legal debate, the expansion, since 1930, of the normative functions of the Federal Government and even of the work of the National Congress – efforts that tried to discipline the social phenomena which overlapped and were surpassed by the accelerated rhythm of time in modernity – ended up constituting sparse, disorderly, antinomic, and excessively numerous legislations (Horta, 1963).

In February 1961, at the request of President Jânio Quadros, the Ministry of Justice and Interior Affairs, Oscar Pedroso d'Horta, began studies for the national legislation, as well as the evaluation of projects to renew the country's codes and federal laws that had already been drafted but were still not evaluated or approved. A few months later, on June 20, the Quadros administration (1961) signed Decree No. 51,005 creating, within the Ministry of Justice, a Code Reform Service and a Legislative Studies Commission to systematize and carry out these efforts to modernize positive law and form a permanent service for examining government bills.[23]

> [...] the implementation of the great work required, from the beginning, difficult and time-consuming studies [....] These complicated preliminary works were carried out by an admirable team of civil servants from the Secretary of State, under the direction and enlightened supervision of the illustrious Professor Alberto da Rocha Barros [...] which resulted in the establishment of the legal field to be reformulated and the creation of the Code Reform Service and Legislative Studies Commission.
>
> (Horta, 1963, p. 33–34)

Nonetheless, Quadros' resignation and the adoption of Constitutional Amendment No. 4 in September of that year, which instituted a parliamentarian regime in Brazil, put the theme of the renewal of the positive order on hold – despite the attempt by then Minister Alfredo Nasser to restructure the Code Reform Service with Decree No. 917, of April 1962. Still under the parliamentary system, this interregnum for the reform was ended by the Minister of Justice and Interior Affairs, João Mangabeira. The minister in fact expanded and systematized the scope of the reform, by defining, in a conclusive way, the service and devoting to it the methodology to be adopted to accomplish the task. Decree No. 1,490, of November 1962, institutionalized this agenda, effectively stipulating the following organization of work:

I The Penal Code and the Law on Criminal Misdemeanors was assigned to Minister Nelson Hungria;
II The Criminal Procedure Code was assigned to Professor Hélio Tornaghi;
III The Penal Executions Code was assigned to Professor Roberto Lyra;
IV The Civil Code was assigned to Professor Orlando Gomes;
V The Code of Obligations was assigned to Professors Caio Mário da Silva Pereira, Alfredo Lamy Filho, and Sylvio Marcondes;
VI The Law of Introduction to the Civil Code and the Law of Obligations were assigned to Professor Haroldo Valladão;
VII The Civil Procedure Code was assigned to Professor Alfredo Buzaid;
VIII The Navigation Code was assigned to Professor Edgardo de Castro Rebello;
IX The Labor Code was assigned to Evaristo de Morais Filho;
X The Labor Judicial Code was assigned to Professor Mozar Victor Russomano;
XI The Code of Minors was assigned to Professor Noé Azevedo;
XII The Federal Accounting Code was assigned to Professor Carlos José de Assis Riberto;
XIII The Military Penal Code and the Military Criminal Procedure Code were assigned to Professor Ivo d'Aquino Fonseca (Campos, 1972; Horta, 1963).[24]

Francisco Luiz Cavalcanti Horta, then Executive Secretary of the Code Reform Service, predicted in mid-1963 that, in one year, all preliminary drafts would be concluded, pointing out that the legislative reform "without equal in our country, and probably in the world" would be concluded soon (1963, p. 38). The path indicated by Horta would be followed, but the process of approving the new codes was interrupted by the 1964 coup. Yet, even considering those who opposed the codification effort, such as Lamy Filho or Caio Tácito,[25] the renewal of the positive order was a consensus among the country's legal elites. Thus, shortly after the coup, the newly "elected" president, Humberto de

Alencar Castello Branco, instructed his Minister of Justice, Milton Campos, to take on the task of managing the plan for renewing the positive order. According to Campos, the task was part of the wide modernization intended by the Castello Presidency.

> Now, President Castello Branco has repeatedly said that the Revolution, represented by him in the government, has a commitment to reforms that must be kept. Not reforms for the simple pleasure of reforming, or for the unpatriotic purpose of inciting unrest [....] But reforms demanding the improvement of Brazilian democracy, by our desire for social, economic, and political progress, by the imperative for the people's welfare, which constitute the dominant objective of the modern state.
>
> (1972, p. 198)

In August 1967, shortly after Arthur da Costa e Silva assumed the Presidency, the Commission for the Coordination and Review of the Codes Project was created, chaired by Alfredo Buzaid (under whose guidance, the Penal, Military Penal, Military Criminal Procedure, and Military Judicial Organization Codes were converted into laws).[26] The discussion about the other codes, however, did not progress until the Costa e Silva administration adopted Decree No. 64,416, of April 1969. Resuming the initiative proposed by the Quadros administration, the decree recreated, as a member of the Ministry's "consultative and deliberative bodies," the Legislative Studies Commission, which would be responsible for "elaborating draft codes, complementary laws, ordinary laws, while also being responsible for issuing an opinion on bills in progress in the National Congress."[27] The commission, with more extensive and permanent tasks regarding the country's legislative life, absorbed the duties of the former Commission for the Coordination and Review of the Codes Project and replaced those responsible for some of the projects (Buzaid, 1974) – presumably lawyers closest to the "Revolution" agenda, such as Miguel Reale (Machado, 2015).

After the coup, this way of conceiving the renewal of the positive order was based, in general, on what Reale had argued regarding the rules of private relations in the Civil Code, namely, on the tutelage of subjectivity, allowing the overcoming of the liberalism of the "autonomy of the will." In other words, it was founded on a legal order by which individual enterprise would be naturally bound to the collective interest and which, furthermore, would organize a normative production in accordance with the "acceleration of history." This was, for instance, precisely Haroldo Valladão's justification for his *Lei geral de aplicação das normas jurídicas* (General Law for the Application of Legal Rules), when advocating the need to establish, in Brazil, just and equitable solutions to the contemporary processes, so that the law would meet "the interests of all and not that of some or small groups, expanding, more and more, to protect the weak, the humble, those who are still on the periphery of our legal order" (1964, p. 11). These ideas were also structuring aspects of the 1967 Constitution and of Constitutional Amendment No. 1, 1969, which reformed it. The 1964 coup, therefore, in the words of those who interrupted the democratic order in 1964, gave a fundamental role to the *legislative policy* of the new regime: to adapt legal institutions to the principles of the "Revolution," which involved correcting the laissez-faire culture. According to then Minister of Justice, Alfredo Buzaid, the positive laws, contingent on political life, were not conceived arbitrarily, but for the "realization of the common good." It was what the Minister alluded to, in a lecture in 1971, at one of the most important intellectual and military institutions of the country, the Brazilian War College:

> In fact, the Revolution did not consist only in overthrowing João Goulart's leftist government, maintaining all the institutions, old political customs, and myths from a priori ideas. It emerges as a philosophy of life, a political doctrine, a new economy, a conception of law. That is why it cannot exclude any area of thought from its reforming mission [....] The Revolution is therefore aware that, to achieve its objectives, it will have to revise the legislation, correcting its defects, filling in the gaps, and replacing it totally or partially, when it no longer adapts to the needs of the people [....]
>
> The Revolution needs to legislate. Law is not just the voice that conveys its desires; it is especially the consolidation of ideas. In establishing the new legal system, the Revolution not only made material progress, in line with development policy, but also moral progress, dignifying the human person. Political, economic, and social transformations have a constant influence on the evolution of law [....] Before the triumph of the Revolution, the influence was partial and moderate. The codes were maintained since they were subject to successive mutilations. Dozens of laws changed their rules, institutes, and perhaps their structure. And the codes began to lose unity and systematicity.
>
> After the triumph, the Revolution returns to the democratic idea of development [....] "To ensure progress," notes Ripert, "it is necessary to continually reform traditional law. An aristocracy can defend and preserve; democracy must inevitably conquer and develop. Hence the incessant transformation of law under the impetus of the democratic idea." Under this inspiration, the revolutionary ideal is sublimated. The new legislation will thus translate what it has already done and what it has already designed and is currently being implemented.
>
> (Buzaid, 1971, p. 9; 13–14)

The second half of the 1960s is fundamentally marked by the promulgation of a great number of laws, decree-laws, decrees, ordinances, and regulations, which came within the scope of the broad national modernization program. In other words, this debate, which had dragged on since the 1950s, by renewing positive law as a way of equating the time of the law to social phenomena, came to an end with the reform of legislative policy under the authoritarian rule. Initially, Castello Branco's measures proceeded to a gradualist plan of economic stabilization in the short term, with contractionary fiscal and monetary policies to combat inflation. Castello not only counted on financial assistance from the U.S. government but also, controlling the political environment, established a new policy on wages and salaries (Dreifuss, 1981; Trubek, 1971). For the modernization of the country's economic and commercial structure, more than 10,000 laws were approved between 1964 and 1970, following the understandings surrounding the Government Economic Action Program (PAEG), created by Roberto Campos and Otávio Gouveia de Bulhões, respectively Ministers of Planning and Economy under Castello Branco. Most of these laws were approved by decree-laws issued by the executive branch, dispensing with the action of Congress.

The PAEG's modernization program was based on a broad program of structural reforms. This included a codification of Tax Law which transformed a mix of revenue devices into an instrument of economic development, by allowing an increase in the state's revenues and investment capacity. It also included an entirely new system of housing, banking, and market financing, opening the way for industrial economic growth with private capital (Trubek, 1971; Briso Neto, 2008; Penholato, 2017). This profound reorganization of the economic and commercial order can be illustrated in the list of measures adopted at that time:

- Law 4,726, of June 13, 1965, and its regulation, of January 19, 1966, restructured the Commercial Boards, abolishing the merchant registration institute, a remnant of "medieval corporatism";
- Law 4,595, of December 31, 1964, offered a complete reformulation of banking institutions, creating the National Monetary Council (CMN) and the Central Bank (BC), bodies of the national financial system. The same law, in Art. 9, gave the BC regulatory powers, with the task of establishing rights and obligations in financial matters. BC Resolution No. 39 was responsible for the modernization of the Stock Exchange in the legal form of civil associations;
- Law 4,728, of July 14, 1965, placed the capital market under the discipline of the CMN and the supervision of the BC and stipulated rules for corporate law and obligations. Furthermore, in the capital market, the law changed the legal regime for public limited companies, in an attempt to encourage the population to purchase securities (taking North American modeling as a reference), and reformulated concepts of private law, including fiduciary alienation, anchored in the institute of trust, which was peculiar to Anglo-American law;
- Decree-Law 254, of February 28, 1967, instituted the new Industrial Property Code to stimulate its power of creation, organization, and invention;

- Decree 57,595, of January 7, 1966, created a uniform law on checks, according to the Geneva Convention, of 1931;
- Decree 57,663, of January 24, 1966, created a uniform law on bills of exchange and promissory notes;
- Decree-Law 73, of November 23, 1966, instituted the National Private Insurance System;
- Law 5,172, of October 25, 1966, instituted the National Tax System, later renamed National Tax Code (Barreto Filho, 1967).

In sum, the dictatorship put into motion, from the executive branch, a profound modernization of the Brazilian institutional order.

However, it was precisely this great legislative agenda carried out by the Castello Branco administration that Brazilian jurists began to criticize, borrowing a term from the Italian Francesco Carnelluti: "legislative inflation," or "legislative elephantiasis," "legislative healer" – to the extent that such a healer, unaware of law as a practice besides its technical function, made laws in large numbers, in a disorderly, erroneous manner and to the detriment of social organization. Indeed, such criticism was directed at a technocracy that, not knowing the system of national ordering (in its hierarchical and organic principle), produced chaotic legislation, threatening the so-called legal security of the country (Silva, 1968).

> In the three years of the revolutionary government, the lawful process in our country had an unusual pace. It seems that the government desired to reform all national legislation from top to bottom and through it, the whole nation [....] The "Official Diaries" were referring to laws and decrees on the most varied subjects, in an inflation only comparable to that of the paper money issues; and the editions of the final days of the revolutionary government, constituted, as it were, truly special collections of legislation.
>
> (Nunes, 1967, p. 347)

This sense of legislative inflation was not a consensual issue for lawyers. There were those who understood it as a "natural consequence" of the rapid development of the country, such as David M. Trubek from the United States Agency for International Development. Despite the recognition of an apparent legislative inflationism, the confusion, and the potential if not real legal insecurity in those years, the whole process would be inherent in underdeveloped countries in a frank developmental process. It was a "natural step" in the transition to the stages of economic and social (and political) life of the (industrialized) capitalist center, represented by the Global North, particularly the United States (Ramos, 1967; Trubek, 1966). In the framework of U.S. international aid for the country, systematized by the Alliance for Progress and supported by the premises of modernization theory, it had become essential, according to Trubek (1966), for an elite group of lawyers to be formed in order to deal with new institutes of commercial law, such as the law on capital markets and on monetary correction. This elite group would join economists and administrators in favor of developmentalism.

This was also the defense made by the University of São Paulo professor Oscar Barreto Filho, in a seminar sponsored by the Debate Forum of the Roberto Simonsen Institute in April 1967. Barreto Filho (1967) argues that the legislative fertility, in Brazil, stemmed from developmentalism, demanding the adaptation of "old structures" to the new national reality. As a whole, one could identify in the country, according to the jurist, what one of the great advocates of modernization theories and advisor to John F. Kennedy, Walt Whitman Rostow, named a *take-off* in his famous 1960s book *The Stages of Economic Growth: an anti-communist manifesto*. The technological evolution of industry and agriculture would bring about changes in the economic structure, which, consequently, would impact the social and political structure of the community. To put it another way, Rostow's work, from the same anti-totalitarian anchor established by a transnational intellectuality, pointed out, as described in modernization theories, the defense of developmentalism as a condition for political maturity and democracy. However, here one could find the authoritarian facet of U.S. "technocosmopolitanism" in its view of modernization theory in the late 1950s and 1960s: to achieve the *end* of political maturity, the *means* – the *transition* – could involve authoritarianism (Gilman, 2003, p. 185–186; Cancelli, 2017).

Nevertheless, even among those who supported the regime established by the 1964 coup, there was criticism of the authoritarian rule's legislative policy. These critics included, for example, Arnold Wald (1965) and Orlando Gomes (1974), other important commercial law specialist in the country, who questioned the reason for that veritable "tetralogy of legal codes" in Brazil, which was especially seen with the Institutional Acts and, shortly afterward, with the 1967 Constitution.[28] Despite the positive view of the 1964 coup, which would be inspiring for the "organization of a new society," the lawyer argued that the legislative attitude of an economic technocracy, which had been formulating laws without knowledge of the constitutional system, ended up putting the security of the national order on hold. As one of its consequences, it was responsible for throwing the lawyer into a "labyrinth of laws," suppressing, after all, his function of disciplining social life. In these terms, it was necessary to return to the ethics of a development law (a "new law"), supported by the thesis, widely disseminated by the French philosopher Raymond Aron, which distinguished "simple" economic growth – the agenda of an immediate technocracy, according to Wald (1967) – from development, or modernization.

In his *Trois essais sur l'age industriel* (1966), Aron, who came to Brazil in 1962 and was also enthusiastic about the Brazilian dictatorship, advocated for "a rationalized administration and legislation, the diffusion of education, the recruitment of businessmen and the formation of necessary investment capital" to achieve a fully modern and industrial society, including a new national culture or mentality (Wald, 1967, p. 422). These would be inescapable factors for the establishment of democratic regimes, of democratization via modernization, as Aron and other intellectuals present at the Congress for Cultural Freedom defended, and which the Brazilian regime should implement (Cancelli, 2012, p. 131).

The ideas developed by these legal intellectuals began to relate to the "failure" of the technocratic thesis. As stated by San Tiago Dantas in 1955, in defense of a profound renewal of the teaching of law, it would be rare for the administrator not to believe in the usefulness of dictating norms, without having to go through the debate with the Legislative, or even more often, in the willingness of such technicians to act outside legal norms, but following administrative techniques. According to Dantas, law, as a tool for social control, was losing its primacy in favor of a *technique*, less ethical and more efficient, such as in management and economics.

> In the study of legal institutions presented in a system, the sensitivity of social, economic, and political relations is easily lost [....] The system has an autonomous logical and rational value, so to speak. The study we do of it, with strictly deductive methods, leads to self-sufficiency that allows the jurist to turn his back on society and to lose interest in regulated matters, as well as the practical scope of his solutions.
>
> (1955, p. 453)

These technobureaucracy elites, following liberal modernization theses, had fulfilled the broadest organizational and decision-making power in the sphere of the economic public and private order. Such elites would have imposed a *materialist conception* of the problems of political life and, thus, a reduction of "the horizons of human life to mediocre objectives of increasing production and income" (Garcia, 1974, p. 273; Ribeiro, 1976).[29] Twenty years later, the diagnosis proposed by Dantas became the very nucleus where legal ideas found a new legitimacy. Indeed, in the mid-1970s, for instance, Alfredo Lamy Filho defended that jurists should restore their leadership role in the world, to make it more "humane" and "supportive": "the priests of that technological creed, so proud of the secrets of the matter that they have unveiled, or the mastery of their sectorial techniques, respond empty-handed to the calls of a humanity that feels it is losing the meaning of life" (1976, p. 17).

Among jurists, the lack of political virtue in the *technocratic* approach regarding social discipline was also underpinning an inclination to the philosophical dimension of law. The former would be in greater harmony with a constant renewal of law under the "constant transformation" of societies. In the late 1950s, Miguel Reale (1959) argued in defense of such a restoration of an intellectual agenda centered on the philosophy of law: the times demanded a renewal of studies in philosophy, since positive law would no longer account for the "social reality." In its "narrow objectivity," positive law had become incapable – with the change in the structures of Western society due to modernity – of avoiding the "divorce" between social phenomena and the science of law. Years later, as this process of moral decay deepened, Reale, along with intellectuals such as Peter Sorokin and Arnold Toynbee, at the invitation of Richard Schwarz, professor of Pedagogy at the University of Munich, took part in the symposium *Human Existence and the Modern World. An International Symposium on Modern Man's Understanding of Himself.* At the event, authors from different "geographical, cultural and intellectual-ideological backgrounds" stressed that a *common humanity* is the "ground-basis of mutual understanding" (Arnold, 1970). Reale's paper (1970) at the event, *O problema do homem nos países subdesenvolvidos* (*The Problem of Man in Underdeveloped Countries*), dealt with the connection between the "singular" and the "universal" as founding values of modern man. It was these values that were informing what Arnold Wald alluded to when he defended, in opposition to technobureaucracy, a "development law":

> The processes of both laws may be similar, but the purposes are different. For development law, the basic idea is to raise the standard of living for man, guaranteeing his dignity, making, in the words of the Stoics, the man the measure of all things. Although contemporary law, maintaining the positivist method, has refuted the metaphysics of positivism, we cannot deny the existence of a movement for the restoration of natural law as a necessary conditioner of the objective norm. [...] the idea of the validity of the norm in itself loses substance, highlighting the crisis that currently goes through legal positivism.
>
> (1967, p. 424)

By opposing such legal *technicality*, legal elites in Brazil could circumvent legislative inflationism as the proper response to the "revolt of facts against the law" and, at the same time, find a renewed political legitimacy, a moral dimension for law – the value of Man. In other words, as asserted by Wald, the law of technocracy was that of public law, in particular of economic law, of state planning and intervention, separate from "naturalistic principles" and thus different from "development law." Therefore, despite still being based on the same technical plan as economic law (by subjugating individual enterprise), it would have a fundamental theological difference: according to the teachings of Pope Paul VI, it was intended for dignity, human welfare, social welfare, and democracy (Wald, 1970).

Gradually, throughout the 1970s, this moral dimension would signify a certain recovery of the value of the individual as the central dimension in politics, concerning, in particular, a formal egalitarianism and market values (Bolsterman, 2012, Introduction). The New Deal order and the confidence in an activist federal government came rapidly to an end. Empires declined and capitalism spread: it was the birth of globalists and neoliberal transition

(Slobodian, 2018; Brown, 2005, chapter 3). Law's moral precepts, to which Brazilian legal thinking referred, would then gradually encounter the transnational idea of human rights in the 1970s, in its peculiar capacity to congregate the wide range of political discontent that exploded in the period – from state institutions to the most basic aspects of private life. In a sense, human rights offered a renewal of political legitimacy in the face of discredit of modernization theories (Guilhot, 2005, p. 122; Dezalay and Garth, 2002, p. 62) Indeed, progressively, in a complex and nonlinear way, human rights allowed the United States to revive its Cold War activism in the world against the totalitarian threat (Hartmann, 2001), contributing decisively to the end of the Cold War itself (Snyder, 2011).

Regarding Latin America and Brazil, the U.S. National Security Complex – the "integral organic links between state" involving state and civil society, (HOU and Parmar, 2019; Parmar, 2012) – was accordingly undergoing a profound reorientation of its hegemonic project. This new *aggiornamento* offered support to new groups and strategies of political development in the region. Although still based on the strategies of training elites and institutional development, the core assumption of the U.S. strategy became a debate on political decompression, which represented a security process of reestablishing the rule of law in the country. Human rights, as Chapter 5 will demonstrate, through organizations such as the International Commission of Jurists, played a role in this process: it became a tool for denouncing authoritarian rule, especially in its violent dimension, corroding the military's legitimacy and pressing for an orderly conduction of the political transition.

In April 1970, Miguel Seabra Fagundes, in his inaugural speech as President of the Institute of Brazilian Lawyers, would have a say on the criticism of the "Liberal State" and the idea of liberalism. Referring to the French political scientist Georges Burdeau, Seabra Fagundes, in a critical position concerning authoritarian rule and the suppression of individual freedoms in Brazil, argued that what was "outdated" was not "political liberalism," which was "increasingly rooted in the soul of man." In another sense, what was outdated was the "Liberal State," the state of "*laissez faire, laissez aller*, a silent spectator even of the suppression of freedom" (1970, p. 405). Eight years later, in an interview with a newspaper (Faria, 2016), Raymundo Faoro, one of the most vocal opponents of the dictatorship and a negotiator of political transition with the military, argued in defense of the reestablishment of the rule of law in Brazil. However, what for Seabra Fagundes would be a "building process" for Faoro (1978) would already be the political maturity of Brazilian political life concerning the Liberal *versus* Social State: "a liberalism more linked to the people, from whom it had distanced itself." The "pernicious" and "individualist" character of the "old liberalism" had become "new freedoms." Furthermore, what had "saved" liberalism was "its extension to all forces of civil society, which gave it topicality and political awareness."

After an interlude, from the 1930s to the mid-1970s, of disciplining classical liberalism and forging national elites, it was possible to Brazilian elites to establish democratic and liberal forms of political organization.

Notes

1 The checks and balances system stipulated that no individual or political organization could take precedence over another individual or political organization. Each branch is subjected to the same scheme of rules and controls.

2 According to Jellinek (1959, p. 125–128), "if the state is a collective unit, an association, and this unit is not a fiction, but a necessary form of synthesis of our conscience which, like all its facts, forms the basis of our institutions, then such collective units are no less capable of acquiring legal subjectivity than human individuals."

3 Alexandre Parodi argued: "It is in an early stage that private activity can be freely exercised in economic matters: the freedom of commerce and industry is one of the aspects of individual freedom; like other freedoms, it can only be restricted by virtue of the law and is protected by the set of legal guarantees that guarantee individual rights. And then [...] that the principle of freedom of trade and industry forbids the state and its decentralized agencies [...] to intervene, with the exceptional weight of collective resources, in industrial or commercial competition" (1935, p. 20–26; Quoted in Venâncio Filho, 1968, p. 7–8).

4 In the period, legal elites sought to define what would inspire, what would be the shaping forces of law, mindful of the "new civilization" that was born with the modernity of the 20th century. Orozimbo Nonato (1958, p. 9), then Minister of the Federal Supreme Court, who was opposed to the ideas that the economic phenomenon had become the sole, direct, and autonomous cause of all legal norms, argued that "[...] law reflects life, and the whole legal system [...] translates a philosophical thought, realizes a political ideal, and serves an economy. And since the feeling of the just should not yield to impositions of another order, the responsibility of the legislator, wise and advanced, is to avoid a mismatch of rhythms and mitigate that 'revolt of facts against the law,' [...] by Morin [...]"

5 The French Declaration states in Article 1: "Men are born and remain free and equal in rights. Social distinctions may be founded only upon the general good."

6 At that time, analyses on the malaise in the legal field followed as an expression of a broader malaise of civilization. According to Alfredo Lamy Filho (1976, p. 7), "the succession of new facts reaches the legal world and causes concern and perplexity in law students focused [...] on the cult of principles, formulas, and solutions that [...] aspired to eternity."

7 In 1941, on the occasion of the 50th anniversary of the National School of Law, Dantas pronounced these words about the profound changes in modern times and the role to be played in them by the jurist. See Nascimento Silva (1970, p. 15).

8 In the legal debate, the Vargas Regime is initially analyzed as a positive movement, insofar as it had reorganized the country's political structure outside the framework of liberalism; the doctrine, however, would indicate that, in a second moment, specifically with the Estado Novo (1937), the regime "had lost itself." See, for example, Wald (1965).

9 As Samuel Moyn describes (2011, p. 62), this intellectuality linked to the ecumenical movement of Christian realism, which included John Foster Dulles, Reinhold Niebuhr, and Gerhard Ritter, sought "[...] an acknowledgment of moral limitations for and about politics [....] the crucial role of human rights as 'the essential hallmark of Western civilization in contrast to "totalitarian state slavery"' meant a transformation of recent political attitudes and called for a reformulation of conservatism." See also Sabella (2013) and Melis (2003).

10 See also Pope John XXIII's *Pacem in Terris* construction: "[...] the common good 'must take account of all those social conditions which favor the full development of human personality'." Available at: www.vatican.va/content/john-xxiii/en/encyclicals/documents/hf_j-xxiii_enc_11041963_pacem.html. Accessed on: December 15, 2020.

11 "Formalism" refers to the interpretation of the law in an *intrinsic way*, excluding any relation with the broad social phenomena. This perspective is concerned with the interpretation and analysis of the law in accordance with the formal requirements founded by the legal *corpus* itself. See Hespanha (2012, p. 422).

12 Represented mainly by the Brazilian Communist Party, which, however, was made illegal by the administration of Eurico Gaspar Dutra, in April 1947 (Munhoz, 2002).

13 Public diplomacy refers to the set of activities aimed at influencing public opinion. Such activities can be divided into four categories: "International Advocacy" and "Public Affairs"; "Government-Administered Economic Relations"; "Cultural Diplomacy"; and "State-Subsidized International News."

14 In 1951, there were 24 headquarters; in 1954, 33. Among them, the Brazilian Association of Democratic Jurists, located in Rio de Janeiro.

15 In 1956, during his visit to Brazil, Van Dal argued that racial discrimination in the United States could be seen as a form of freedom of expression. Van Dal's justification on the racial issue and the appearance of this theme in the jurist's speech highlighted in the Brazilian media were part of a broader strategy of U.S. intelligence, particularly developed by the USIA. See Cattai (2019).

16 In 1958, 42 Brazilian intellectuals also founded the Brazilian Association of the Congress for Cultural Freedom, the CCF's Brazilian headquarters (Cancelli, 2012, p. 72–73). Van Dal's visit to Brazil occurred in June 1956. The lawyer had already visited Argentina, Uruguay, Guatemala, and Cuba. After Brazil, he would leave for Lima. In April 1961, the CIA coordinated the creation of a headquarters in Ecuador (Agee, 1975, p. 167).

17 Levi Carneiro belonged, also, to the Brazilian Association of the Congress for Cultural Freedom.

18 UMA OPINIÃO. 1956. In *Correio da Manhã*. 2.° Cad. July 7, p. 3. In 1997, on a Brazilian interview show, Roberto Campos, one of the main people responsible for the dictatorship's program to modernize the country's economic order, stated that, at that time, "[...] the choice was between fierce and ideological authoritarianism, which would take [...] years to self-destruct, and right-wing authoritarianism, which was ashamed and embarrassed [...]; the choice was between left-wing authoritarianism and right-wing authoritarianism. And right-wing authoritarianism is much more biodegradable, lasts much less and is less violent than left-wing authoritarianism." In this sense, a transitory "compression" would be necessary to guarantee a secure modernization process. The interview is available at: www.youtube.com/watch?v=8247O1l6QPE. Accessed on: March 6, 2018.

19 The family issue was the most controversial of the Civil Code Project presented by Orlando Gomes. The new code had intended, among other issues, to modify the current legal regime concerning marriage and family law. The opposition to this part of the new code came from Deputy Arruda Câmara, which attracted attention from the national press concerning changes in the "cultural bases of our society and the scale of values that dominate it." See, in this regard, Wald (1969).

20 Here, one can find the revival of an old dispute on the motif of "coding." The "controversy" between jurists Anton Friedrich Justus Thibaut and Friedrich Carl von Savigny, in the 19th century, involved the necessity of producing a general and unified Civil Code for all German states. The former wanted to harmonize positive law with the traditional teachings of rationalistic natural law, thus giving support to the codification of German Law. The latter, who was linked to the renewing movement of romanticism, believed that said code was unnecessary and defended spontaneous law, arising from the "spirit of the peoples," from habits that gradually translate into law, the result of the continuous adaptation of the jurists' knowledge to the constant historical-social changes. On this, see Reale (1961) and Costa (2008, p. 206–207).

21 Reale was in line with his 1968 three-dimensional theory of law, which had a great impact on Brazilian legal thinking. According to the theory, law is composed of the combination of three aspects: facts ("social reality"), values (the values sought by society, as an ideal of Justice), and norms (the validity and organization of the legal system). Thus, the construction of law should take place in a direct relationship between the first two aspects, composing the basis on which the rules would come to be organized. See Cella (2001).

22 This understanding that the Estado Novo broke with the positive initiatives of the "1930 Revolution" was, indeed, common ground to legal elites. In 1943, the *Manifesto dos Mineiros* (Mineiro Manifesto) was based on the "tradition of the people from Minas Gerais, which in the empire would have been expressed with the liberal revolution of 1842, reaffirmed in the ideals based on the institution of the Republic, and inscribed in the Revolution of 1930; however, these ideas had been distorted in the 'present chapter' of Brazilian political life, since it had moved away 'from historical spontaneity and [created the conditions that] transformed it[self] into a simple lever of the fascist government'" (Dutra, 2014, p. 454).

23 See Decree No. 51,005, of 20 July 1961. Available at: www2.camara.leg.br/legin/fed/decret/1960-1969/decreto-51005-20-julho-1961-390625-publicacaooriginal-1-pe.html. Accessed on: February 9, 2020. See also, Wald (1969).

24 In the first half of 1963, some Preliminary Drafts had already been published. Each of them would be printed and distributed to courts, schools of law, councils of the bar association and institutes of lawyers, and associations of the Public Ministry. The suggestions that emerged from this "debate" would be appreciated by the Review Commissions (composed of three members). See also Decreto do Conselho de Ministros No. 1,490, of November 8, 1962. Available at: www2.camara.leg.br/legin/fed/decmin/1960-1969/decretodoconselhodeministros-1490-8-november-1962-352031-publicacaooriginal-1-pe.html. Accessed on: February 10, 2019.

25 Tácito (1971b, p. 409) stated that the function of producing regulations should be questioned, since they would be too static to account for the acceleration of time. However, approaching Reale, he affirmed that it was not a question of denying law, but of reconciling acquired values with the innovations necessary for a society in transformation.

26 Respectively, Decree-Laws 1,004–69, 1,001–69, 1,002–69, and 1,003–69. In addition to these codes, others were approved, as will be mentioned later. Such are the cases, for example, of the Tax Code (Law No. 5,172), the Brazilian Air Code (Decree-Law No. 32), and the Industrial Property Code (Decree-Law No. 254).

27 Decree No. 64,416, of April 28, 1969. Available at: www2.camara.leg.br/legin/fed/decret/1960-1969/decreto-64416-28-abril-1969-405956-publicacaooriginal-1-pe.html. Accessed on: February 9, 2018.

28 Gomes (1974, p. 8) stated that "the national interest in accelerating development has exaggerated, however, the constructive function of law with the adoption of copious technical means and abundant instruments that lead to condemnable nationalization and promote reckless legislative inflation." Regarding Decree-Law 200/1967, which reformed the "public administration," Celso de Mello (2010, p. 156) argues that the decree-law "resents both terminological improprieties and flaws in its systematic purposes, leading one to believe that it was prepared by people with zero or very little legal training, as apparently was the case at the time of the military dictatorship [....]"

29 Manoel Ribeiro argued: "When, however, administration overrides political power, with the formation of technocracy, with the supremacy of technocrats, with a philosophy which is that of not having a philosophy; when administration overrides political power with the formation of a dominant techno-structure, we cannot claim the inversion as healthy. This prevents the development of human values, of political values, subjecting us all to the 'straitjacket' of technocratic solutions, which are often inhumane" (1976, p. 28).

Bibliography

Agee, P. (1975). *Inside the Company: CIA Diary*. Allen Lane: London.

Arnold, W. (1970). "Human Existence and the Modern Word. An international Symposium on modern Man's understanding of himself," *Philosophy and History*, Vol. 3, No. 2, pp. 180–181. https://doi.org/10.5840/philhist19703278

Aron, R. 1966. *Trois essais sur l'age industriel*. Collections Preuves: Plon.

Barreto Filho, O. (1967). "Os novos institutos do Direito Comercial,"*Revista dos Tribunais*, São Paulo, Ano 56, Vol. 382, agosto.

Bessner, D. (2018). *Democracy in Exile: Hans Speier and the Rise of the Defense Intellectual*. Ithaca and London: Cornell University Press.

Bird, K. (1992). *The Chairman: John J. McCloy & the Making of the American Establishment*. New York: Simon & Schuster.

Borstelmann, T. (2012). *The 1970s: A New Global History from Civil Rights to Economic Inequality*. New Jersey: Princeton University Press.

Bresciani, M. S. M. (2005). *O charme da ciência e a sedução da objetividade. Oliveira Vianna entre intérpretes do Brasil*. São Paulo: UNESP.

Brinkley, A. (1995). The End of Reform: New Deal Liberalism in Recession and War. New York: Alfred Knopf.

Briso Neto, J. L. P. (2008). *O conservadorismo em construção: o IPES e as reformas financeiras da Ditadura Militar* (1961–1966). Dissertação de Mestrado. Campinas: Unicamp.

Britto, L. N. (1966). "Legislação e Poder Executivo," *Rev. Dir. Públ. e Ciência Política* – Rio de Janeiro – FGV, Vol. IX, No. 1 – Jan./Mar.

Brown, W. (2005). *Edgework: Critical Essays on Knowledge and Politics.* New Jersey: Princeton University Press.

Bu, L. (1999). "Education Exchange and Cultural Diplomacy in the Cold War," *Journal of American Studies*, Vol. 33. No. 3. http://10.1017/S0021875899006167

______ (2003). *Making the World like US: Education, Cultural Expansion, and the American Century*. New York: Praeger.

Busetto, A. (2002). *A democracia cristã no Brasil: princípios e práticas.* São Paulo: Editora UNESP.

Buzaid, A. (1971). A renovação da ordem jurídica positiva. Ministério da Justiça: Brasília.

______ (1974). *O Ministério da Justiça – Relatório de 1969 a 1974*. Armário de obras raras: Brasília.

Campos, F. (1941). *Educação e Cultura*. 2.ª Edição. Rio de Janeiro: José Olímpio.

Campos, M. (1972). *Testemunhos e ensinamentos*. Rio de Janeiro: Livraria José Olympio Editora.

Cancelli, E. (1994) *O mundo da violência: a polícia na Era Vargas*. 2ª. ed. Brasília: Editora Universidade de Brasília.

______ (2012). *O Brasil e os outros: o Poder das Ideias*. Porto Alegre: EDIPUCRS.

______ (2017). *O Brasil em Guerra Fria Cultural: o pós-guerra em releitura.* São Paulo: Intermeios.

Cassin, R. (1963). "Reflections on the Rule of Law," *Journal of the International Commission of Jurists*, Vol. IV, No. 2, Summer.

Cattai, J. (2019). *Guerra Fria e Propaganda: a U.S. Information Agency no Brasil.* Curitiba: Appris.

Cella, J. R. G. (2001). *Teoria Tridimensional do Direito de Miguel Reale*. Paraná: Juruá Editora.

Chaves, W. and Cattai, J. (2019). "Transição política" e ditadura no Brasil: os anos 1970 e seus agendamentos políticos e intelectuais," *Revista Brasileira de História*, Vol. 39 , Issue no. 82, pp. 199–219. https://doi.org/10.1590/1806-93472019v39n82-10

Christian, M., Kott, S. and Matějka, O. (2017). "International Organizations in the Cold War: the circulation of experts beyond the East-West divide," *Acta Universitatis Carolinae Studia Territorialia*, Vol. 1, Year XVII, issue No.1, pp. 35–60. http://doi.org/10.14712/23363231.2017.17

Comparato, F. K. (1965). "O indispensável direito econômico," *Revista dos Tribunais,* Vol. 353, São Paulo, Ano 54, Março.

Costa, A. A. (2008). *Direito e Método: diálogos entre a hermenêutica filosófica e a hermenêutica jurídica*. Tese de doutoramento em Direito. Universidade de Brasília.

Cox, R. W. (contribution by Timothy J. Sinclair). (2001). "On Thinking About the World Order." In Cox, Robert W. (contributed by Timothy J. Sinclair). *Approaches to World Order*. New York: Cambridge University Press.

Craig, C. (2003). *Glimmer of a New Leviathan: Total War in the Realism of Niebuhr, Morgenthau, and Waltz*. New York: Columbia University Press.

Cull, N. (2008). *American Propaganda and Public Diplomacy 1945–1989: the US Information Agency and the Cold War*. Cambridge: Cambridge University Press.

Dallari, D. de A. (1973). *Elementos de Teoria Geral do Estado*. 2.ª Edição. São Paulo: Saraiva.

Dantas, F. C. de S. T. (1955). "A educação e a Crise Brasileira" (aula inaugural dos cursos da Faculdade Nacional de Direito, 1955), *Revista dos Tribunais*, São Paulo.

_____ (1958). "Em defesa do Direito," *Revista Forense*. Vol. 175. Rio de Janeiro. Ano 55. Janeiro-fevereiro.

Dezalay, Y. and Garth, B. (Eds). (2011). *Lawyers and the Rule of Law in an Era of Globalization*. New York: Routledge.

Dezalay, Y. and Garth, B. G. (2002). The Internationalization of Palace Wars: Lawyers, Economists, and the Contest to Transform Latin American States. Chicago, IL: University of Chicago.

Dreifuss, R. A. (1981). *1964: A conquista do Estado: ação política, poder e golpe de classe*. Petrópolis: Vozes, 3 ed.

Dutra, P. (2014). *San Tiago Dantas: a razão vencida*. (O ideólogo) Vol. I (1911–1945). São Paulo: Editora Singular.

Fagundes, M. S. (1956). "Reformas essenciais ao aperfeiçoamento das instituições políticas brasileiras," *Revista Forense,* Rio de Janeiro, Vol. 163, Ano 53, janeiro-fevereiro.

_____ (1963). "Da Intervenção do Estado na Ordem Econômica, em face da Constituição Federal," *Arquivos do Ministério da Justiça e Negócios Interiores*, Ano XXI, No. 86, junho.

_____ (1970). "A legalidade democrática," *Revista Forense*, Vol. 231, Rio de Janeiro, Ano 66, julho-agosto-setembro.

Faoro, R. (1978). "Faoro em nome da lei," *Jornal da Tarde*, May 6, São Paulo. Interview for José Eduardo Faria.

Faria, D. (2006). *O mito modernista*. Uberlândia: EDUFU.

Faria, J. E. (2016). "Juristas fora da curva: três perfis," *Revista Direito GV*, São Paulo, Vol. 12, No. 2, pp. 272–310, Maio-Ago.

Foucault, M. (2009). *Security, Territory, Population*. Lectures at The Collège De France, 1977–1978. (Ed. M. Senellart). Translated by G. Bruchell. New York: Palgrave Macmillan.

Friedrich, C. J. and Brzezinski, Z. (1965). *Totalitarian Dictatorship and Autocracy*. 2a. Ed. Cambridge, MA: Harvard University Press.

Gans, J. (2019). *White House Warriors: How the National Security Council Transformed the American Way of War*. W.W. Norton & Company: New York.

Garcia, D. S. (1974). "O Direito e a Tecnologia," *Revista dos Tribunais*, São Paulo, Maio.

Garth, B. G. (2000). "James Willard Hurst as Entrepreneur for the Field of Law and Social Science," *Law and History Review*, Vol. 18, No. 1, Spring. https://doi.org/10.2307/744348

Gilman, N. (2003). *Mandarins of the Future: Modernization Theory in Cold War America*. Baltimore: Johns Hopkins University Press.

Gomes, O. (1974). "Desenvolvimento econômico e evolução jurídica," *Revista Forense,* Rio de Janeiro, Ano 71, Out-Nov-Dez.

Grémion, P. (1995). I*ntelligence de l'anticommunisme: Le Congrès pour la liberté de la culture à Paris (1950–1975)*. Paris: Fayard.

Guilhot, N. (2005). The Democracy Makers: Human Rights and the Politics of Global Order. New York. Columbia University Press.

Gusmão, P. D. (1956). "Direito como cultura," *Revista Forense,* Rio de Janeiro, Vol. 164, Ano 53, Março-Abril.

Gygi, F. (1962). "The Rule of Law in the Contemporary Welfare State," *Journal of the International Commission of Jurists*. Geneva: International Commission of Jurists. Vol. IV, No. 1, Summer.

Halévy, D. (1949). *Essai sur l'accélération de l'histoire*. 2nd Ed. Paris: Plon.

Hamby, A. L. (1972). "The Vital Center, the Fair Deal, and the Quest for a Liberal Political Economy." *The American Historical Review*, Vol. 77, No. 3, pp. 653–678. http://dx.doi.org/10.2307/1870345

Hartmann, H. (2001). "US Human Rights Policy under Carter and Reagan, 1977–1981," Human Rights Quarterly. Vol. 23, No.2, pp. 402-430 https://doi.org/10.1353%2Fhrq.2001.0017

Hespanha, A. M. (2012). *Cultura Jurídica Europeia: síntese de um milênio*. Coimbra: Almedina.

Horta, F. L. C. (1963). "Aspectos da reformulação e atualização do Direito Positivo Brasileiro," *Arquivos do Ministério da Justiça e Negócios Interiores*, Brasília, Ano XXI. No. 86, junho.

Huo, S. and Parmar, I. (2019). "'A new type of great power relationship'? Gramsci, Kautsky and the role of the Ford Foundation's transformational elite knowledge networks in China," *Review of International Political Economy*, June. http://doi:10.1080/ 09692290.2019.1625427

Iber, P. J. (2015). *The Imperialism of Liberty: Intellectuals and the Politics of Culture in Cold War Latin America*. Department of History. University of Chicago.

ICJ. International Commission of Jurists. (1952). *Complete Report – Discourses and Protocols*. Published by the International Commission of Jurists. Buitenhof, The Hague, Netherlands.

ICJ. International Commission of Jurists. (1954). For the Rule of Law. *Bulletin of the International Commission of Jurists*. No. 1. ICJ: The Hague.

ICJ. International Commission of Jurists. (1961). *African Conference on the Rule of Law: a Report on the proceedings of the Conference*. Lagos, Nigeria, January 3–7, 1961. Geneva: International Commission of Jurists.

Jellinek, G. (1959). *Teoría General del Estado*. Ed. Albatros: Buenos Aires.

Judt, T. (2008). *Pós-guerra: uma história da Europa desde 1945*. (Trad. José Roberto O'shea). Rio de Janeiro: Objetiva.

Kennedy, D. (2006). "Three Globalizations of Law and Legal Thought: 1850–2000," in Trubek, D. M. and Santos, A. (Eds). *The New Law and Economic Development: a Critical Appraisal*. New York: Cambridge University Press.

Kinzer, S. (2013). *The Brothers: John Foster Dulles, Allen Dulles, and Their Secret World War*. New York: Henry Holt and Company.

Koch, S. (2004). *Double lives: Stalin, Willi Munzenberg and the seduction of the intellectuals*. New York: Enigma Books.

Kornhauser, A. M. (2015). *Debating the American State: Liberal Anxieties and the New Leviathan, 1930–1970*. Philadelphia: University of Pennsylvania Press.

Lalive, J. F. (1959). "Editorial: The Rule of Law in a Changing World," *Journal of the International Commission of Jurists*. See II, no. 1, spring-summer.

______ (1960). "Editorial: Contemporary problems of the Rule of Law," *Journal of the International Commission of Jurists*, Vol. II, No. 2, winter, 1959 / spring-summer.

Lamounier, B. and Meneguello, R. (1986). *Partidos Políticos* e *Consolidação Democrática*: O *caso brasileiro*. São Paulo: Brasiliense.

Lamy Filho, A. (1970). "A Reforma da Lei das Sociedades Anônimas," *Revista Forense,* Rio de Janeiro, Ano 1967, jul-set.

______ (1976). "Pressupostos e objetivos da reforma da lei de sociedades por ações," *Revista Forense,* Rio de Janeiro, Ano 72, Vol. 255, Julho-Agosto-Setembro.

Latham, M. E. (2000). Modernization as Ideology: American Social Science and 'Nation Building' in the Kenney Era. Chapel Hill and London: The University of North Carolina Press.

Lima, H. (1954). "O Estado da Constituição de 1946." In *Estudos sobre a Constituição Brasileira*, Rio de Janeiro, FGV.
Lipset, S. M. (1959). "Some Social Requisites of Democracy: Economic Development and Political Legitimacy," *The American Political Science Review*, Vol. 53, No. 1. Mar., pp. 69–105.
Machado, R. C. (2015). *Alfredo Buzaid e a contrarrevolução burguesa de 1964: crítica histórico-imanente da ideologia do direito, da política e do Estado de Justiça*. São Paulo. Pontifícia Universidade Católica de São Paulo. Mestrado em História.
Marsh, N. S. (1957). "Editorial: Domestic jurisdiction and International Concern," *Journal of the International Commission of Jurists*, Vol. 1, No. 1, Autumn.
______ (1958). "Editorial: The Rule of Law: Form and Substance," *Journal of the International Commission of Jurists*, Vol. 1, No. 2, Spring-Summer.
Medeiros, J. (1969). "A Filosofia do Direito e o Direito Natural," *Revista Forense*, Rio de Janeiro, Ano 65, Vol. 228, Outubro-Novembro-Dezembro.
Melis, D. V. (2003). "Strengthened and Purified Through Ordeal by Fire': Ecclesiastical Triumphalism in the Ruins of Europe." In Bessel, R. and Schumann, D. (Eds). *Life After Death: Approaches to a Cultural and Social History of Europe During the 1940s and 1950s*. German Historical Institute / Cambridge University Press.
Mello, C. A. B. (2010). *Curso de Direito Administrativo*. 27a Edição. São Paulo: Malheiros Editores.
Mello Franco, A. A. (1957). *Estudos de Direito Constitucional*. Inprenta: Rio de Janeiro, Revista Forense.
Menezes, D. (1962). "Democracia e Liberdade no 'Contrato Social' de Rousseau." In Cavalcanti, T., Menezes, D., Bonavides, P. *et al. Estudos em homenagem a J. J. Rousseau*. Instituto de Direito Público e Ciência Política. Rio de Janeiro: Editora FGV.
Moreira, M. S. de C. F. (1970). *O moderno e suas diferenças*. 1970. Tese (Livre--docência) – FFLCH, Universidade de São Paulo. São Paulo.
Mota Filho, C. (1965). "A Reforma Eleitoral," *Arquivos do Ministério da Justiça e Negócios Interiores*, Brasília, Ano XXIII, No. 94, junho.
Moyn, S. (2011). "The First Historian of Human Rights," *The American Historical Review*, Vol. 116, No. 1, February.
______ (2018). *Not Enough: Human Rights in an Unequal World*. Cambridge, MA: the Belknap Press of Harvard University Press.
Munhoz, S. (2002). "Ecos da Emergência da Guerra Fria no Brasil (1947–1953)." In *Diálogos*, Maringá, DHI/UEM, Vol. 6, pp. 41–59.
Nader, P. (2003). *Introdução ao Estudo do Direito*. 23ª Ed. Rio de Janeiro: Forense.
Nascimento Silva, L. G. (1970). "O papel do jurista em um mundo em transformação," *Revista Forense*, Rio de Janeiro, Ano 67, Abr-mai-jun.
Nazo, N. (1958). "O Direito em um mundo em transformação," *Revista dos Tribunais*, Vol. 278, São Paulo, Ano 47, Dezembro.
Nonato, O. (1958). "A crise do Direito e o dever dos juristas," *Revista Forense*, Vol. 180, Rio de Janeiro, Ano 55, Novembro-Dezembro.
Nunes, R. (1967). "Considerações Gerais sobre a legislação revolucionária," *Revista dos Tribunais*, Vol. 386, São Paulo, Ano 56, dezembro.
Ortega y Gasset, J. (1994). *The Revolt of the Masses*. New York: W. W. Norton & Company.
Parmar, I. (2012). Foundations of the American Century: The Ford, Carnegie, and Rockefeller Foundations in the Rise of American Power. New York: Columbia University Press.

Parodi, A. (1968). "La vie publique et l avie économique. Encyclopédie Française." – *Tome X: L'Etat Moderne*. Paris: Encyclopédie Française, 1935, pp. 20–26. Cited in Venâncio Filho, A. *A intervenção do Estado no domínio econômico: o Direito Público Econômico no Brasil*. Rio de Janeiro: Fundação Getúlio Vargas.

Penholato, D. (2017). José Garrido Torres nas Sombras do Poder: Um Economista na Construção do Projeto de Modernização de 1964. Dissertação (Mestrado) – FFLCH, Universidade de São Paulo, São Paulo

Piettre, A. (1964). "La Liberté Economique et son évolution. Encyclopédie Française." In *L'Etat*. Tome X. Paris: Encyclopédie Française.

Porto, M. M. (1959). "O Efêmero e o Eterno no Direito," *Revista dos Tribunais*, São Paulo, Ano 48, Dezembro.

Pruden, C. (1998). *Conditional Partners. Eisenhower, the United Nations, and the Search for a Permanent Peace*. Lousiana State University Press.

Ramos, J. N. (1967). "O Código Tributário Nacional," *Revista de Direito Público*. Vol. 1. São Pulo: Instituto de Direito Público.

Reale, M. (1959). "A Filosofia do Direito e as Formas de Conhecimento Jurídico," *Revista dos Tribunais*, São Paulo, Dezembro.

______ (1961). "As Faculdades de Direito na História do Brasil," *Revista dos Tribunais*, Vol. 306, São Paulo, Ano 50, abril.

______ (1970). *Problemas de nosso tempo*. São Paulo: Editorial Grijalbo.

______ (1976). "Considerações gerais sobre o projeto de Código Civil," *Arquivos do Ministério da Justiça e Negócios Interiores*, Brasília, Ano 33, No. 137, janeiro-março.

Ribeiro, M. (1976). "Poder Executivo e Administração Pública," *Revista de Direito Administrativo*, Rio de Janeiro – Fundação Getúlio Vargas, Ano XVI, V. 126, out./dez.

Rodríguez-Garavito, C. (2011). "Toward a Sociology of the Global Rule of Law Field: Neoliberalism, Neoconstitutionalism, and the Contest over Judicial Reform in Latin America." In Dezalay, Y. and Garth, B. (Eds). *Lawyers and the Rule of Law in an Era of Globalization*. New York: Routledge.

Romano, R. (1979). *Brasil: Igreja contra Estado*. São Paulo: Kairós Livraria e Editora.

Sabella, J. L. (2013). *The Politics of Original Sin: Reinhold Niebuhr's Christian Realism and its Cold War Realist Reception*. Doctoral Thesis. Boston College. Department of Theology.

Saunders, F. S. (1999). *The Cultural Cold War: the CIA and the World of Arts and Letters*. NY: The New Press.

Schlesinger Jr., A. M. (1948). "Not Left, Not Right, But a Vital Center," *The New York Times*. April 4.

______ (1949). *The Vital Center: The Politics of Freedom*. Boston: H. Mifflin Company.

Silva, J. (1968). "Considerações em torno da Inflação Legislativa," *Revista dos Tribunais*, São Paulo, Janeiro.

Simpson, C. (Ed.) (1998). *University and Empire: Money and Politics in the Social Sciences During the Cold War*. The New Press: New York.

Slobodian, Q. (2018). Globalists: The End of Empire and the Birth of Neoliberalism. Cambridge, MA: Harvard University Press.

Sluga, G. (2011). "René Cassin Les droits de l'homme and the Universality of Human Rights, 1945–1966." In Hoffmann, S. L. (Ed). *Human Rights in the Twentieth Century*. New York: Cambridge University Press.

Smith, A. (1977). *The Wealth of Nations – An Inquiry into the Nature and Causes of the Wealth of Nations*. Chicago: University of Chicago Press.

Snyder, S. (2011). *Human Rights Activism and the End of the Cold War: A Transnational History of the Helsinki Network*. Cambridge: Cambridge University Press.

Souza, M. C. C. (1990). *Estado e partidos políticos no Brasil (1930 a 1964)*. São Paulo: Alfa-Omega.

Spektor, M. (2018). "The United States and the 1964 Brazilian Military Coup," *Oxford Research Encyclopedia of Latin American History*. https://doi.org/10.1093/acrefore/9780199366439.013.551

Spengler, O. (2016). *Decline of the West*. Vol. 1 and Vol. 2. (Translated by David G. Payne). Random Shack.

Staar, R. (1991). *Foreign Policies of the Soviet Union*. Hoover Institution Press Stanford University: California.

Tácito, C. (1952). "O poder de polícia e seus limites," *Revista de Direito Administrativo*, Rio de Janeiro, FGV, Vol. 25.

______ (1971a). "O Desafio no Ensino do Direito," *Revista Forense,* Rio de Janeiro, Ano 67, Vol. 233, março.

______ (1971b). "O Estado e a Empresa," *Revista Forense,* Rio de Janeiro, Ano 67, jul-set.

Tolley Jr, H. B. (1994) The International Commission of Jurists: Global Advocates for Human Rights. University of Pennsylvania Press: Philadelphia

Toynbee, A. (1946). *Civilization on Trial*. London: Oxford University Press.

Trindade, W. L. (1976). "O Superdireito das normas de aplicação e de interpretação," *Arquivos do Minstério da Justiça*, Brasília, Ano 33, No. 137, janeiro-março.

Trubek, D. (1966). "Problemas jurídicos da Cooperação Internacional," *Revista dos Tribunais,* São Paulo, Novembro.

______ (1971). "Law, Planning, and the Development of the Brazilian Capital Market: A Study of Law in Economic Change," *Yale Law School Studies in Law and Modernization*, No. 3, April.

Valladão, H. (1962). "A forma jurídica do desenvolvimento econômico e social," *Revista Forense,* Rio de Janeiro, Ano 59, abril, maio, junho.

______ (1964). "Lei geral de aplicação das normas jurídicas," *Revista Forense,* Rio de Janeiro, Ano 61, Vol. 208, outubro-novembro-dezembro.

Van Dal, A. J. M. (1955). *Under False Colors: A Report on the Character of the International Association of Democratic Lawyers*. The International Commission of Jurists. Buitenhof, The Hague, Netherlands.

Wald, A. (1965). "A função do advogado no processo revolucionário brasileiro," *Revista dos Tribunais,* São Paulo, Ano 54, Vol. 356, junho.

______ (1966). "Novas Dimensões do Direito de Propriedade," *Arquivos do Ministério da Justiça e Negócios Interiores*, Brasília, Ano XXIV, N.º 99, setembro.

______ (1967). "O Direito do Desenvolvimento." In *Revista Forense,* Rio de Janeiro, Ano 64, outubro-novembro-dezembro.

______ (1969). "A elaboração e revisão dos projetos dos códigos," *Revista Forense*, Rio de Janeiro, Vol. 228, Ano 66, outubro a dezembro.

______ (1970). "A Introdução do Leasing no Brasil," *Revista dos Tribunais,* São Paulo, Maio.

Wertheim, S. (2020). *Tomorrow, the World: The Birth of U.S. Global Supremacy*. Cambridge, MA: The Belknap Press of Harvard University Press.

2 The executive and the judiciary

Constitutional review and the contours of individual freedom

By the end of the 19th and beginning of the 20th century, *police power*, the principle of public law relative to state intervention in the public domain, was based on guarantees of public safety and public health. As described by Michel Foucault (2008, chapter 1), this corresponded to *government reason*, emerging in the mid-18th century and known as *liberalism*. Based on the assumption that self-limitation would be in the best interest of the nation's wealth and prosperity, this regime informed the relations between law and government action. Developed at the end of the 19th century in particular by German jurists such as Otto Mayer, founder of modern German administrative law, and Fritz Fleiner, both widely referenced in Brazilian legal debates of the 20th century, the police power doctrine established that "definitely, the result of each application of police power will never be anything other than this: *that this man does not disturb*" (Mayer, 1949, p. 35). In sum, police activities – in their primary sense as equivalent to the administration of the city (*politia*, from Latin; *polis* and the Greek *politeia*) – corresponded to state action to enforce the individual's duty not to disturb the good order of public affairs.

A power, in other words, of balance, prevention, and correction of conflicts between individuals, informed by the citizen's revolt against the power of the monarch, described in the principles of the *Declaration of Independence of the United States* and the *Declaration on Human and Citizen Rights*: "freedom consists in doing everything that is not harmful to others." In the modern evolution of this governmental regime, therefore, one can find the imposition of a series of regulatory mechanisms capable of guiding "good government" under the auspices of liberal forms: a method that accepts the belief that there must be a limitation to its powers and that such limitation would ensure the activities of its citizenship and, thus, the prosperity of the nation (Foucault, 2008, chapter 1). In sum, this limitation on government practices described the restrictions imposed on police power, including in the domain of law (Foucault, 2008; 2009).

To assure individual rights (to life, freedom, property) over state power, the processes of formalization of social relations by law, in the post-French Revolution, split the sovereign power unified in the figure of the monarch with a divine mandate, between legislative, executive, and judiciary – therefore

DOI: 10.4324/9781003123941-3

accepting Montesquieu's formula for a tripartition of powers and reciprocal control between them: the basic premises of the concept of rule of law. As noted in regards to G. Jelinek, rule of law stipulated that the relationship between the government and the individual would be mediated by law, limiting state action to a principle of legality – in sum, as expressed by the Brazilian jurist Caio Tácio (1952), a restriction to government action, imposing a "negative" role to government action and centering the search for public "good order" on the guarantees of individual freedoms.

By the late 19th century and especially after the outbreak of World War I, however, the premise of this "negative" police state as a bulwark against state authority was under attack throughout the West. In Brazil, anti-liberalism had become not only the inclination of "politicians of centralizing and authoritarian tendencies," but a *locus* where a national intellectual field articulated their political engagement in the first half of the 20th century. These intellectuals expressed a common gospel regarding political life in the country: the incompatibility between liberal institutions and ideals ("advanced") and the Brazilian reality ("archaic") (Bresciani, 2005, p. 298; 2010). To respond to growing inequality, mass poverty, disease, urbanization, and the extraordinary challenges of geographic mobility, Brazilian elites led an effort to modernize the country's governance. In particular, liberal state organization had to evolve in favor of rising interventionism: for the "common good," public authority should play a central role in restricting and conditioning the exercise of individual freedoms (Meirelles, 1957).

In fact, in the North Atlantic, this new functioning of the binomial state-individual, regulated, fundamentally, by police power, had been reorganized since the mid-19th century as an effect of the revolutions of 1848 and the rise of the social question. In the United States, for instance, this went through the dispute of the antinomic institutions of *due process of law*, whereby it was stipulated that certain fundamental rights were above state control and, consequently, police power. Both represent expressions of the opposition concerning social issues between private enterprise and public interest whose final word was left to the judiciary, especially to the Supreme Court through the control of constitutionality (judicial review) (Swisher, 1946; Pinto, 1951). Indeed, the first quarter of the 20th century marked a period known as the "government of judges." Introduced in 1921 by Edouard Lambert in his study *Le government des judges et la lutte contre la legislation sociale aux Etats-Unis – L'experience americaine du contrôle judiciaire de la constitutionalité des lois*, the term meant to signify an unconstrained system of judicial review, not even by constitutional amendment. In such a system, the Supreme Court would act as a loyalist in the balance between those interests, exerting considerable influence over the country's political life (Davis, 1987).

However, as the prestige of liberal capitalism – of the "captains of industry" – diminished, especially with the increasingly acute social conflict (the upsurge of the organized working class and the first signs of economic exhaustion, which finally broke out with the crisis of 1929) a sense of the need for state intervention gained strength. The "business affected with a public interest" formula emerged, that is, the idea that certain sectors of the economy are linked by their characteristics to vital collective interests and, consequently, manipulation of those sectors affects the entire social group (Tácito, 1971, p. 327). This new moral gospel assumed a central political position with the policies advocated by the British economist John M. Keynes and with Franklin D. Roosevelt's New Deal. Within this process, for example, the Theodore Roosevelt (1901–1909) and, later, Taft administrations (1909–1913) with the support of antitrust regulations (the Sherman Act of 1890) intervened against monopolies in the oil sector. In 1911, Standard Oil, owned by the Rockefellers, was forced to split up (Tota, 2014, p. 26–31). "The regulation of economic power relations by antitrust legislation," Belgian public law specialist Fritz Gygi said many years later, demonstrates that "freedom of contract and freedom of association are no longer to be regarded as a purely private matter" (1962, p. 7–8). By the same token, reflecting on the police power doctrine, Brazilian jurist Caio Tácito Sá Viana Pereira de Vasconcelos (1952, p. 7–8) argued that a conviction was being formed that the choice was not between freedom and authority, but between public and private control of the economic order.

Efforts to regulate state intervention, however, would be systematized only after the post-World War I period. National legal systems in the West began to be profoundly modified to accept such expanded functions of the state power, particularly in the economic domain. The premise was that it was the responsibility of public authority to form a cohesive program to attend to the "social issue," representing another moral assumption of power and governance, its organization, and exercise. In the first half of the 20th century, constitutions, starting with Mexico in 1917 and Weimar in 1919, abandoned the legal typology, as expressed by the Spanish jurist Laureano Luíz Rodó (1954), that had led public authority to abstain from legal discipline, ensuring the primacy of individual guarantees and rights. Jurists had the grand ambition of transforming legal forms into a true *program*, whose "management" would be the responsibility of the federal government and public administration. Indeed, in Brazil, technical institutions were created to produce data, diagnoses, and intervention strategies by public authority and the training of elites capable of conducting the country's institutional life.

Under the Getúlio Vargas regime in the 1930s, in particular, after the "Estado Novo" coup of 1937, Articles 168 to 173 of the 1934 Charter and Law n. 284, of October 8, 1936, created the Federal Council for Civil Public Service. Later, inspired by the U.S. model, the Council was replaced by the Administrative Department of Public Service (DASP), with Article 67 of the 1937 Constitution and Decree-Law n. 579, of July 30, 1938. The reforms consolidated the professionalization of public administration by establishing access to civic services through public tenders and the structuring of careers and the rights and obligations of civil servants. With broad attributions, such as rationalizing and controlling the civil servants in their functions and organizing the country's administrative structure, DASP was, for a time, responsible for the preparation of the federal budget (Bercovici, 2010, p.79; Wahrlich, 1983). The creation of state institutions between 1937 and 1945 was unprecedented. In 1937 the Brazilian Council of Geography and the Technical Council for Economics and Finance were created; in 1938, the National Petroleum Council and the National Mate Institute; in 1940, the Commission for the Defense of the National Economy, National Salt Institute, and National Engine Factory; in 1941, the National Steel Company, National Pine Institute; in 1943, the Coordination of Economic Mobilization, the National Alkali Company, Central Brazil Foundation, Volta Redonda Steel Plant; and, finally, in 1944, the National Council for Industrial and Commercial Policy and the Wheat Expansion Service (Ianni, 1977, p. 47–48; Brinkley, 1995, p. 21–23).

Along with this expansion, a doctrinal effort began in legal thought concerning the discipline responsible for this institutional evolution: public administrative law, followed by the birth, in the Global North, of *public administration* as a field of study.[1] One of the central points of this exertion – and one that can be seen in the evolution of Brazilian legal thought – was the conceptualization of police power, the main instrument of the state in the process of discipline of individual interests (Fagundes, 1965). After World War II, Caio Tácito, following this doctrinal effort, defended the notion that the modern concept of police power "goes beyond conservative boundaries to recognize the state with a broader and more active role in promoting general well-being." Therefore, Tácito argued, this modern concept establishes not only public order but also, even principally, economic and social order, with "norms largely exercised through police power that limit individual freedom" (1952, p. 3).

Accordingly, this debate gained significant stress and doctrinal energy after World War II, due especially to the 1946 Constitution's restoration of rule of law principles, maintaining, however, the centrality of "social justice." In other words, it re-established, to some extent, individual guarantees and rights, which Vargas' anti-liberal program had disorganized in favor of an expanding public administration. By the early 1940s, liberal premises start gaining momentum within opposition to the dictatorship. An important incentive took place at the protest at the 1943 National Legal Congress, with the publication, in October of that year, of the *Mineiros' Manifesto* (Mattos, 2011, p. 45–75) and, even more incisive, pro-democracy mobilizations at the São Paulo Law School (Dulles, 1984). Liberal opposition, as described in Chapter 1, also underwent a gradual development from the shift of secular Catholicism in Brazil toward liberal conventions that were influenced, to a large extent, by the philosophy of Jacques Maritain.[2] Indeed this led to the creation in 1945 of the Christian Democratic Party, based on a political *third way* inspired by the social doctrine of the Catholic Church. With increasing anti-dictatorship sentiments in Brazil, this party came to represent an alternative solution to the antinomy of liberal capitalism and soviet collectivism.

Informed by this liberal mobilization, the 1946 Constitution swung the pendulum between the individual and public authority in favor of the former.[3] The Constituent Assembly of that year demarcated *rule of law* with strict separation of powers, thereby containing the expansion of the federal government and maintaining the normative function of the National Congress. *Federalism* was reasserted by regulating and restricting the cases in which the union was able to intervene in states and municipalities,[4] which were guaranteed greater autonomy, particularly due to the expanded possibilities of intervention in the economic order with the systematization of taxes and the creation of mixed or public companies. This reassertion of federalism also provided a new expression to the administration of justice by ending the Federal Court of 1st Instance, which guaranteed the interests of the Union in federated entities, and revalued the role of regional courts. Federal Supreme Court competencies subsequently expanded, especially with the *mandado de segurança*, an ordinary appeal, increasing opportunities for filing extraordinary appeals with the Supreme Court.

Nevertheless, soon after, juridical thought came to establish a relative consensus on the problematic role of the new Constitutional order insofar as it would represent an "obstacle" to economic and social development. Accompanying a broader modernization agenda and a transnational debate in the United States and Western Europe, legal ideas in Brazil focused on the role to be played by public administration and the legal contours of individual freedom. To that extent, Brazilian elites reinstated their criticism of laissez-faire liberalism present in national political thinking since the early 20th century.

State expansion: public administration and the totalitarian threat

From the Acropolis, in a passionate defense of ancient Greek man and his legacy for contemporary times, the French writer André Malraux spoke to his audience about the central problem of that century: finding ways to *reconcile individual freedom with social justice*.

> Ancient Greece will tell you: I sought the truth and found justice and freedom, I invented the independence of art and spirit. For the first time, I erected, in front of their gods, man prostrate everywhere for four millennia. And, at the same time, I erected him in front of the despot! It is a simple language, but we still hear it as an immortal language. It has been forgotten for centuries and threatened every time it has been found. Perhaps it has never been needed more. The main political problem of our time is to reconcile social justice and freedom; the main cultural problem is to make the greatest works accessible to the greatest number of people.[5]
>
> (1959)

At the end of World War II, with the Axis forces defeated, discussions emerged of this reconciliation vocalized by Malraux in the late 1950s. Envisioning a great Atlantic civilization between the United States and Europe, formed from a common history, destined to a common future and confronted by a common enemy, the United States structured a political agenda in opposition to the aspirations of rupturing the secular order advocated by the Soviet system (Allardyce, 1982, p. 695). Scholars, in particular on the liberal left, interpreted the communist bloc as an approximation to Nazism, that is, both represented forms of totalitarianism. In fact, since 1941 totalitarianism was used to link German Nazism and Soviet Communism, becoming, after the war, the dominant foundation of U.S. political thinking on dictatorships. After 1945, totalitarianism became not only the main public and academic discourse in the country but also a useful bridge between the United States and its allies and supporters in the Cold War. At the heart of the revival of totalitarianism as a political rallying point was George Orwell's *Nineteen Eighty-Four* (1949), Arthur Schlesinger Jr.'s *The Vital Center: The Politics of Freedom* (1949), and the classics *The Origins of Totalitarianism* (1951) by Hannah Arendt, and Carl Friedrich and Zbigniew Brzezinski's *Totalitarian Dictatorship and Autocracy* (1956) (Alpers, 2003, chapter 9). The centrality of totalitarianism as a Cold War theoretical anchor reached decisively into Brazilian political thought in the period, directly and indirectly informing the modernization process in the country (Cancelli, 2017, chapter 3). This took place as a U.S. hegemonic project, particularly as an expression of the network composed of state agencies, philanthropic foundations, and major U.S. universities (Parmar, 2012; Chaves, 2018).

It was in this milieu that the Harvard historian Arthur Schlesinger Jr. (1949) made his moral argument against the totalitarian threat into a defense of a renewed liberalism as a "fighting faith" against totalitarianism (Forrester, 2019, chapter 1). As mentioned before, the historian advocated for a deepening of democracy residing in the unification of the non-communist left, the center, and the non-fascist right into what he called a "vital center." This anti-totalitarian apology, indeed a vague concept (Alpers, 2003, p. 252), was at the core of the U.S. political establishment after World War II. In 1950 its main political institution for intellectual and artistic elites around the world was based on this assumption: the *Congress for Cultural Freedom*. André Malraux was one of its first promoters (Saunders, 1999, p. 48).

Schlesinger Jr.'s "fighting faith," however, was not only a call to fight against the Soviet Union, it was also a call against unrestrained or monopolistic capitalism. It had a moral dimension by which he and other Americans for Democratic Action (ADA) liberals in the Democratic Party stressed the limitations of human nature and the naïve belief in progress and human perfectionism of popular-front liberals. Internally, ADA was able to isolate Communists and pro-Communists such as Henry Wallace from the liberal community, supporting Harry S. Truman and his Fair Deal agenda (Powers, 1995, p. 201). In other words, the liberal mainstream came to favor a "mixed economy," a "middle way," a "strong political center," distinguishing themselves from fascism, communism, and socialism, with their complete economic control, detailed planning, and massive bureaucracy. They envisioned, particularly with Schlesinger's vital center, an "effort to establish a mixed economy that would preserve the essentials of capitalism while mitigating its abuses" (1948, p. 1). The widespread political gospel of this new liberalism – encompassing Reinhold Niebuhr's moral theory and John M. Keynes's economical thinking – found its way under the Truman administration (1945–1953) despite being largely blocked by a Republican majority in Congress (Hamby, 1972, p. 657).

Regarding U.S. foreign policy, this vital center liberalism paved the way for a broad dissemination of modernization theories. Assuming an essential pattern of development and modernization (based on what liberals wished the United States to be), theorists such as Edward Shils, Gabriel Almond, Lucian Pye, Karl Deutsch, and others proposed some degree of economic cooperation under the state baton on a national level in Latin America and the rest of the developing world (Gilman, 2003, p. 3). Indeed, as part of the anti-totalitarian psychological warfare, the Department of State developed a sophisticated international aid program dedicated to the development of economic infrastructures and the training of technical and intellectual elites who could lead, within the technicist rationality of social sciences, state institutions and agencies (Dezalay and Garth, 2002; Ioris, 2017).

United States aid to Brazil had been ongoing since the beginning of World War II (Tota, 2000), but gained systematization with the *Point IV* program, launched in 1949 by the Truman administration; more precisely, with the *Basic Technical Cooperation Agreement* between the governments of Brazil and the United States, signed in December 1950. At that time, the predominant assessment of elites on the public administration processes was that there was a profound inadequacy of the state apparatus for economic development programs devoted to industrialization. Indeed, this assessment led to the creation by Luiz Simões Lopes of the Getúlio Vargas Foundation in 1944. Lopes saw the need for creating a qualified workforce and institutions dedicated to public administration in the country: "an entity designed to improve the intellectual level of Brazilians in the field of social sciences, with a preponderance for public and private administration" and for something connected to administration, but practically inexistent in Brazil: economics (D'araujo, 1999, p. 13). In this post-World War II, the modernization of public administration in Brazil was structured on three fronts: the *administrative processes*, the *institutional structure* and, the development of elites to conduct this new public authority structure.

Between 1950 and 1964, different administrations tried to modernize the administrative process. The Vargas administration (1950–1954) formed in 1952 a group composed of Simões Lopes, Roberto Campos, and Sebastião Santana e Silva to study the federal administration. This resulted in Law n. 3,563, of August 31, 1953. Introduced to the Chamber of Deputies, it proposed an administrative reform based on the *centrality of a general coordination and planning body*. The proposal was not accepted and subsequently the Kubitschek administration (1956–1961) took another look at the reform, focusing on a "parallel administration" and, thus, on development, thereby avoiding a more global administrative reform (Bercovici, 2010). In 1956, the Kubitschek administration created by decree the Commission for Studies and Administrative Projects (CEPA), integrated by the DASP's technicians – Lopes, Campos, and Santana e Silva –, who worked throughout on Kubitschek's economic program – the *five-year plan*;[6] shortly thereafter, the Bureaucratic Simplification Commission (COSB),[7] which proposed to modify administrative processes, including the delegation of power and structures and routines of ministries. As occurred to the Vargas administration, those tentatives also did not evolve. A few years later, João Goulart's administration (1961–1964) would revive these initiatives by appointing Ernani do Amaral Peixoto the Extraordinary Minister for Administrative Reform on January 23, 1963. The plan was to modernize federal public services by implementing administrative planning in all sectors of the executive branch. The commission presented four projects, the most important being Bill 1482, the *Organic Law of the Federal Administrative System*.

None of these attempts at reform were ever realized, however, due in large extent to resistance in the National Congress. Nonetheless, these proposals and diagnoses for the improvement or modernization of public administration, particularly the *administrative processes*, would be taken up again under the dictatorship. The previous studies came together with works organized within the scope of the think tank Institute for Research and Social Studies (IPES). After analyzing the government's administrative reform project, IPES proposed to decentralize the planning and execution of resources, taking advantage of broad possibilities for administrative cooperation at the federal, state, and municipal levels; and the creation of a top body to guarantee the elaboration and coordination of the action plans and return of the merit and competition system for any public office (Bortone, 2014, p. 47 and 59–60). Funded a few months after the coup in 1964, the Special Commission for Administrative Reform Studies (COMESTRA), led by Roberto Campos and formed by elite members such as Carlos Medeiros Silva and Luis Simões Lopes, became the leading agency in this reforming effort. In February 1967, the Castello Branco administration enacted Decree-Law n. 200 that modernized the country's public administration. According to Campos, the Minister of Planning at the time, state planning was not intended to interfere in private enterprise, but rather to offer discipline to public investments and rationalize government action, making it possible to operate with predictability and security (Salinas, 2010). Soon thereafter, the formulations of the Decree-Law n. 200 were absorbed by Article 163, of the 1967 Constitution. It stated:

> Private companies have preference, with encouragement and support from the State, to organize and explore economic activities.
>
> § 1 – Only to supplement private enterprise, the State will directly organize and explore economic activities.
>
> § 2 – In the exploration, by the State, of economic activity, public companies, autarchies, and mixed-capital companies shall be governed by the rules applicable to private companies, including as to the right to work and obligations. § 3 – A public company that exploits non-monopolized activities will be subject to the same tax regime applicable to private companies.
>
> (Brasil, 1967a; FGV.RAP, 1967)

Following the anxieties and malaise of this era of "permanent crises," in particular, the U.S. and U.N.-led determination concerning development efforts (such as the legal-institutional organization of the public administration in Brazil) avoided the tendency toward centralization – as it seems to be the case of the general coordination and planning body proposed by Vargas, a vestige of DASP's "totalitarian stigma" (Bittencourt, 1947, p. 362) –, founding, on the contrary, a decentralized and disarmed state authority (Sinclair, 2020).

Along with the modernization of the administrative processes, U.S. elites were also occupied in training local elites around the world, which took place through strategic institutions and programs such as the Fulbright academic exchange (1946) and the Foreign Leader Program (1948) (Scott-Smith, 2008). For Latin America and Brazil, the training of technical and intellectual elites took place especially with the International Cooperation Administration (ICA). Widely disseminated by the U.S. Information Agency in the Brazilian print media (Cattai, 2019, p. 73), ICA's programs not only offered scholarships at U.S. universities but also subsidized the creation in Brazil and throughout the Global South of research, teaching, and dissemination centers for this "modern knowledge" of public administration. Based on highly comparative academic studies in the United States, public administration involved "surveying, mapping, collecting, counting, recording and standardizing" as fundamental premises to modern state intervention (Sinclair, 2020, p. 57).

As a result of two meetings attended by technical elites from FGV and the Brazilian Federal Government, representatives of the UN and professors from U.S. universities, the Brazilian School of Public Administration (EBAP) was founded in April 1952 and became the model case adopted by U.S. philanthropic foundations, universities and government agencies, and by the United Nations in their efforts to train local elites in Latin America (Tickner, 1956; Fischer, 1984). Under the U.N. Technical Assistance Administration, which lasted until 1959, the agreement provided for the visit of U.S. teachers to Brazil, the development of new curricula, methods, and teaching techniques; the installation of libraries and research services; the monitoring by U.S. teachers at the School of the Administrative Department of Public Service to improve the work of the civil service; the use of the FGV-Rio structure and the FGV-SP School of Administration as initial training centers for the program; training Brazilian teachers to prepare high school and university students in public and business administration; and granting scholarships to Brazilian students to take advanced courses in the United States.[8]

Complementary to Point IV's *Basic Technical Cooperation Agreement*, in May 1953 the Eisenhower and Vargas administrations signed an *Agreement on Special Technical Services*. Under the aegis of the agreement, a new project – designated as PBA-1 – was arranged in March 1959 between the Brazilian Ministry of Education and Culture, DASP, FGV, the Universities of Rio Grande do Sul and Bahia,[9] and the ICA's Institute of Inter-American Affairs and the United States Operation Mission (USOM) (Jacobs, 2004, p. 112). The PBA-1 was a "program for teaching public and business administration," that saw a growing need for qualified human resources in an industrial economy within "a process of accelerated development and expansion," seeking to promote "the intensification and gradual expansion of educational resources that Brazil has in the area of public and business administration" (Fischer, 1984, p. 282).

By the mid-1950s, the importance and successes of these programs for the U.S. international aid agenda were already being noticed. Elwyn A. Mauck, then director of the Division of Public and Business Administration at ICA, reported in a communication with the Department of State in September 1956 that the development of the "Belo Horizonte Project," dedicated to technical training of all public administration employees in the capital of Minas Gerais in municipal finances, and the creation of the São Paulo School of Business Administration of the Getúlio Vargas Foundation (EAESP-FGV), the cornerstone in this international aid effort to train elite cadres in the field of administration, were models of success in regard to the aid agenda.[10] Furthermore, the training of cadres capable of supplying the demand for a highly qualified workforce to lead the development program was also central to the agenda of U.S. philanthropy in Brazil. The most important of these philanthropic institutions was undoubtedly the Ford Foundation. Ford's grant strategy in the period focused on training, through academic and technical exchanges, "a new generation of economists and civil servants (and, to a lesser extent, scientists, educators, and engineers) who could lead the country on the path of progress" (Brooke and Witoshynsky, 2002, p. 169).

The Brazilian dictatorship did not interrupt such efforts. As with the modernization of administrative processes, the training of human resources continued under authoritarian rule. On April 15, 1964, for instance, through an agreement with ICA, EBAP hosted the former Center for Administrative and Social Research, then the Research Center (CPqA), which was responsible for research, editorial activities and cooperation, and technical assistance in the area of public administration (FGV.EBAP, 1964a). Immediately after this reorganization, the research center signed agreements with U.S. international aid, managed at the time by the United States Agency for International Development (USAID), which replaced ICA and the Ford Foundation.

> CPqA is currently carrying out four different programs. The first carried out in partnership with USAID, consists of the translation and publication of foreign books on public administration, which will constitute a special series called "Administration for Development." The second program, sponsored by the Ford Foundation, foresees the elaboration of genuinely Brazilian literature on public administration, in the form of books, monographs, and cases. The third concerns the development of research activities directly related to the teaching of the School, that is, as a method of teaching and measuring school performance. Finally, the fourth and final program consists of coordinating the participation of EBAP professors and the staff of the Center itself in technical assistance services provided by the Foundation to other entities, by agreement or accord.
>
> (FGV. EBAP, 1964b, p. 10–11)

Along with training elites, over the course of the 1940s and 1950s the commissions formed between the governments of Brazil and the United States led to the creation and renewal of instruments for planning and regulation of the economic order by the public administration. Some of the more prominent commissions formed were the Superintendence of Currency and Credit (SUMOC), 1945, the National Economic Council (CNE), 1949, later the Brazilian Institute of Economics (IBRE), 1951, the National Bank for Economic Development (BNDE), 1953, and the Foreign Trade Portfolio of Banco do Brasil (CACEX), 1953, which would come to subsidize industrialization programs based on import substitution industrialization (Dreifuss, 1981; Penholato, 2017; Geddes, 1990). Those efforts attempted to expand competencies based on economic and administrative techniques that modernization theories were outlining and developing for the "underdeveloped" regions. The general idea was to make the state, specifically the executive power, an intervention complex, especially in the domestic economy. This, however, implied involving it in tasks of normalization of economic relations, a function kept by the legislative power, according to the liberal premises instituted in 1946 and submitted to the control by the judiciary. The intervention, in this sense, should be carried out following the constitution's precepts – an issue that particularly interests us in this chapter.

In Brazilian legal thinking, the problem was that the legal order of the 1946 Charter was motivating a constitutional crisis. For instance, in the mid-1950s, the then Minister of Justice and Interior Affairs, Nereu Ramos, and the jurist Miguel Seabra Fagundes defended the notion that the imposition of the dynamics of modernity made institutional instruments of government detach from "reality." They were warning that the serious crisis of the country's political-constitutional institutions would bring down "moral standards in the practice of the regime" and would give subsidies to opponents of free institutions to convince the masses that the best way out for social change would be via dictatorial government (Fagundes, 1956, p. 9–10). The executive power was expected to give direction to the new modernizing dynamics in such an organic and secure manner that it would not lead to a totalitarian outburst. However, the executive's superposition over the other powers and the political dimension of the individual was another facet of the malaise in the Brazilian legal debate.

Amidst all the practical issues discussed by legal elites in Brazil, these issues were above all structural. That was precisely the focus of the International Commission of Jurists regarding the modernization in the Global South. From the 1950s through the early 1960s, the ICJ directed the debate, gathering local elites from around the world at their conventions and distributing publications through its national headquarters, alerting that the defense of individual rights should not focus on criticism of the countries where such rights were blatantly disrespected. In other words, the focus should not be communist countries. Maintaining the totalitarianism threat on the political horizon, the controls of this expanded administration should be arranged to ensure that the political order benefits individuals (ICJ, 1956, p. 5). The legal debate, therefore, sought to formulate a third way: neither an uncontrolled administration of total powers, nor another, unable to carry out and give meaning to modernization, but rather a path of conciliation. For this reason, the significance of this debate could be found in André Malraux's discourse: the great question of the century was to find ways to reconcile individual freedom with social justice; or, more properly, in the terms of one of the main Brazilian commercial law specialist, Arnold Wald (1967, p. 423): "the fundamental problem existing in the contemporary world … stems from the conflict between the totalitarian vocation of economic dirigisme and the survival of the private company, between collectivist tendencies of all kinds, and respect for the individual…."

Within the fundamentally Cold War debate in post-war Brazil, legal ideas structurally turned to discuss police power's indoctrination and jurisprudence. In this context, police power came to be understood as the central legal instrument responsible for regulating the "individual-state" relationship.

The principle of legality: public administration and the rule of law

In 1948, one of the most important administrative law journals in Brazil (*Revista de Direito Administrativo*), founded by the Getúlio Vargas Foundation, published in its 14th volume a judgment issued by a judge from Rio Grande do Norte state, Miguel Seabra Fagundes. The judgment was on a *mandado de segurança* required by a transport company against the

State Traffic Inspectorate. The company complained that the obstacle to the circulation of vehicles at certain times and along certain routes, issued by the Inspectorate, violated a pre-existing basic right (the very substance of the *mandado de segurança*)[11] "... because it is an act of trade practiced honestly, without offending the law regulating its exercise ...." In his decision, Seabra Fagundes (1948, p. 56) accepted the *mandado de segurança*, insofar as the Inspectorate hurt competition between companies and, in effect, the public interest that should "... prevail over any other."

Seabra Fagundes' decision was important because it gave substance to the jurisprudence of judicial control over police power, specifically its discretionary power. The judge attested that whatever the public administration's prerogatives were to regulate the economic order, its purpose should always be to favor the common good. The judgment was therefore supported by the transport company's claim that the economic freedom was exercised in the public interest (Meirelles, 1957).

In public law, police power is divided between "linked or regulated power" and "discretionary power." In positive law, the former corresponds to the competence given to the public administration to practice a specific administrative act, previously circumscribed by the law. In this sense, before this act, the law determines the content, the mode, and the form of its commitment.

> In these acts, the law fully links its implementation to the information contained in its text. Therefore, such acts are linked or regulated, which means that, in practice, the public administrator is entirely bound by the statement of the law, in all its specificities. In this category of administrative acts, the administrator's freedom of action is minimal, as he will have to stick to the detailed enumeration of the positive law on how to execute them effectively.
>
> (Meirelles, 1957, p. 13)

In these terms, as further explained by the jurist Hely Lopes Meirelles, the principle of legality, the administrative act stipulated by law, imposes on the administrator the strict observance of the referred rule, determining that any measure of public authority outside of this scope is an illegal action. The control of such activities, their observance of the law, is the responsibility of the judiciary. According to Hely Lopes, the jurisprudence of the linked or regulated administrative act in Brazilian courts consequently was considered a "firm" and "consensual" issue (1957, p. 14; Fagundes, 1950)

In contrast, discretionary power corresponds to that which is granted by law to the practice of administrative acts whereby public authority is permitted to choose its convenience, opportunity, and content (Meirelles, 1957). Discretionary power thus became the one that conformed to the predictability of expanding the powers of the executive, largely justified in this debate due to the difficulty of the legislative branch to act as a normative body following the modern dynamics. Here, precisely, one finds the idea behind the renewal of the positive law order that imposed limits to its competence: the question of time, the vertigo of modernization, the "fast rite of time" determining a new agency of human processes and relations in the social order. In other words, the law, according to one of the principal Spanish public law specialists, Laureano Luíz Rodó, unable to deal with the minutiae of social life, the multiplication of the acts of this expanded public authority under the aegis of modern social dynamics, "had retreated." In an article published by the *Revista de Direito Administrativo* concerning discretionary power, Rodó argued that the legal regulation of administrative activity is restricted: "it cannot go any further than what is categorically predictable." Legal rules should always maintain a certain margin of appreciation, for on every occasion they rely on circumstances that are "indeterminate and fluctuating" whenever they suffer the impact of social life, "molding themselves and assuming different coloring, according to the circumstances." Here, Rodó considered that if the normative effort was structured in rigid concepts it would, certainly, collapse when in contact with life in its natural "movements." The fundamental assumption concerning discretionary power was that it entails a "faculty of free appreciation, of self-determination," allowing it to act by its judgment. Thus, the discretionary power – "a way of acting with discretion – is the art of choosing the best, the art of appreciating and evaluating everything in view of its purpose" (Rodó, 1954, p. 44–45).

Indoctrinating police power, particularly the controls over "discretionary power," had become one of the most complicated and important issues and focal point of the debates on public administrative law precisely because this device was at the foundation of state intervention (Leal, 1948; Tácito, 1952). In the doctrinal debate of public law, it became essential to examine the nature of the administration's acts: as its activities multiplied, the state abandoned the exclusively legal purpose of its actions to dedicate itself to the purposes of social welfare. The law declared itself, as mentioned, powerless to describe administrative life in its complexity, paving the way for the expansion of the public authority's discretionary activity. Indeed, only this typology of decision-making would permit public authority to organize economic and social life in favor of the general interest (Rodó, 1954).

After 30 years of this doctrinal evolution, Hely Lopes Meirelles, possibly the most important Brazilian jurist regarding public administrative law, followed the steps of Caio Tácito, Laureano Rodó and argued that regarding public administration controls there was no scope for the judiciary to pronounce on *administrative merit* – convenience, opportunity, and fairness of the government's action. In so doing, the judiciary would be passing over to the executive competencies of the administration and thereby not favoring its own jurisdictional competence to verify the conformity of the administrative act with the law (Meirelles, 1973; Fagundes, 1951, p. 1). In other words, the objective of administrative activity differed from the legal objective, which is to safeguard the public interest, making discretionary power an attribute of the administration for the fulfillment of its initiatives (Rodó, 1954). In this, moreover, the Brazilian doctrine would consensually find what the main German jurists were arranging. "The discretionary power has, more or less," Fritz Fleiner argued, "the scope of making it possible for the administration to adjust its activity to the requirements of individual circumstances, so that it is always most effective and most useful for the public purpose it deals with" (Fleiner, 1933, p. 6; Ponde, 1951).

Following the evolution of the doctrine on discretionary power, it became important to describe the *autonomous nature of the administration*. Together with a formulated control for what would be a free executive will, the doctrine underlined the understanding that this autonomous action by the administration is not legal and, consequently, demanded *jurisdictional restraint*. In other words, the doctrine moved the discretionary act to legality, effectively imposing legal limits on its exercise. The doctrine distanced itself, which is important to note, from the view that identified state with law, by which all state activity would simply be the law in action. This understanding was inscribed in the understanding, guided largely by Austrian jurists such as Hans Kelsen and Edmund Bernatizik, that legal norms hold validity in and of themselves, intrinsic to the text of the law, and their evaluation is not fit for anything outside it. As far as discretionary power is concerned, its control would not fit, since the administrative act would be nothing more than a power to interpret and, therefore, execute the law (Rodó, 1954). Ultimately, such an understanding established every state as based on rule of law, including totalitarian states.

In these terms, this freedom of action recognized, in particular, by the executive power marked the difficulty and the hermeneutical effort of the legal field, here and in other parts of the Atlantic world, such as Rodó's Spain, Fleiner's Germany, and Bartolome Fiorini's Argentina, to explain that one should not confuse this power with arbitrariness or illegality. On the contrary, in this distinction lay the fundamental role of *control* of the administrative act by the judiciary. In other words, in this doctrinal process, if, on the one hand, discretionary action as an attribute of the administration was brought to law, on the other, a control function was created between the government branches: administrative acts were subject to the control of the judiciary, assuring their operationalization within the principle of legality and guaranteeing their democratic legitimacy. In doing so, the government action could circumvent the "collectivization" principles advocated by the socialist legality.

This was an inclination of Brazilian doctrine already present, even before the 1948 court decision of Miguel Seabra Fagundes, in a 1941 work authored by the judge himself and titled "The Control of Administrative Acts by the Judiciary," and in texts that preceded it, like the books of jurists José Matos de Vasconcelos, "Direito Administrativo," [Administrative Law] 1936, Tito Prates da Fonseca, "Direito Administrativo," 1939, José de Castro

Nunes, "Do Mandado de Segurança," 1937, and José Guimarães Menegale, "Direito Administrativo e Ciência da Administração," [Administrative Law and Administrative Sciences] 1939 (Fagundes, 1948; Meirelles, 1988). Even dissonant voices, such as those of Themístocles Cavalcanti and Vitor Nunes Leal, were reassessing their positions in this immediate post-war period in favor of controlling the discretionary acts of the administration (Cavalcanti, 1938, p. 102–103; Leal, 1946).

The construction of jurisprudence in public law could be supported, as shown in the justification of the judgment by Seabra Fagundes (1948), by foreign doctrine, in which German authors such as Mayer and Fleiner were prominent. Such inclination and the acceptance of the control institutions in the different justice administration systems worldwide had, moreover, in the prominent International Commission of Jurists (ICJ) a *locus* of anchoring and systematization. By the beginning of the Cold War era the organization had established itself as the most important institution for the defense of human rights and the premises of rule of law. These premises, during more than a decade of activity, constituted the basis for an agenda dedicated to offering parameters and legal direction for the modernization process undertaken in the underdeveloped countries and the post-colonial world (Tolley, 1994). In a way, the ICJ invested itself within the framework of the State Department's anti-totalitarian agenda with the task of producing a legal doctrine in line with the efforts envisioned in modernization theories.

Among other aspects, the legal elites gathered by the Commission of Jurists turned to the discussion of the activities of executive power and the functions of controlling its acts. In this sense, it became important to stipulate a principle of legality in response to the expanded prerogatives of the state: the prevision that such prerogatives be practiced under the law and, thus, be subject to the control of the law. This doctrinal effort received an important boost with the publication of the *New Delhi Declaration*, resulting from the ICJ convention held in January 1959 in the Indian capital. It stipulated, in line with the social rights declared in the Universal Declaration of Human Rights (Moyn, 2018, p. 90), that the rule of law depended not only on the provision of safeguards against abuses by the executive branch but also on the existence of governments capable of guaranteeing adequate social and economic conditions for life in society. This involved the delegation of normative functions from the legislative to the executive branches of government. Aware of the demands for development that came mainly from the post-colonial countries, the International Commission of Jurists sought, in terms of this expanded concept of rule of law, to bring modernization programs within the framework of the so-called free world (Marsh, 1959; Moesley, Harrigan, and Toye,1991, p. 3).

At the beginning of the following decade, the Commission, in a very sophisticated and attentive work in particular on Latin America, dedicated itself to scrutinizing the norms for controlling administrative acts. In the

Journal, the Commission's periodical publication – which, as well as its archives, had "subscriptions to one hundred newspapers, journals, and periodicals" around the world (Tolley, 1994, p. 100) –, the Belgian Fritz Gygi published in 1962 a long and dense article. Gygi, one of the most important European legal scholars of the period, took stock of the premises for rule of law and its adequacy to the legal forms of the welfare state. In this sense, the jurist described the transition from the legal system proper to the laissez-faire society, in which the legal scope of the state's action was reduced to regulating social obligations for freedom, to that of this modern society, in which the legislator was led to grant discretionary powers to the administration – given the greatly expanded role of its activities, claiming, accordingly, greater freedom and speed of movement. "It is not the fact," Gygi stressed, "that administrative acts are remotely related to some legal provisions which make the legality principle an important feature of the rule of law, but the inclusion in the law and unmistakable provisions as to what the duties of administrations are, and how and within what limits it is to go about them." The Belgian went further to say that to respect the rule of law it is not only necessary to ensure legality, but the "correct implementation of legislation" which depends on "additional institutions," particularly the judicial review of administration. "This can only be effective," Gygi concluded, "if the legality principle has first committed the administration in judicially controllable form to the observance of fixed rules of conduct" (1962, p. 27).

When in December 1962 the Commission of Jurists met at a new international convention in the city of Petrópolis, Rio de Janeiro, this reconciliation was brought to the fore in the analysis of the executive. It was considered necessary to guarantee certain freedoms to public administration for it to carry out economic and social development, but at the same time also to ensure the protection of individual rights. The "Rio Resolution," the resulting report of the ICJ's International Congress in Brazil, stipulated that this discretionary power should be subject to examination by the courts. Here, the parameter brought by the commission was comprised of values of natural justice: the principles that, despite the legal order organized by the constitutions and codes, there are human rights evident in and of themselves and that do not depend on their existence in positive law (Congresso Internacional de Juristas. Resolução do Rio, 1963, p. 27).

Doctrine and jurisprudence in the country leaned in the direction of the understanding defended by Gygi and the legal elites gathered in Brazil, among them Themístocles Cavalcanti, Miguel Seabra Fagundes, and Miguel Reale. The main Brazilian jurists to take part in this debate – Seabra Fagundes, Vitor Nunes Leal, Hely Lopes Meirelles, Castro Nunes, and Caio Tácito – called the "the common good" the "legal destination" that all administrative acts must have merit and political reason. In other words, reflecting the structure of legal ideas in the period, the common good guides the best use for administrative procedure in the relationship between individual right (subjective) and collective interest in the search for political fulfillment (Rodó, 1954, p. 42).

However, insofar as this common good was not precisely stipulated in positive law, the limitation the administration had to respect was an *extrinsic* one, based on the moral virtue of that time and the "good conduct" of the public administration. Therefore, on a more complex level regarding the linked administrative act, the discretionary act had, besides the legal aspects, the merit aspects. Thus, legal authority distinguished the administrative act's motive and object from its legality in such a way that the *autonomous nature of administration* had a non-legal aspect, and therefore one that the legal authority – courts and judges – had nothing to do with.

> [....] the merit of the administrative act constitutes an aspect of the Administration's procedure, in such a way related to circumstances and assessments only perceptible to the administrator, given the inquiry processes available to him and the nature of the function he exercises, that the judge is unable to know [....]. The merit is in the political sense of the administrative act. [....] In other words: every administrative measure must take into account the meaning of the act as a procedure that serves the public interest, and, at the same time, adjusts it to private interests. That is why it always expresses a comparative judgment.
>
> (Fagundes, 1951, p. 1–2)

As explained by Fritz Gygi, however, Brazilian doctrine began to describe, in addition to extrinsic limitation, an internal control over the discretionary act. This power/function – the theme of the thesis in administrative law that Caio Tácito defended[12] in 1951 at the State University of Guanabara (today, UERJ) – "...is not only subject to external limits, such as competence, form and material existence of motives, but also internal limits... that concern the observance of the legal purpose" (Tácito, 1952, p. 9). As a result, Brazilian jurists sought the French principle of *détournement de pouvoir* – the "misuse of power," more precisely, "misuse of purpose" – as an internal limit (Queiró, 1947). It was to this legal norm that Seabra Fagundes had supported his judgment, marking a jurisprudence of control of the administrative act: the discretionary action, in the case of the Transport Company, was illegal because it had demonstrated "misuse of purpose" (Fagundes, 1948). It ceased to aim for the purpose for which it was intended, the sense of bringing about a reconciliation between the "common good" and the subjective right of the individual to serve the merely private interest of a second Transport Company.

The evolution of the doctrine of control of the executive by the judiciary, together with the recognition of the principle of legality, sought to place the rule of law as a condition for these discretionary actions by public administration. The doctrine of control sought to re-insert expanded public authority into the framework of democratic and anti-totalitarian forms of government.

Nonetheless, the legal debate in Brazil was also concerned with a broader issue regarding the organization of the administration of justice. In particular, there was a diagnosis on the need to reform the judiciary. Indeed, the "crisis of the Federal Supreme Court," the growing docket, year by year, of cases not judged by the court was a clear indication to legal elites that the Federal Supreme Court (STF) was no longer effectively fulfilling its role of controlling and guaranteeing the individual rights against state authority. Reform, then, became essential to ensure the balance of the binomial state-individual in the face of the modernization process.

Reforming the judiciary: the "crisis of the Supreme" and the control of public administration

The impositions of modernity had also arrived at the judiciary, particularly in the form of a "crisis" of its highest institution: the Federal Supreme Court. Following the proclamation of the Republic and the federative regime instituted by Decree n. 1, of November 15, 1889, the provisional government of Marshal Deodoro da Fonseca enacted Decree n. 848, on October 11, 1890, stipulating the duality of the Brazilian justice system: alongside the state judiciary, it created the justice of the Union, with the Federal Justice of 1st Instance, divided between the federal judges and courts and distributed throughout the country, and the Federal Supreme Court at its summit. Influenced by U.S. legal modeling, the highest court in the country was entrusted with guarding the tenets of the constitution: the protection of individual freedoms and rights; the federative balance; to discipline jurisprudence; and the unity of national positive law.

As part of its tasks, the 1891 Constitution attributed two fronts to the court: an *original* competence and an *appealable jurisdiction*. The first concerned the competence to prosecute and judge causes of greater interest and seriousness (involving the president of the republic, in the case of common crimes; conflicts between the union and states, as well as between these and foreign nations). The second, to judge, as the last instance of the justice system, the causes appealed against lower court decisions rendered by federal courts and by states courts.[13] The competence to judge *appeals* was, in turn, divided by *ordinary* paths, proceeding through the lower courts until they reached the Supreme Court, and by the *extraordinary* path, an innovation that borrowed from U.S. modeling and whose purpose was to ensure the primacy of federal law by invoking the case by a justice of the STF or by the attorney general of the republic, at that time appointed among one of the members of the court itself.[14] To meet the nature of the federative regime (which, on the one hand, authorized the legislative duality, produced in the spheres of the states and the union, and, on the other hand, the duality of justice, one federal and the other state), the extraordinary appeal imposed the recognition of the sovereignty of the union and federal laws to the entire territory of the republic.

> If the Constituent Congress had not included among the attributions of the Supreme the power to annul [....] sentences, each State would embark

> on a sovereign unity in the application of the law and there could appear as many ways of pronouncing the law as there were local justices.
>
> (Buzaid, 1960, p. 342)

During the First Republic (1889–1930), the relationship to the Federal Supreme Court in the cases raised – through appeals or the original via – remained in balance. Moreover, the modeling of the administration of justice continued analogous to the federalist system instituted in 1891. After the 1930 coup and the Vargas regime's concentration of powers in the executive, the relationship between the entry of lawsuits and those judged became increasingly deficient: 150, in 1935; 230, in 1936; 242, in 1937; 210, in 1938; 286, in 1939; 804, in 1940; 1,047, in 1941; 1,113, in 1942; and 1,124, in 1943 (Buzaid, 1960, p. 346). In 1964, the Supreme Court would judge 7,000 cases, against 3,511, in 1950 (Wald, 1965a, p. 4), reaching almost 10,000 in 1968 (Baleeiro, 1973, p. 9).

This expansion of the public administration came to re-articulate, on the one hand, relations that were previously articulated privately and whose discipline the state abstained from carrying out, and, on the other, the federalist organization of administration, favoring, above all, the concentration of powers in the union. Such centrality of the union concerning the states and municipalities can be seen in the evolution of the tax income of the federated entities: between 1930 and 1946, the Union's income grew in the proportion of 598%; that of the states, 112%; and that of the municipalities, 217% (Meirelles, 1963). The growing empowerment of the state authority at the federal level, at the expense of individual rights and federated entities, led to an increase in rights claims through the judicial system, specifically those rights ensured in the form of concessions of *habeas corpus* and what would become, from 1934,[15] the *mandado de segurança* (Buzaid, 1960; Costa, 2006).

Reacting to the Vargas dictatorship, the legal order of the 1946 Constitution was based on the resumption of some liberal premises. For what we are specifically interested in, the Constituent of that year maintained, in its fundamental lines, the expanded scope guaranteed by the 1934 Charter, in which it was possible to file an extraordinary appeal. Moreover, the lawmaker prescribed to the Federal Supreme Court the authority to judge not only extraordinary but also ordinary appeals for *mandados de segurança* and *habeas corpus*, formerly decided by local or federal courts, when the request was not granted. Despite the creation in 1946 of the Federal Court of Appeals (TFR), based on the need to "unburden" the Supreme Court,[16] the imbalance and *deficit* of processes judged by the STF continued to increase throughout the 1950s and early 1960s.

This led to the deepening of what legal elites called the "crisis of the Federal Supreme Court" (Medeiros, 1944; Fagundes, 1954). The Constitutional Amendment of 1926, the first systematic effort to modernize the Brazilian legal order, restricted the circumstances in which *habeas corpus* could be appealed to the Supreme Court. Thus, according to the Special Commission of the National Congress, the amendment was justified because the text of the 1891 Constitution had "raised numerous and notable controversies and so facilitated the appeals of the judges of the States to the Federal Supreme Court such that the accumulation of service has disturbed the regularity of its functions" (Meirelles, 1963, p. 4).

By the early 1940s, jurists such as José Saboia Viriato de Medeiros and Levi Fernandes Carneiro had been arguing that the Brazilian Supreme Court "suffers from a plethora of cases submitted to its judgment." The ministers, said Carneiro (1943, p. 1), were increasing their efforts, multiplying the sessions and decisions handed over, reaching high numbers – "nonetheless, the cases received by the Court rose even higher." Naming such a crisis was a way of recognizing the modern challenge of shaping the judiciary into an organic system and maintaining the expanded competence of the Supreme Court as the guarantor of the foundational clauses of liberalism – the *habeas corpus* and *mandado de segurança* – without impeding state economic development. In other words, meeting the divided demands of the political dimension based on the individual, protected from illegal action or abuse of state power, and the politics of economic development, which at times meant circumventing certain individual guarantees and the independence of the judiciary.

Since the early 1940s and intensifying throughout the 1950s, the legal field was dedicated to discussing the crisis of the Brazilian Supreme Court.[17] An important systematization aimed at responding to the crisis took place with the appointment of Nereu de Oliveira Ramos in March 1956 for a special committee of jurists. Such committee, which took place a few months after Juscelino Kubitschek assumed the presidency, had the purpose of responding to the criticism that a significant part of the legal elites had been making regarding the ungovernability of the Greater Law of 1946 (Meirelles, 1963, p. 2; Fagundes,1956) by presenting a constitutional reform draft proposal. One of the topics of the preliminary draft, led by Carlos Medeiros Silva, dealt with the "jurisdiction of the Federal Supreme Court, particularly in regards to the extraordinary appeal." The committee proposed abolishing the possibility of ordinary appeal to reach the Supreme Court and the reduction of the scope of admission of extraordinary appeal by the STF (Lima, Dantas, Medeiros Silva, *et al*, 1956, p. 40).

In an inaugural class given at the University of São Paulo Law School in April 1960, Professor Alfredo Buzaid diagnosed the need to deepen the measures to restrict the functions of the Supreme Court (Buzaid, 1960, p. 357). He further argued that the nodal point for the STF crisis rested on the liberal formula, that is, the laissez-faire culture of the 1946 Charter. In his long assessment of the Supreme Court, from its founding to that moment of crisis, he emphasized that the hybridity of the court – as a constitutional court and as an appellate court of the highest instance – made it impossible to carry out so many tasks by a single tribunal of 11 ministers. In other words, while the constitutional process had not discussed increasing the number of justices, as was done, for example, in Mexico, the function of verifying the constitutionality of laws and normative acts of the legislative and executive branches remained with the Supreme Court. Despite his support for the restrictive tendency of the powers of the Supreme Court, Buzaid doubted that the legislature could eliminate the ordinary appeal for *mandado de segurança* and *habeas corpus*. He thus presented as a possible solution to the "permanent crisis" the creation of a new court: a tribunal with exclusive appellate function to judge the claims processed through appeals, thereby reserving the Supreme Court for the other assignments, including declarations of unconstitutionality.[18]

The assessment of the "Supreme Court crisis" and consequent "ungovernability of the country" within the framework of the 1946 Charter was commonplace among Brazilian legal elites. Yet despite this and the urgency required of the situation, proposed legal solutions did not reach a consensus. The urgency resumed with the end of the parliamentary system and return of João Goulart to the presidency after the national referendum in January 1963 on the political system to be adopted. That same month, the Brazilian Congress for the Definition of Basic Reforms met under the arches of the University of Sao Paulo Law School. The discussion focused on structural reforms in favor of resolving the impasse of the national plan for modernization. The prominent Brazilian constitutionalist, José Horácio T. Meirelles, described the situation as a "…total crisis, manifesting itself in so many crises and partial collapses" (1963, p. 2). Sponsored by the newspapers *Correio da Manhã* and *Folha de S. Paulo* and with support from the Institute of Brazilian Lawyers (IAB), the meeting, in many ways a locus for gathering political and intellectual elites against the Goulart administration, discussed the detailed formatting of reforms of all three branches of government and the functionality of the state in a new legal order.

The congress was divided into five commissions, focused on specific themes, each organized by a president, a secretary, and a general rapporteur. Additionally, each commission received theses produced by their participants. Before going to the plenary for a vote, the theses were reviewed and filtered by technical commissions. The first of the five commissions – chaired by Minister Antônio de Sampaio Dória with Professor Alfredo Cecílio Lopes as secretary and report by Judge Oswaldo Aranha Bandeira de Mello – took up the question of the modernization of the judiciary with the theme entitled "Constitutional, Political-Party, and Electoral Reforms."

The discussions about the judiciary focused on examining the competencies of the STF. The thesis presented by the constitutionalist José Horácio Teixeira Meirelles addressed constitutional control over the public administration's acts. He indicated the fragile role of the judiciary in the examination of the expanded powers of the union, making Brazilian federalism closer to the existing geopolitical organization in the Soviet Union than the United States. In these terms, he pointed out what would be the flawed system of constitutional control of laws in Brazil: a fundamental instrument to ensure the unity of positive law and the legal security of the national system and to impose discipline for the profusion of legislation without the proper techniques and pertinence to the law. Thus, Teixeira Meirelles, in an "early" criticism of legislative production in Brazil (1963, p. 2–51), noted that weak constitutional controls had been allowing the approval and application of several norms in contrast to Brazilian major law and, therefore, to the detriment of it.

Teixeira Meirelles then proposed the creation of a constitutional court, whose exclusive competence would be to verify the constitutionality of laws. The unburdening of the Supreme Court, in these terms, would be due to the diminution of the court's competence exclusively to regulate constitutional unity and federal law, as had happened with the Federal Constitutional Court of Germany (*Bundesverfassungsgericht*) and with the French Constitutional Council (*Conseil Constitutionnel*), created with the same purpose, respectively, in 1951 and 1958. Promptly rejected by the rapporteur, Judge Oswaldo Aranha, who stood for the maintenance of Brazilian "tradition" – the system of declaration of unconstitutionality by all courts, with the Supreme Court being the last instance –, the president of the commission proposed to divide the discussion about the judiciary into two parts: (a) should constitutional courts be created or not; and (b) evaluate the competences of the Supreme Court.

In the same vein as Oswaldo Aranha, the plenary rejected (with the exception of its proponent, Teixeira Meirelles) the creation of constitutional courts. The question then turned to how to reduce the attributions of the STF regarding extraordinary appeals to constitutional matters. In this area, Miguel Seabra Fagundes came up with a detailed proposal:

> On the one hand, there is the unity of the interpretation of the Constitution and federal law. On the other hand, that of ensuring effective protection for the individual, before justice, through the various instances. [....] In his [Seabra Fagundes'] view, the Supreme Court would hold its current ordinary jurisdiction, except in the case of habeas corpus. As for extraordinary appeals, it would only function as a constitutional court, that is, when the text of the constitution was at stake. ... Thus, all other jurisdictions of the Supreme Court would be transferred to three regional courts, which ordinary law would organize, and to which it would assign jurisdiction and guidelines, according to the convenience of the local population.
>
> These courts, then, would not be what the Federal Court of Appeals is today. These courts would also be courts of extraordinary litigation – extraordinary litigation under federal law is not constitutional – and courts of ordinary litigation for habeas corpus and *mandado de segurança*. The result will be that the Federal Supreme Court will have its functions reduced, in terms of the original jurisdiction, to those matters that, due to their nature, should not fall outside the jurisdiction of the Federal Supreme Court. [....] Then, practically, the service volume of the Supreme Court would drop vertically.
>
> (Congresso Brasileiro para Definição Das Reformas de Base, 1963, p. 22)

Thus presented, Seabra Fagundes' suggestion was accepted to avoid the accumulation of claims in the Supreme Court, but without prejudice to its essential functions. In October 1963, Seabra Fagundes defended the same position before the Federal Council of the Brazilian Bar Association, which, gathering representatives from all states, unanimously approved the proposal as part of its judiciary reform project (Fagundes, 1966).[19]

These proposals for restructuring the judiciary to resolve the "crisis of the Supreme" were not put into effect, however, and instead the debate resumed in the immediate post-coup environment of 1964. This took place when the Castello Branco administration signaled, through his minister of justice, Milton Campos, his inclination to reform the judiciary and that he was open to "society's proposals" (Campos, 1965, p. 9; Wald, 1965a; 1965b).

The 1964 coup and the reform of the judiciary: aligning with developmentalism

> Between 1965 and 1966 President Castello Branco issued no less than three institutional acts, 36 complementary acts, 312 decree-laws, and 3746 punitive acts. The so-called exclusion clause hovered above all, that is, the device that eliminated certain acts of revolutionary power from examination even of the judiciary and, therefore, of any other authority.
>
> (Bonavides and Andrade, 1991, p. 432)

In June 1965, the ministers of the Federal Supreme Court, especially in the figure of their president, Ribeiro da Costa, delivered the project for judiciary reform to the minister of justice, Milton Campos. In its project, the Supreme Court made a critical assessment of proposals previously presented, resuming the legal debate before the coup.[20] The first and most important aspect highlighted in the project referred to the "crisis" of the court, noting that the issue was not a reality exclusive to Brazil. The ministers attested that the burden of the highest courts was a "universal phenomenon," including the United States, whose justice system inspired the Brazilian organization in the late 19th century. However, in the United States the crisis was practically resolved with the 1925 reform (*Judiciary Act*), whereby it became the Supreme Court's exclusive competence to decide which cases to judge based on the fundamental repercussions they would have or not for the unity of law in the country. Following this understanding, the Brazilian project indicated that the flexibility (or rather, the decrease) of the Supreme Court's attributions should rely on the decrease of its responsibilities, preserving its historical tasks as the arbiter of the constitution and federal law, the insurer of the federative pact balance, the harmony between state powers and the integrity individual rights.

Nonetheless, a reform of the most important Brazilian legal institution also involves reforming the entire justice system. One of the questions rested on the re-establishment of the Federal Court of 1st Instance, extinguished by the 1937 Constitution, which would better correspond to the federative idea. In this regard, the project accepted such re-establishment, but demanded the clear definition of its competence to avoid jurisdictional conflicts which would result in the congestion of the Supreme Court and risk disrupting the unity of the legal order (Ribeiro Costa, Mota Filho, Leal, *et al,* 1965). Another issue raised in the project rested on the imperative to relieve the Federal Court of Appeals by increasing the number of judges and transferring part of its attributions to another federal court of appeals, to be created.

In this sense, the "crisis of the Supreme" would not be resolved with the disciplinary action of its competencies and with a profound modification in the structure of the justice system in the country. In the STF project, the question was, rather, one of technique. The project listed measures adopted that would have softened the work of the court, such as the creation, in late 1963, on the initiative of Minister Victor Nunes Leal, of the "Predominant Jurisprudence Summary,"[21] and the institution of monetary correction and restrictions on *mandado de segurança* by civil servants. It furthermore stipulated disciplinary measures, by relevance, in response to the claims raised to the Supreme Court, especially of extraordinary appeals, which caused a greater burden on the tribunal (Ribeiro Costa, Mota Filho, Leal, *et al,* 1965; Valladão, Gil, and Basílio, 1965).[22]

Resuming some of the positions previously defended, the STF indicated a way to overcome its crisis, thus re-establishing the integrity of the justice system. This took place especially with the recreation of the Federal Court of 1st Instance (repositioning in favor of the federal government the interests of the union in the states)[23] while preserving its position as the ultimate guardian of the constitution, of the unity of law and legal certainty and individual rights and safeguards. To a certain degree, legal elites (Valladão, Gil, and Basílio, 1965),[24] including the ministers, were in agreement with the understanding that the modernization effort required state intervention under the auspices of the federal government. This is true not only regarding the reform project but mostly the decisive support and legitimization of the 1964 coup by the Supreme Court and by institutions of the legal elite such as the Brazilian Bar Association and the Institute of Brazilian Lawyers (Mattos, 2011, chapter 3). Nonetheless, although it was not truly included in legal thinking until the coup, except by the suggestion of the conservative Alfredo Buzaid, one issue rapidly entered the political debate after 1964: the increase in the number of ministers. However, an important part of the legal elites opposed the Castello Branco administration's proposal – justified as a way of enabling the STF to act *pari passu* with the "acceleration of the pace of history" – to increase the number of the court justices and the creation of a "sub-plenary."[25]

In early September 1965, the president of the STF, Ribeiro da Costa, declined an invitation by the president of the Senate, Auro de Moura Andrade, for the court to appoint a representative to the Mixed Commission of Deputies and Senators in charge of discussing the institutional reform, including of the judiciary. As indicated by an article very critical of the Castello

Branco administration that appeared in the newspaper *Correio da Manhã* on September 2nd of that year, the Supreme Court had already delivered a project to the federal government. Furthermore, the article noted that the "good constitutional norm" – the respect for the rule of law premise of the separation of powers – required keeping the reform initiative with the Court. In any case, the participation of one minister in the Mixed Commission would be problematic, since all the members of the court would not be present for deliberation in case of a controversial matter (Wald, 1965a, p. 6).

Later that month, Victor Nunes Leal published an article in *Revista dos Tribunais* where he dedicated himself to examining the issue of increasing the number of ministers in the Supreme Court, although he indicated that this hypothesis had already been discarded in the STF project that he subscribed to. At the outset, Leal's analysis placed the referred increase between two intentions: the Court's greater efficiency and the possible modification of its jurisprudence (in other words, of its political inclination). In short, the argument for efficiency, according to Leal, was unsustainable because the volume of cases to judge was not the determining factor for the number of ministers, but the opposite. In this sense, the Court is an arbiter of state powers and the limitations imposed by the constitution, a fundamental pillar of individual freedoms and rights. Leal also argued that the Supreme Court of the United States had only nine members and did a satisfactory job: the theme of the crisis at the top of the judiciary lay, as pointed out in the STF's own proposal for reform, in the technical organization of that power. In Leal's argument (1965), the hypothesis remained that the Castello Branco administration wanted in fact to modify the Court's jurisprudence (see Tables 2.1–2.3).[26]

By the same token, Arnold Wald, in an article published by *Correio da Manhã*, noted that the issue was a revival of the discussion that took place in the United States in the mid-1930s. Wald recalled that the Franklin D. Roosevelt administration, in an attempt to expand the state's intervention

Table 2.1 Federal Supreme Court composition on March 31, 1964

Minister	*Nominated by President*	*Nomination Date*
Alvaro M. Ribeiro da Costa	José Linhares	January 26, 1946
A. C. Lafayette de Andrada	José Linhares	November 1, 1945
Hahnemann Guimarães	Eurico Gaspar Dutra	October 24, 1946
Luis Gallotti	Eurico Gaspar Dutra	December 9, 1949
Cândido Motta Filho	Juscelino Kubitschek	April 13,1956
Antônio Martins Villas Boas	Juscelino Kubitschek	February 13, 1957
Antônio G. de Oliveira	Juscelino Kubitschek	October 2, 1960
Vitor Nunes Leal	Juscelino Kubitschek	November 26, 1960
Pedro R. Marcondes Chaves	Jânio Quadros	April 14, 1961
Hermes Lima	João Goulart	June 11, 1963
Evandro C. Lins e Silva	João Goulart	August 14, 1963

with New Deal policies, had several of its initiatives reversed by the Supreme Court, specifically because its members were inclined toward the supremacy of individual freedoms and guarantees, including in the economic order. In Wald's terms, the "government of judges in the United States at that stage proved to be a dangerous obstacle to the constructive New Deal policy, nullifying important U.S. Congressional laws that ensured the country's economic development and the effective distribution of social justice." (1965a, p. 6). Roosevelt's "court-packing" project, in this sense, was an attempt to modify the Supreme Court's jurisprudence – an attempt also recalled in the STF's project and Leal's article. Indeed, Roosevelt's plan to reshape the Supreme Court was born of fears, among liberals, of invalidation of the New Deal agenda by the tribunal, which did indeed occur from the spring of 1935 on. The Castello Branco administration used similar arguments to the Roosevelt administration when emphasizing the Court's "congestion" and "delays." The court-packing plan, however, not only was defeated by U.S. Congress in July 1937 but also gave the opposition a powerful rhetorical argument of impending dictatorship to use against FDR. By the early 1940s, such rhetoric became so profound that the New Deal agenda became the "anti-totalitarian" struggle – leaning not to the Right, nor the Left, but a Vital Center (Brinkley, 1995, p. 18–21; Alpers, 2003, chapter 3). It is interesting that the legal opposition to the Castello Branco plan revived Roosevelt and not the Vargas regime. In February 1931, Vargas reduced the number of Brazilian Supreme Court ministers from 15 to 11 and compulsorily retired 6 members: the attorney general, Antônio Joaquim Pires de Carvalho e Albuquerque, and Ministers Edmundo Muniz Barreto, Pedro Afonso Mibielli, Godofredo Cunha, Geminiano da Franca, and Pedro Joaquim dos Santos. He appointed two new members: João Martins de Carvalho Mourão and Plínio Casado (Costa, 2006, p. 70–71; Recondo, 2018, p. 12–13). With this compulsory retirement, the Vargas administration was able to reshape the Court's jurisprudence.

Victor Nunes Leal, in his analysis, wondered about the possibility that Castello's intention, after all, was to modify the court's jurisprudence, which the minister himself, however, said was not a plausible hypothesis. Not least because, he warned, this would jeopardize the independence of the judiciary and separation of powers. Apart from that, public opinion in countries like the United States had rejected such initiatives (Leal, 1965; Baleeiro, 1973). By the same token, on October 20, the president of the Supreme Court, Ribeiro da Costa, in an article entitled "Uselessness of the Increase of Ministers of the Supreme Court," published in *Correio da Manhã*, reacted to the intention of increasing the number of ministers:

> Nothing is more blunt, absurd, weird, and shocking regarding the basic principles of the constitution than considering to increase the number of judges of the Supreme Court without the judges having expressed this need through a message addressed to the National Congress. [....]. It is time for the military to realize that in democratic regimes they do

> not have the role of mentors of the Nation, as they recently did, with an astonishing breach of sacred duties, the sergeants urged by Jangos and Brizolas. Civil activity belongs to civilians, military to military personnel who, under their sacred commitment, swear allegiance to the laws of the Constitution.
>
> (Costa, 1965. Cited in Rodrigues, 2002, p. 335)

A week later, on the 27th, Castello Branco enacted Institutional Act n. 2, a discretionary "revolutionary" legal instrument to put into motion the authoritarian modernization project. The AI-2 determined, following the Supreme Court's project, the re-establishment of the Federal Court of 1st Instance, the increase in the number of judges of the Federal Court of Appeals from 9 to 13 and, despite opposition not only from the STF but also from jurists such as Arnold Wald, increased the number of Supreme Court judges from 11 to 16 ministers. Moreover, STF gained a third sub-plenary collegiate of five members each, besides the plenary (Costa, 2006, p. 166–168; Gaspari, 2002, p. 257 e 271). Furthermore, it excluded from judicial review – a strategy also stipulated in the Institutional Act n. 1, of April 1964 – the acts practiced by the Supreme Command of the Revolution and by the federal government within the scope of Institutional Acts and their complementary acts. Among these acts was the competence to suspend, for six months, constitutional guarantees of vitality and stability of public servants, including those in the legal authority, and to dismiss, transfer or retire (Brasil, 1965b).

Shortly afterward, Castello Branco complemented the reform of the judiciary with Constitutional Amendment n. 16, approved by the National Congress on November 26, 1965. The amendment limited the appeals

Table 2.2 Brazilian Federal Supreme Court composition after Institutional Act n. 2

Minister	*Nominated by President*	*Nomination Date*
Alvaro M. Ribeiro da Costa	José Linhares	January 26, 1946
A. C. Lafayette de Andrada	José Linhares	November 1, 1945
Hahnemann Guimarães	Eurico Gaspar Dutra	October 24, 1946
Luis Gallotti	Eurico Gaspar Dutra	December 9, 1949
Cândido Motta Filho	Juscelino Kubitschek	April 13,1956
Antônio Martins Villas Boas	Juscelino Kubitschek	February 13, 1957
Antônio G. de Oliveira	Juscelino Kubitschek	October 2, 1960
Vitor Nunes Leal	Juscelino Kubitschek	November 26, 1960
Pedro R. Marcondes Chaves	Jânio Quadros	April 14, 1961
Hermes Lima	João Goulart	June 11, 1963
Evandro C. Lins e Silva	João Goulart	August 14, 1963
Adalício Coelho Nogueira	Castello Branco	November 25, 1965
José Eduardo do Prado Kelly	Castello Branco	November 25, 1965
Oswaldo Trigueiro de A. Mello	Castello Branco	November 25, 1965
Aliomar de Andrade Baleeiro	Castello Branco	November 25, 1965
Carlos Medeiros Silva	Castello Branco	November 25, 1965

brought against the decisions of the STF's collegiate to cases of divergence between them, eliminating infringing and nullified embargoes. It also established the irrevocability of the decisions of the electoral and labor courts for the STF, except in the case of *habeas corpus, mandado de segurança* and unconstitutionality of law; the delimitation of the competence of the plenum, with several causes being transferred to the sub-plenary collegiate, such as *habeas corpus* and *mandado de segurança*; and, finally, it extended the representation of the attorney general of the republic, before the Supreme Court, against the unconstitutionality of law (or normative act), in thesis, to federal norms titles.[27] In sum, it approved a profound reorganization of the Brazilian justice system.

It is important to note that the Brazilian legal system started to accept a generic system of constitutionality control – one *diffuse* and the other *concentrated.* With the proclamation of the Republic and the 1891 Charter, a diffuse control was instituted whereby, from a judge of the 1st instance to the members of the STF, any magistrate had the power to declare the unconstitutionality of a law or normative act. However, such control required the existence of a specific case, such that the declaration of unconstitutionality served only for one specific judgment and the law or normative act concerning other cases remained valid. These were the cases, for example, of disputes between the executive and the legislative branches over a normative act or law approved by the latter, but vetoed by the former.

Constitutional Amendment 16, of 1965, later incorporated into the 1967 Constitution, introduced a novelty to this system by extending this constitutionality control, instituting the Supreme Court's *concentrated* control of constitutionality. Through representation of the attorney general's office, directly and exclusively to the Supreme Court (for that reason *concentrated*), it became possible to invalidate in thesis – without the need for a specific case – a federal law or normative act of *erga omnes* effect (in other words, invalidating the law for all cases and not just for the parties involved, as in the *concentrated* case).[28]

> Now, in any case, as long as there is the unconstitutionality of a federal or state legislative act or normative act, the attorney general may request the supreme court's pronouncement, arguing unconstitutionality. [....] This, in my view, is the most important power conferred by the 1967 Constitution to the federal supreme court: to declare the unconstitutionality of a federal or state law or normative act proposed by the attorney general, to invalidate legislative norms voted by Congress and by the assemblies with the sanction of the president of the republic, or governor, or even the decree-laws issued by the latter (Const., art. 58), provided they are contrary to the constitution. ... Generally, this high authority [attorney general] will take such an initiative at the request of the head of the federal executive, as it has so often taken at the request of state governors, as to state laws, when there is a veto and the veto is rejected [by Congress].

> The supreme court … judges in thesis and its pronouncement is brought to the attention of the senate to suspend the validity of the law (Const., Art. 45, paragraph IV).
>
> (Oliveira, A. G., 1968, p. 7)

Regarding the "crisis of the Supreme," the cases to be judged by the court continued to increase in the following years, despite the reforms. Not long before, between early 1967 and late 1969, other norms, mostly issued by the minister of justice and interior affairs, Carlos Medeiros Silva (Baleeiro, 1973), were promulgated in an attempt to solve the issue. Medeiros Silva abolished the ordinary appeal of injunctions against the *mandados de segurança* by other courts, as suggested in 1960 by Alfredo Buzaid, reducing the scope of extraordinary appeals.[29] This allowed the Supreme Court, in its bylaws, the power to stipulate the process and judgment of the causes of its competence and the very range of extraordinary appeals (Oliveira, 1968; Baleeiro, 1973). According to Aliomar Baleeiro, minister appointed after the AI-2, those norms demonstrate the confidence of the constituent legislator "… in the experience and knowledge of the ministers themselves for this meritorious work, the performance of the high and complex powers and competencies that were reserved by the Constitutional Instrument" (1973, p. 9).

Contrary to what Baleeiro was advocating – supported by the evaluation made by the ex-president of the STF, Antônio Gonçalves de Oliveira, of the set of reforms from 1964 to 1969 –, in January 1969 the Artur da Costa e Silva administration compulsorily retired three ministers based on Institutional Act n. 5 of December of the previous year: Victor Nunes Leal, Hermes Lima, and Evandro Lins e Silva. Following this, in February, Costa e Silva enacted the Institutional Act n. 6, reducing the number of members from 16 to 11, as in the period between 1931 and 1965. The composition of the STF on March 31, 1964 was almost entirely modified by the beginning of 1969. The reorientation of jurisprudence, as intended in the 1930s by FDR and by Vargas, was thus successfully carried out under the post-1964 authoritarian rule.[30]

An illustrative case shows the political inclination of the STF after these developments. On March 10, 1971, the Supreme Court's plenary judged complaint 849, filed by the organized political opposition in Congress, the Brazilian Democratic Movement (MDB), against Attorney General Xavier de Albuquerque, who had ordered the filing of the unconstitutionality petition of Decree-Law n. 1,077. Issued on January 26, 1970, by the Médici administration, the decree had instituted prior censorship in the disclosure of books and periodicals considered harmful to national security. Albuquerque had justified his position on the basis that – as stipulated by the Brazilian legal order after the coup – it was his private competence, as attorney general, to offer a cause of constitutionality control to the STF. The structural aspect of this claim was that it would open up the possibility of expanding, beyond the attorney general's office, the institutions that could submit an unconstitutionality claim before the Supreme Court. In this case, a political

Table 2.3 Brazilian Federal Supreme Court composition after Institutional Act n. 5

Minister	*Nomination Date*	*Leave STF*	*Reason*
Alvaro M. Ribeiro da Costa	January 26, 1946	December 5, 1966	Length of service
A. C. Lafayette de Andrada	November 1, 1945	February 3, 1969	Retired by decree
Hahnemann Guimarães	October 24, 1946	September 20, 1967	Illness
Luis Gallotti	December 9, 1949	August 16, 1974	Length of service
Cândido Motta Filho	April 13,1956	September 13, 1967	Length of service
Antônio Martins Villas-Boas	February 13, 1957	November 15, 1966	Length of service
Antônio Gonçalves de Oliveira	October 2, 1960	January 18, 1969	Renounced
Vitor Nunes Leal	November 26, 1960	January 16, 1969	Retired based on AI-5
Pedro R. Marcondes Chaves	April 14, 1961	June 5, 1967	Length of service
Hermes Lima	June 11, 1963	January 16, 1969	Retired based on AI-5
Evandro Cavalcanti Lins e Silva	August 14, 1963	January 16, 1969	Retired based on AI-5

party, the MDB. The Federal Supreme Court's plenary, however, chose to keep the competence restricted to the attorney general, capable, as affirmed in the scope of the commission gathered to reform the 1967 Constitution, of preventing abuses (of individual freedoms) (STF, 1971, p. 2).[31]

Since 1964 the measures concerning the judiciary allowed for a response to the "crisis of the Supreme," at the same time that they were able to circumvent the resistance to the "revolutionary" program at the top of the judiciary. In other words, a modernization agenda was indeed implemented – even if it meant a limitation (or a political "compression") of individual guarantees and the role of the Supreme Court in deciding on the constitutionality of public administration acts. The comprehensive modernization of the country's public administration (of all executive apparatus and its logic of action), whose central character, in Castello's words, was to "... ensure the public sector to operate by the efficiency of a private company" (Campos, 1994, p. 697), was enacted by Castello Branco in the second half of the 1960s using the decree-law instrument (n. 200/67). The basic assumption of Brazilian legal elites concerning the contours of the Social State in the country was that the private company should constitute the basic unit of national life (Paiva, 1960; Barreto Filho, 1970). This non-state dimension of "Modern State" in Brazil could also respond to the transnational anxieties regarding state-led intervention. Anti-totalitarianism played its role.

However, the encouraging anti-totalitarian reconciliation between individual freedom and social justice, as André Merloux advocated in his speech at the Acropolis, had transformed by the late 1950s and early 1960s to prominently favor a *secure* modernization. The Global North, especially U.S. power – through modernization theories, international aid, psychological warfare, and the Congress for Cultural Freedom – supported a stable industrial development, even if it meant contributing decisively to an authoritarian regime. In the Brazilian debate, by the same token, authoritarianism became a "lesser evil" compared to João Goulart's "totalitarian threat," an "adequate" torsion to what would be the lack of political maturity of Brazilian elites. The formula used by Belgian jurisconsult Jean Dabin, remembered by one of the most important constitutionalists in Brazil, José Horácio Teixeira Meirelles (1963, p. 51), was "well suited" to such a view of Brazilian political life: "if the democratic regime is ideal, it is only accessible to an elite of peoples, and after a long learning." Brazil, to the country's elites, was not one of them.

Notes

1 By this time the American Society for Public Administration and the *Public Administration Review* had been created. In 1926, the Social Science Research Council (SSRC) was established as the Advisory Committee on Public Administration to promote studies in the field. See Roberts (1994) and Fischer (1984).

2 Maritain, a French Catholic philosopher, had an important reception in Brazilian Catholic circles. Since he left *L'Action Française* in 1928, he had been approaching liberal positions and criticizing totalitarianism. In 1942, Alceu translated and wrote the Preface to "A noite da agonia." In 1945, Alceu participated in the I Brazilian Congress of Writers, an important landmark in the re-democratization of the country. On this liberal repositioning of Alceu and Catholic intellectuals in Brazil, see Cury (2010, p. 22) and Dutra (2014, p. 439–440).

3 The titles relating to the economic and social order, first established in Brazilian positive law with the 1934 Charter and inspired by the Weimar Constitution, were kept in 1946. With these titles, Brazilian elites sought to order the expansion of public administration activities so that they could answer this "social question."

4 Unlike the constitutions of 1891, 1934, and 1937, the 1946 Charter did not admit enforcement of federal laws among the cases in which federal intervention in states was permitted.

5 Speech made in Athens by Mr. André Malraux (French Minister of State for Cultural Affairs), May 28, 1959. Available at: www2.culture.gouv.fr/culture/actualites/dossiers/malraux2006/discours/a.m-athenes.htm. Accessed on: August 18, 2017.

6 CEPA was created by Decree 39,555 August/1956 to advise the presidency in matters concerning administrative reform projects, especially regarding the simplification of administrative processes. CEPA published the results of its four years of activity in four volumes, namely: (a) Reorganization of the Presidency of the Republic; (b) Creation of New Ministries; (c) Rules for Budget Preparation, Execution, and Control; (d) Final Report on the Activities of the Commission for Studies and Administrative Projects of the Presidency of the Republic. See MINISTÉRIO DO PLANEJAMENTO E COORDENAÇÃO GERAL (1969, p. 12).

7 COSB was created by Decree 39,510 July/1956 to: "a.) Study the means of decentralizing services, by delegating competence, establishing responsibility, and rendering accountability to the authority; b.) promote measures with the ministries regarding the examination of the current situation (1956) of the offices and routines that deserve immediate corrective measures." See MINISTÉRIO DO PLANEJAMENTO E COORDENAÇÃO GERAL (1969, p. 9–11).

8 This strategy can be seen earlier, in the 1930s, concerning the "modernization" of social sciences in Brazil. The Rockefeller Foundation ensured the creation of libraries, modified curricula, research premises and sent professors from the United States, such as Donald Pearson (Cancelli, Chaves, and Mesquita, 2019); Roberts (1994, p. 221–228).

9 The University of Bahia's School of Administration focused on training in public and business administration. In 1964, the school's first diplomas were awarded. Beginning in 1964, with the auspices of Ford Foundation, the school's public administration sector developed a research program under the direction of Professor José Rodrigues Senna, focused on three areas: state and municipal administration; political and social processes; and teaching methodology and materials. Along with it, the Public Service Institute was founded as its auxiliary institution, in an agreement between the government of Bahia, SUDENE, and USAID. At the University of Rio Grande do Sul, the Administration Institute was created as part of the School of Economic Sciences. The director of this school, Professor Pery Diniz da Silva, and Professor Luiz Felipe Silva intended to create a curriculum common to economics and public administration. In 1966, undergraduate courses in administration were approved, which was possible due to scholarship holders who had graduated from U.S. universities with USAID's resources having returned to Brazil. See FGV.EBAP (1964); Jacobs (2004).

10 Elwyn A. Mauck. "Public and Business Administration Division Monthly Report, August 1956." AIRGRAM Rio de Janeiro/International Cooperation Administration. RG 59. National Archives Records Administration.

11 In Brazilian doctrine, *mandado de segurança* is recognized as an "extension" of *habeas corpus.* Indeed, "the doctrinal and jurisprudential contribution that garnered the most attention in international legal circles was the so-called 'Brazilian doctrine of *habeas corpus,*' which extended it to other civil and political rights, in addition to freedom of movement." This doctrine would come to fruition in the constitutional consecration of the *mandado de segurança*, which always constitutes itself by the premise of being a certain right with the Constitution of 1934. It is important to understand that it constitutes a legal institution concerned with individual rights and is guaranteed by the STF (1965, 465).

12 Miguel Seabra Fagundes, Themístocles Cavalcanti, Carlos Medeiros Silva, Oscar Tenório, and Roberto Lyra were on the examining board. See Tácito (1951).

13 According to the 1891 Constitution:

"Art 59 – The Federal Supreme Court is responsible for:

I - process and judge originally and privately:

- a the President of the Republic in common crimes, and the Ministers of State in the cases of art. 52;
- b Diplomatic Ministers, in common crimes and those of responsibility;
- c the causes and conflicts between the Union and States, or between States with each other;

d disputes and claims between foreign nations and the Union or States;
e conflicts between Judges or Federal Courts between themselves, or between them and those of States, as well as those of Judges and Courts of a State with Judges and Courts of another State;

II - judge, as to appeals, the issues resolved by the Judges and Federal Courts, as well as those dealt with in this article, § 1, and art. 60;

III - review the processes, ended, pursuant to art. 81.

§ 1. - From the judgments of the State Courts, ultimately, there will be an appeal to the Federal Supreme Court:

a when questioned about the validity, or the application of federal treaties and laws, and the decision of the State Court is against it;
b when the validity of laws or acts of the Governments of States is challenged under the Constitution, or of federal laws, and the decision of the State Court considers those acts, or those contested laws, to be valid;

§ 2. - In cases where State laws are to be applied, the Federal Court will consult the jurisprudence of the local Courts, and vice versa, the State Courts will consult the jurisprudence of the Federal Courts, when they are to interpret Union laws" (Brazil, 1891).

14 The first attorney general of the republic was also the STF Minister, José Júlio de Albuquerque Barros, Baron of Sobral. He held the position from March 3, 1891, until his death on August 31, 1893.
15 Regulated in 1936 by Law 191.
16 The TFR was effectively installed under Law n. 33, of May 13, 1947. In order to meet the purpose of "clearing up" the Supreme Court, the new court was given original jurisdiction to judge writ of mandamus against an act of minister of justice. State, the court itself, or its president; and, as an appellate jurisdiction, to judge the causes decided at first instance when there is an interest of the union or crimes committed against its goods, services, and interests.
17 Until 1960, only Law 3,396, promulgated by the National Congress, constituted an attempt to respond to the so-called STF congestion (Buzaid, 1960, p. 357).
18 Buzaid (1969, p. 372) offered a solution for the filing of an extraordinary appeal: make such an appeal conditional on the deposit of a certain amount, whatever the nature of the case, reverting in favor of the defendant if the appeal was not recognized or dismissed.
19 The think tank Institute of Research and Social Studies (IPES) published in 1963 an account on the Basic Reforms. IPES affirmed the need to create high courts as a way to relieve the claims submitted to the Supreme Court but maintaining its fundamental competencies (IPÊS, 1963, p. 30).
20 There were four other projects, as described in the STF project: (1) of the Federal Council of the OAB, in 1963, whose rapporteur was Miguel Seabra Fagundes; (2) of the São Paulo Lawyers Association, 1964; (3) suggestions contained in articles by Professor José Frederico Marques, from 1964; and (4) an unsigned project.
21 The Súmula concisely catalogs, by numbers, the subjects in which the STF had set an interpretation for certain federal provisions, with the effect of preventing the court from judging the same theme repeatedly (Baleeiro, 1973, p. 8).
22 In addition, the STF project stipulated the creation of a Superior Council for the Judiciary with the function of administrative and financial coordination of the Federal Court of 1st Instance and its disciplinary regulations.

23 The IAB Project underlined the issue of the judiciary's organicity. The IAB Commission brought as the main element of the organic unit of the judiciary because it sought to end the municipal-oriented organization of the 1946 Charter, restricting executive power. The Federal Court of 1st Instance would favor the increase of the powers of the union. See Valladão, Gil, and Basílio (1965).

24 The Nereu Ramos Commission, the Brazilian Congress Committee for the Definition of Basic Reforms, and the OAB Federal Council project made no mention of increasing the number of STF ministers. In August 1965, a round table organized by IDPCP, also carried out a project in which the increase in the number of Justices was not mentioned. The round table was attended by Lamy Filho, Caio Tácito, Flávio Novelli, and Seabra Fagundes, as members of the directing council and, as guests, Alcino Salazar, Caio Mário Pereira, Frederico Marques, Ulhôa Canto, Levy Carneiro, Mário Pessoa, and Miguel Reale (FGV.IDPCP, 1965).

25 In early 1931, Vargas modified the structure of the Supreme Court by creating two collegiate inside the court. Additionally, to the plenum, the court also began to meet in two collegiate bodies with five ministers each (Costa, 2006, p. 70).

26 In 1975, a new discussion to reform the judiciary would be held. In the project presented by the STF, the hypothesis of increasing the number of justices was raised as a way to relieve the Court, but it was promptly rejected (Falcão, 1975, p. 12).

27 Since the Charter of 1891 in Brazil, as in the United States, there existed *diffuse control of constitutionality*. Judges from the 1st Instance to the Supreme Court were responsible for considering cases of *concrete* violation of constitutional rights. The 1934 Constitution brought innovation to diffuse control by instituting interventionist representation, entrusted to the attorney general and for which it was stipulated that federal intervention required prior judicial assessment. The 1946 Constitution also adopted the model of interventional representation. Brasil. Constitutional Amendment 16 (Brasil, 1965a).

28 It should be noted that this *erga omnes* effect has become an assignment of the Federal Senate since the 1934 Charter – maintained by the following constitutions. In the 1967 Constitution, for example, Art. 45, paragraph IV established that it was up to the Senate to "*suspend the execution, in whole or in part, of a law or decree declared unconstitutional, by a final decision of the Federal Supreme Court*"; as for the diffuse control of constitutionality, Article 111 stipulated that "only by the vote of the absolute majority of its members, the courts may declare the unconstitutionality of a law or act of the public authority." Still in the 1967 Charter, concentrated control appeared in Art. 114, in the section of the Supreme Court, letter l – "the representation of the attorney general, due to the unconstitutionality of a federal or state law or normative act."

29 The extraordinary appeal was considered responsible for the crisis of the Supreme Court. The 1967 Charter ceased to include extraordinary appeal when the decision of last resort by other courts or judges is contrary to the letter of a federal treaty or law. Otherwise, it became possible to file an extraordinary appeal only when the contested decision was contrary to a provision of the constitution or to deny the validity of a federal treaty or law. It is worth that placing a limitation on extraordinary resources was proposed by Miguel Seabra Fagundes, elucidated earlier, on the occasion of the Brazilian Congress for the Definition of Basic Reforms. On this change in the 1967 Constitution, see Oliveira (1968) and Baleeiro (1973).

30 The president of the STF at the time, Antônio Gonçalves de Oliveira, resigned after the retirement of the three justices, and Lafayette de Andrada retired. The composition of the Supreme Court on March 31, 1964, was almost completely modified in early 1969, with "... ministers of the regime's confidence." Costa (2006, p. 173).

31 Xavier de Albuquerque was appointed attorney general in 1969 by President Costa e Silva. He became a justice in 1972. The "High Level" Commission had in mind strengthening the executive and reorganizing the individual's liberal sense in favor of general welfare as the premise for the constitutional reform enshrined in the 1969 Amendment. The Commission was formed by President Costa e Silva, Vice President Pedro Aleixo, Ministers Rondon Pacheco, Luiz Antônio Gama e Silva, Hélio Brandão, Carlos Medeiros Silva, Themístocles Cavalcanti, and Jurist Miguel Reale. See Comissão de "Alto Nível" (1982a); Comissão de "Alto Nível"; (1982b); Comissão de "Alto Nível" (1982c). The role of the attorney general, who would be responsible for "avoiding abuse," can be found specifically in Volume II, p. 356.

Bibliography

Allardyce, G. (1982). "The Rise and Fall of the Western Civilization Course," *The American Historical Review*, Vol. 87, No. 3, pp. 695–725. http://doi:10.2307/1864161

Alpers, B. L. (2003). *Dictators, Democracy, and American Public Culture: Envisioning the Totalitarian Enemy, 1920s-1950s*. University of North Carolina Press.

Baleeiro, A. (1973). "O Supremo Tribunal Federal," *Revista Forense,* Rio de Janeiro, Vol. 242, No. 2, Ano 69.

Barreto Filho, O. (1970). "Novos rumos para a sociedade anônima: as empresas no contexto social," *Revista dos Tribunais,* São Paulo, Ano 59, Vol. 419, Setembro.

Bercovici, G. (2010). "O direito constitucional passa, o direito administrativo permanece": a persistência da estrutura administrativa de 1967. In Teles, E. and Safatle, V. (Eds). *O que resta da ditadura: a exceção brasileira.* São Paulo: Boitempo.

Bittencourt, L. (1947). "O D.A.S.P. como imperativo democrático e técnico," *Revista de Direito Administrativo,* Rio de Janeiro – FGV, Vol. 7, No. 1.

Bonavides, P. and Andrade, P. (1991). *História Constitucional do Brasil.* 3.ª Ed. Rio de Janeiro: Paz e Terra.

Bortone, E. (2014). "O Instituto de Pesquisas e Estudos Sociais (Ipes) na construção da Reforma do Estado Autoritário (1964–1968)," Tempos Históricos, Vol. 18, No.1.

Brasil. 1891. Constituição de República dos Estados Unidos do Brasil de 1891.

Brasil. 1965a. Emenda Constitucional N° 16, de 26 de novembro de 1965.

Brasil. 1965b. AI-2. Ato Institucional N° 2, de 27 de outubro de 1965.

Brasil. 1967a. Constituição da República Federativa do Brasil de 1967.

Brasil. 1967b. Decreto-Lei N° 200, de 25 de fevereiro de 1967.

Brasil. 1969. Ministério do Planejamento e Coordenação Geral. Reforma administrativa em marcha: atividades em 1967 e 1968. Rio de Janeiro.

Bresciani, M. S. M. (2005). *O charme da ciência e a sedução da objetividade. Oliveira Vianna entre intérpretes do Brasil.* São Paulo: UNESP.

______ (2010). "Projetos políticos nas interpretações do Brasil da primeira metade do século XX," *Revista de História* – edição especial, São Paulo, pp. 187–215. https://doi.org/10.11606/issn.2316-9141.v0ispep187-214

Brinkley, A. (1995). *The End of Reform: New Deal Liberalism in Recession and War.* New York: Alfred Knopf.

Brooke, N and Witoshynsky, M. (Eds). (2002). *Os 40 anos da Fundação Ford no Brasil: uma perspectiva para a mudança social*. São Paulo: EDUSP/Rio de Janeiro: Fundação Ford.

Buzaid, A. (1960). "A crise do Supremo Tribunal Federal," *Revista da Faculdade de Direito*. Universidade de São Paulo, Vol. 55.

Campos, M. (1965). "Reforma Do Poder Judiciário," *Correio da Manhã*, Janeiro 1, Rio de Janeiro, Ano LXIV, Caderno 1.

Campos, R. (1994). *A lanterna na popa: memórias*. Rio de Janeiro: Topbooks.

Cancelli, E. (2017). O Brasil em Guerra Fria Cultural: o pós-guerra em releitura. São Paulo: Intermeios.

Cancelli, E., Mesquita, G., and Chaves, W. (2019). *Guerra Fria e Brasil: Para a agenda de integração do negro na sociedade de classes*. São Paulo: Alameda.

Carneiro, L. (1943). "Ainda a Crise do Supremo Tribunal Federal," *Arquivos do Ministério da Justiça*, Rio de Janeiro, Vol. 1, No. 2, agosto.

Cattai, J. (2019). Guerra Fria e Propaganda: a U.S. Information Agency no Brasil. Curitiba: Appris.

Cavalcanti, T. (1938). *Instituições de Direito Administrativo*. 2.ª Ed. II Vol., Rio de Janeiro: Livraria Editora Freitas Bastos.

Chaves, W. (2018). A questão negra: a Fundação Ford e a Guerra Fria (1950-1970). Curitiba: Prismas.

Comissão de 'Alto Nível'. (1982a). *Estudo para a Reforma da Constituição de 1967*. Vol. I, Presidência da República, Arquivo Brasília.

Comissão de 'Alto Nível'. (1982b). *Estudo para a Reforma da Constituição de 1967*. Vol. II, Presidência da República, Arquivo Brasília.

Comissão de 'Alto Nível'. (1982c). *Estudo para a Reforma da Constituição de 1967*. Vol. III, Presidência da República, Arquivo Brasília.

Congresso Brasileiro Para Definição Das Reformas De Base. (1963). Rio de Janeiro, 1963, Sessão 3ª.

Costa, E. V. (2006). *O Supremo Tribunal Federal e a construção da cidadania*. 2.ª Ed. São Paulo: Editora Unesp.

Costa, R. (1965). "Inutilidade do aumento de ministros do STF," *Correio da Manhã*. 20 de outubro, Ano LXV. Cited in Rodrigues, L. B. (2002). *História do Supremo Tribunal Federal.* Tomo 4. Vol. 1. Rio de Janeiro: Civilização Brasileira.

Cury, C. (2010). *Alceu Amoroso Lima*. (Coleção Educadores). Recife: MEC, Fundação Joaquim Nabuco; Editora Massangana.

D'araujo, M. C. (Ed). (1999). *Fundação Getúlio Vargas: Concretização de um ideal*. Rio de Janeiro: Editora FGV.

Davis, M. H. (1987). "A Government of Judges: An Historical Re-View." In *The American Journal of Comparative Law,* Vol. 35, No. 3, pp. 559–580. http://doi:10.2307/840481

Dezalay, Y. and Garth, B. G. (2002). *The Internationalization of Palace Wars: Lawyers, Economists, and the Contest to Transform Latin American States*. Chicago, IL: University of Chicago.

Dreifuss, R. A. (1981). 1964: A conquista do Estado: ação política, poder e golpe de classe. Petrópolis: Vozes, 3 ed.

Dulles, J. W. F. (1984). *A Faculdade de Direito de São Paulo e a resistência anti-vargas (1938–1945)*. Trans. Vanda de Andrade. Rio de Janeiro: Editora Nova Fronteira; São Paulo: Editora da USP.

Dutra, P. (2014). *San Tiago Dantas: a razão vencida*. (O ideólogo) Vol. I (1911–1945). São Paulo: Editora Singular.

Fagundes, M. S. (1948). "Poder Discricionário da Administração – Abuso desse poder – mandado de segurança – direito líquido e certo," *Revista de Direito Administrativo*, Rio de Janeiro – FGV, Vol. 14.

______ (1950). *O Controle dos Atos Administrativos pelo Poder Judiciário*. 2ª. Edição. Rio de Janeiro: José Konfino.

______ (1951). "Conceito de mérito no Direito Administrativo," *Revista de Direito Administrativo*, Rio de Janeiro – FGV, Vol. 23.

______ (1954). "A Organicidade e o Funcionamento do Poder Judiciário," *Revista Forense*, Rio de Janeiro, Vol. 51, No. 155, setembro-outubro.

______ (1956). "Reformas essenciais ao aperfeiçoamento das instituições políticas brasileiras." *Revista Forense*, Rio de Janeiro, Vol. 163, Ano 53, janeiro-fevereiro.

______ (1965). "Da Contribuição do Código Civil para o direito administrativo," *Revista Forense*, Rio de Janeiro, Vol 209, Ano 62, janeiro-fevereiro-março.

______ (1966). "A Reforma do Poder Judiciário e a Reestruturação do Supremo Tribunal Federal," *Revista Forense*, Rio de Janeiro, Ano 63.

Falcão, D. A. (1975). "Reforma do Poder Judiciário (Relatório elaborado pelo Supremo Tribunal Federal)," *Revista Forense*, Rio de Janeiro, Vol. 251, Ano 71, julho-agosto-setembro.

FGV.RAP. Decreto-Lei N. 200 de 25 de fevereiro de 1967 (Documentação) (1967). *Revista de Administração Pública*, Rio de Janeiro – FGV, Vol. 1, No. 1.

FGV.EBAP. (1964a). "O QUE OS OUTROS ESTÃO FAZENDO." *Boletim do Centro de Pesquisas Administrativas da EBAP*, Rio de Janeiro – FGV, Vol.1, No. 1.

______ (1964b). "ATIVIDADES DO CPqA," *Boletim do Centro de Pesquisas Administrativas da EBAP*, Rio de Janeiro – FGV, Vol.1, No. 1.

FGV.IDPCP. (1963). "Congresso Internacional de Juristas. Resolução do Rio," *Rev. Dir. Públ. e Ciência Política* – Rio de Janeiro – Vol. VI, No. 1 – jan/abril.

FGV.IDPCP. (1965). "Relatório – Mesa-Redonda Sobre 'Reforma Do Poder Judiciário'," *Rev. Dir. Publ. e Ciência Política*, Rio de Janeiro – FGV, Vol. VIII, No. 2. maio-agosto.

Fischer, T. (1984). "Administração pública como área de conhecimento e ensino: a trajetória brasileira,"*Revista de Administração de Empresas,* São Paulo, Vol. 24, No. 4, pp. 278–288. https://doi.org/10.1590/S0034-75901984000400038

Fleiner, F. (1933). *Instituciones de Drecho Administrativo*. Trans. Sabino A. Gendin. Madrid: Editorial Labor.

Forrester, K. (2019). *In the Shadow of Justice: Postwar Liberalism and the Remaking of Liberal Philosophy*. Princeton: Princeton University Press.

Foucault, M. (2008). The Birth of Biopolitics. Lectures at The Collège De France, 1978–1979. (Ed. M. Senellart). Translated by G. Bruchell. New York: Palgrave Macmillan.

______(2009). Security, Territory, Population. Lectures at The Collège De France, 1977–1978. (Ed. M. Senellart). Translated by G. Bruchell. New York: Palgrave Macmillan.

Gaspari, É. (2002). *A ditadura envergonhada*. São Paulo: Cia das Letras.

Geddes, B. (1990). "Building 'State' Autonomy in Brazil, 1930–1964," *Comparative Politics*, Vol. 22, No. 2.

Gilman, N. (2003). Mandarins of the Future: Modernization Theory in Cold War America. Baltimore, Johns Hopkins University Press.

Gygi, F. (1962). "The Rule of Law in the Contemporary Welfare State," *Journal of the International Commission of Jurists*. Geneva: International Commission of Jurists. Vol. IV, No. 1, Summer.

Hamby, A. L. (1972). "The Vital Center, the Fair Deal, and the Quest for a Liberal Political Economy," *The American Historical Review*, Vol. 77, No. 3, pp. 653–678. http://dx.doi.org/10.2307/1870345

Ianni, O. (1977). *Estado e planejamento econômico no Brasil (1930–1970)*. Rio de Janeiro: Civilização Brasileira.

ICJ. (1956). "The Aftermath of the Athens Congress," *Bulletin of the International Commission of Jurists*, No. 5, International Commission of Jurists, The Hague, Netherlands, June.

Ioris, R. (2017). *Qual desenvolvimento? os debates, sentidos e lições da Era Desenvolvimentista*. Jundiaí: Paco Editorial.

IPÊS – Instituto de Pesquisa e Estudos Sociais. (1963). *Reformas de Base: posição do IPÊS*. Rio de Janeiro.

Jacobs, C. C. (2004). *A participação da Usaid na Reforma da Universidade Brasileira na década de 1960*. Mestrado em Relações Internacionais. Universidade Federal do Rio Grande do Sul.

Leal, V. N. (1946). "Atos administrativos – Exame da sua validade pelo poder judiciário," *Revista de Direito Administrativo*, Rio de Janeiro – FGV, Vol. 3.

______ (1948). "Poder Discricionário e Ação Arbitrária da Administração," *Revista de Direito Administrativo*, Rio de Janeiro – FGV, Vol. 14.

______ (1965). "Supremo Tribunal Federal: a questão do número de juízes," *Revista dos Tribunais,* São Paulo, Vol. 359, Ano 54, setembro.

Lima, H., Dantas, S. T., Medeiros Silva, C. *et al.* (1956). "Anteprojeto de Emenda Constitucional," *Revista Forense*, Rio de Janeiro, Vol. 167, Ano 53, setembro-outubro.

Malraux, A. (1959). Discours prononcé à Athènes par Mr André Malraux, Ministre d'Etat du Gouvernement de la République Françaisele 28 mai 1959.

Marsh, N. (1959). *The Rule of Law in a Free Society. A Report on the International Congress of Jurists*, New Delhi, India, January 5–10. 1959. The International Commission of Jurists, Genève, Switzerland.

Mattos, M. A. V. L. (2011). *Os cruzados da ordem jurídica*. Tese FFLCH, Universidade de São Paulo, São Paulo.

Mayer, O. (1949). *Derecho Administrativo Alemán*, Vol. II, Depalma, Buenos Aires.

Medeiros, J. S. V. (1944). "A Alteração da Competência do Supremo Tribunal Federal," *Arquivos do Ministério da Justiça*, Rio de Janeiro, Vol. 2, No. 10, dezembro.

Meirelles, H. L. (1957). "Os Poderes do Administrador Público," *Revista dos Tribunais,* São Paulo, Vol. 266, Ano 46, dezembro.

______ (1958). "Os Poderes do Administrador Público," *Revista Forense*, Rio de Janeiro, Vol. 177, Ano 55, maio-junho.

______ (1973). "A Administração Pública e seus controles," *Revista de Direito Administrativo*, Rio de Janeiro – FGV, Vol. 114.

______ (1988). *Direito Administrativo Brasileiro*. 33.ª Edição. São Paulo: Editora Revista dos Tribunais.

Meirelles, J. H. T. (1963). "Reforma Constitucional, político-partidária e eleitoral." (Tese), *Congresso Brasileiro para Definição das Reformas de Base*, Rio de Janeiro, Vol. 5.

Moesley, P., Harrigan, J., and Toye, J. (1991). *Aid and Power: The World Bank and Policy-based Lending*. London: Routledge.

Moyn, S. (2018). *Not Enough: Human rights in an unequal world.* The Belknap Press of Harvard University Press: Cambridge, Massachusetts; London, England.

Oliveira, A. G. (1968). "Novos Aspectos da Competência do Supremo Tribunal Federal," *Revista Forense*, Rio de Janeiro, Vol. 224, Ano 64, out-dezembro.

Paiva, A. (1960). "As sociedades de economia mista e as empresas públicas como instrumentos jurídicos a serviço do Estado," *Revista Forense,* Rio de Janeiro, Vol. 192, Ano 57, nov-dezembro.

Parmar, I. (2012). Foundations of the American Century: The Ford, Carnegie, and Rockefeller Foundations in the Rise of American Power. New York: Columbia University Press.

Penholato, D. (2017). *José Garrido Torres nas Sombras do Poder: Um Economista na Construção do Projeto de Modernização de 1964*. Dissertação (Mestrado) – FFLCH, Universidade de São Paulo, São Paulo.

Pinto, R. (1951). *La crise de l'etat aux Etats Unis*. Paris: LGDJ.

Ponde, L. (1951). "Princípios gerais do recurso administrativo," *Revista de Direito Administrativo*, Rio de Janeiro, Vol. 23, pp. 17–24, Dec. http://dx.doi.org/10.12660/rda.v23.1951.11832

Powers, R. G. (1998). Not Without Honor: the History of American Anticommunism. New Heaven and London. Yale University Press.

Queiró, A. R. (1947). "A teoria do 'desvio de poder' em direito administrativo," *Revista de Direito Administrativo*, Rio de Janeiro – FGV, Vol. 7.

Recondo, F. (2018). *Tanques e Togas: o STF e a Ditadura Militar*. Cia das Letras: São Paulo.

Ribeito Costa, A. M., Mota filho, C., Leal, V. N. *et al.* (1965). "Reforma Judiciária," *Revista Forense*, Rio de Janeiro, Vol. 212, out-nov-dez.

Roberts, A. (1994). "Demonstrating Neutrality: The Rockefeller Philanthropies and the Evolution of Public Administration, 1927–1936," *Public Administration Review*, Vol 54, No. 3, pp. 221–228. http://doi:10.2307/976724

Rodó, L. L. (1954). "O Poder Discricionário da Administração – evolução doutrinária e jurisprudencial," *Revista de Direito Administrativo*, Rio de Janeiro – FGV, Vol. 35.

Salinas, N. C. (2010). "Reforma administrativa de 1967: a reconciliação do legal com o real," Mota, C. G. and Salinas, N. C. (Eds) *Os juristas na formação do Estado-Nação brasileiro: 1930-dias atuais*. São Paulo: Saraiva.

Sartre, J. P. (1987). "Justicia y Estado." In Sartre, J. P. *Political Writings: The Intellectual and the Revolution*. Madrid: Alianza Editorial. Buenos Aires: Losada.

Saunders, F. S. (1999). *The Cultural Cold War: the CIA and the World of Arts and Letters*. NY: The New Press.

Schlesinger Jr., A. M. (1948). "Not Right, Not Left, But a Vital Center," *New York Times Magazine*, Sunday, April 4.

______ (1949). *The Vital Center: The Politics of Freedom*. Boston: H. Mifflin Company.

Scott-Smith, G. (2008). *Networks of Empire: The US State Department's Foreign Leader Program in the Netherlands, France, and Britain 1950–1970*. Brussels: Peter Lang.

Sinclair, G. F. (2020). "Forging Modern States with Imperfect Tools: United Nations Technical Assistance for Public Administration in Decolonized States," *Humanity: An International Journal of Human Rights, Humanitarianism, and Development*, Vol. 11, No. 1, Spring, pp. 54–83. https://doi.org/10.1353/hum.2020.0007

STF. (1965). "Reforma Judiciária," *Revista Forense*, Rio de Janeiro, Vol. 212, Ano 61, out-nov-dez.

______ (1971). *Reclamação n. 849*, Distrito Federal, Março 10.

Swisher, C. B. (1946) [1943]. *The Growth of Constitutional Power in the United States*. Chicago: University of Chicago Press.

Tacito, C. (1951). *Desvio de poder em matéria administrativa*. Rio de Janeiro: Imprenta.
______ (1952). "O poder de polícia e seus limites," *Revista de Direito Administrativo*, Rio de Janeiro, FGV, Vol. 27.
______ (1971). "O Desafio no Ensino do Direito," *Revista Forense*, Rio de Janeiro, Vol. 233, Ano 67, março.
Tickner, F. J. (1956). "Public Service Training in the Past Decade," *Public Administration*, Vol. 34, No.1, pp. 27–38. https://doi:10.1111/j.1467-9299. 1956.tb01171.x
Tolley Jr, H. B. (1994). The International Commission of Jurists: Global Advocates for Human Rights. University of Pennsylvania Press: Philadelphia.
Tota, A. P. (2000). *O imperialismo sedutor: a americanização do Brasil na época da Segunda Guerra*. São Paulo: Cia das Letras.
______ (2014). *O amigo americano: Nelson Rockefeller e o Brasil*. São Paulo: Companhia das Letras.
Valladão, H., Gil, O., and Basílio, C. S. F. (1965). "A reforma do Poder Judiciário da União," *Revista dos Tribunais*, São Paulo, Vol. 360, Ano 54, outubro.
Vyshinsky, A. Y. (Ed.) (1948). *The Law of the Soviet State*, Translated by Hugh W. Babb. New York: The Macmillan Co.
Wahrlich, B. M. de S. (1983). *Reforma administrativa na Era de Vargas*. Rio de Janeiro: Ed. FGV.
Wald, A. (1965a). "Projetos de Reforma Judiciária," *Correio da Manhã*, Março 21, Rio de Janeiro, Caderno 2, Ano LXIV.
______ (1965b). "Respeito à Lei." *Correio da Manhã*, Setembro 2, Rio de Janeiro, 1.º Caderno, Ano LXV.
______ (1967). "O Direito do Desenvolvimento," *Revista Forense*, Rio de Janeiro, Ano 63, out-nov-dezembro.

3 The executive and the legislative

Normative function and the separation of powers

Lewis Mumford, the historian of technology and cities, described the rise of an abstract time in the early 20th century. The time of the clock, the key machine of the modern industrial age, imposed a new framework for human existence, by reorganizing organic functions and swallowing man (1955, p. 17). Brazilian legal thinking not only reproduced Mumford's diagnoses in modern times (Mota Filho, 1960) but also found by this same token a way of evidencing the malaise regarding the executive branch's "hypertrophy." Opposed to the liberal state's legal formalism, the executive's hypertrophy expressed assumptions concerning the state-individual binominal contrary to the Brazilian tradition of civil law. To the detriment of this tradition, state intervention threatened the separation of powers and the rule of law. Nonetheless, as if it were an inexorable march toward modernization, the 1934 Constitution recognized the initiative of submitting bills to the executive branch (Trigueiro, 1959). Indeed, by the time Mumford was publishing his book on *Technics and Civilization*, the Brazilian constitutional order, inspired by Weimar, was including, for the first time, the title "On Economic and Social Order," thus allowing a broader action on the part of the state.

Yet, even considering the growing regulatory power by the executive since the birth of the Brazilian Republic, in the eyes of the Getúlio Vargas authoriatiran project this state-led economic power was not enough. To a great extent, since in the constitutional order there remained the concept, alluded to by Soriano de Souza in the early 1890s, that "regulation is *quasi-law*, it is a compliment or extension of the law, but it is not law, nor should it depart substantially from it. Law is the work of the legislative branch" (1893, p. 313). In other words, the Brazilian legal order maintained the post-French 1830 revolution juridical assumptions that established a clear distinction between *law* and *regulation*, between the legislative, responsible for innovating the juridical order, and the executive, the mere applier of the law.

In this sense, the new 1934 constitution re-established the legality of political life, restricting the discretionary powers of the regime instituted in October 1930. Indeed, a month after the coup, Vargas introduced a decree allowing the new administration to "exercise with discretion, in all its fullness, the functions and attributions of not only the executive but also the legislative

DOI: 10.4324/9781003123941-4

branch," until the election of a Constituent Assembly and the reorganization of the country's juridical legitimacy (Brasil, 1930a). In December, the new administration established a Legislative Commission of jurisconsults, sociologists, and thinkers to develop a vast program of reform of the country's legal order, including a revision of the Civil Code of 1916 – "the codes of the codes" in the Brazilian tradition (Brasil, 1930b). However, this reform would not be completed as intended by Vargas, partially because of the method adopted by the commission and partially because of the liberal precepts of the 1934 Constitution (Campos, 2001, p. 145).

It was in this sense that Vargas tried to neutralize the liberal aspects of the 1934 charter, so that the legal order could correspond to the state of social surveillance and the project of an "organic society," which required legal measures and a modernized police force (Cancelli, 1994). Shortly thereafter, deepening this understanding of the interventionist prerogatives of the executive branch, the organic jurist to Vargas' regime, Francisco Campos, argued in favor of the formulas of legislative delegations adopted in England and the United States. Contrary to the famous statement by John Locke, that "the legislative cannot transfer the power of making laws to any other hands: for it being but a delegated power from the people, they who have it cannot pass it over to others", Campos argued that

> [....] today there is no important piece of legislation that has not been the initiative of the government or is not the result of a delegation from the legislative branch. [....] In the United States, a country where there has always been court prevention against delegation, legislation by the executive, or delegated legislation, constitutes today the most important mass of legislative production.
>
> (Campos, 2001, p. 55)

The New Deal's tendencies became, in particular, a model for Brazilian constitutionalists (Teixeira, 2018), because the presidential system was a common form of government between the United States and Brazil. There was, as put by another conservative jurist, Carlos Medeiros Silva (1952, p. 3), an inadequacy in looking, "pure and simple," to the doctrines in the parliamentarian system regarding the concept of normative competencies. In sum, contrary to parliamentarianism, in a presidential regime, there is no subordination or hierarchy between powers. Campos was therefore attentive to the fact that, in 1933, when Franklin Delano Roosevelt took office, the U.S. Congress immediately transferred legislative powers to the president, allowing the new administration to put forward the interventionist policies of the New Deal – attributions of enormous breadth, which had never existed before in peace times. It was foreseen that not only the competence of the decrees by the executive but their establishment – given a greater celerity between the promulgation of norms and the new arrangements of social dynamics – would be converted into laws if, within a period of sixty days, Congress did not decide otherwise.

The fulfillment of the Vargas program of reforming the country's legal order involved the promotion of another constitution, organized by Francisco Campos and promulgated on November 11, 1937, following a new organization of the regime after a new coup and the establishment of the "Estado Novo" as an openly authoritarian regime. The new charter – following a different political scope from that engendered by FDR – gave the head of state, in addition to Congress, the *original attribution* of producing law, disregarding the "legislative delegation" that Roosevelt had used with the New Deal policies (Leal, 1945). By 1945, Getúlio Vargas had introduced 10,000 decree-laws (Sampaio, 1959) and was able to accomplish the reform of the positive order initiated in 1931. Among others, there was the approval of the Penal Code (1941), the Penal Procedure Code (1941), the Civil Procedure Code (1939), the Mines Code (1940), the Traffic Code (1941), the Consolidation of Labor Laws (1943), and the modernization of the country's public administration (Trigueiro, 1959; Pauperio, 1962; Gil, 1969).

Shortly after the establishment of the Estado Novo, which put Congress in recess,[1] Campos justified such measures given what would be the "inability of the legislative branch to legislate [...], a fact definitely acknowledged not only by political science but also by the experience of representative institutions." The Minister of Justice affirmed the prominence assumed by the executive branch with the Vargas administration and that, in effect, the legislative action of Congress had lost "its exclusively political character," becoming "a technique that requires the combination of various knowledge and techniques" (Campos, 1938, p. 5–22). Even earlier, in 1936, in a speech at the National Congress of Judicial Law, Campos proposed a "rational organization of the legislative service," for which the creation of "a center of studies, information, and investigations contributed with the function of verifying the gaps and defects in the legal system, the flaws in its functioning, or the inadequacies or incompatibilities of the law with social life" (CONGRESSO Nacional de Direito Judiciário (Campos), 1936, p. 809–810, cited in Silveira, 2016, p. 449).

The rise of a new public law, of state intervention, and the malaise that it cast on the Brazilian legal tradition were in line with the new rite of time under urban and industrial life. Indeed, the acceleration of the pace of history, as asserted by Nuno Pinheiro (1922), Mumford (1955), and many years later by Lamy Filho (1970), for instance, deepened what was a broader crisis in the traditional process of legislative formulation. The diagnosis in Brazil, as well as in the Global North, was that the legislative branches would not be materially equipped for a normative production capable of meeting the new social dynamics engendered by industrialism and urbanization. In this sense, the legislative started to impose an obstacle not only to modernization but also to the most basic capacities of political institutions to reproduce governance: the disciplining of social relations by law. By this token, in his speech installing the Legislative Commission, in May 1931, Vargas said that the provisional government was a proper moment to reform the legal and, thus, social order, since it was possible to legislate "without the delaying obstacles of the constitutional periods, the long altercations of Congress, the demands of politics, and the factionalism of the parties" (Vargas, 1935, p. 54).

The political-intellectual debate started to raise awareness of the "Crisis of Parliaments," regarding in particular the delegation of powers from the legislative to the executive. Indeed, despite the thorough renewal of the Brazilian legal order under the authoritarian Vargas regime (1930–1945), this "pressing issue" remained a major question in the country's political life between 1946 and 1964. Since the removal of Vargas from office, in 1945, and the subsequent promulgation of the 1946 Constitution, a debate was established in Brazil about *legislative delegation*: the transfer of the National Congress' normative function to other branches of the state, particularly to the Office of the President. The central aspect of this debate was the doctrinal formulation of one of the most important instruments of modern public law, legislative delegation, which guaranteed the expansion of the executive's role as the promoter of laws, but in a way that operates within the premises of the rule of law.[2]

The inescapable problem in legal thinking, however, was that Article 36 of the 1946 Constitution, which stipulated *harmony* and *independence* between the powers, also determined a *strict separation* between them. In other words, an orthodox organization prevented public administration from putting into motion an organic program for national development and modernization. Thus, despite the evolution of the doctrine regarding police power, which allowed intervention by the public administration while preserving the order of the rule of law, the *strict separation* among powers proposed by Locke and Montesquieu imposed a rigorous setback to the realization of the Social State as foreseen by the "programmatic constitution" of 1946. It was thus in this regard that legal thinking in Brazil would articulate the "Crisis of Parliaments," concerning specifically the loss of their typical legislative function. Therefore, the legal field in the country advocated an arrangement among branches of the state based on cooperation, or, to a lesser extent, the establishment of another system of government: the parliamentarian . In both cases, the separation of powers would be based on the competence of inspection and reciprocal control among the legislative executive, and judiciary – in Montesquieu's phrase, *le pouvoir arrête le pouvoir* (power checks power) (Rangel, 1966, p. 364).

In sum, the "Crisis of Parliaments" and the "hypertrophy" of the executive were both concerned with the same question: the masses and modern time. Following the lead of the previous chapter, in which I discussed the modernization of public administration and the renewal of the judiciary, this chapter analyzes the response of legal thinking to such a "Crisis," underlining the role played by U.S. actors in this process.

In March 1956, upon taking office, the Minister of Justice and Interior Affairs, Senator Nereu Ramos, who was appointed by Juscelino Kubitscheck, announced plans to form a Committee for Studies on Constitutional Reform. The intent was to respond to the serious crisis in which the country's political-constitutional institutions would find themselves, jeopardizing the "regime's moral standards" (Fagundes, 1956, p. 9–10). In October 1955, in a lecture at that ministry, Miguel Seabra Fagundes established the main line reasons for such a crisis: despite the "influx of the machine" and "the vertigo of scientific progress," the state was not *yet* in charge of social life, thus remaining only as an arbitrator, which was typical of the political organization envisaged by the liberal model (1956, p. 9–10).

One of the central points in the studies of constitutional reform, which were carried out by the commission appointed by Ramos and formed by San Tiago Dantas, Carlos Medeiros Silva, Antônio Gonçalves de Oliveira, Francisco Brochado da Rocha, and Hermes Lima, concerned legislative elaboration, involving the *delegation of powers* and the renewal of the operating structure of the two chambers of Congress. This was perhaps, as Fagundes argued in his 1955 lecture, the most relevant aspect to be faced in a preliminary reform project, since its solution would mean a first step toward addressing several other problems of the constitutional order, such as the powers of the Supreme Court and budgeting, with a special focus on financial balance and deficit coverage (Fagundes, 1956; Lima, Dantas, Medeiros Silva, *et al*, 1956, p. 7–8).

In addition to Fagundes (former Minister of Justice and Interior Affairs of the Café Filho administration in 1954–1955), the congressmen Bilac Pinto and Afonso Arinos, along with Pontes de Miranda, João Mangabeira, and Carlos Medeiros Silva (1953), defended the modification of the 1946 Constitution. The major issue in the constitutional reform draft, completed in April 1956, was precisely the 1946 Constitution's Article 36, Paragraph 2, which prohibited any delegation of function from one branch to another. This would be, as put by the jurist and Catholic intellectual, Afonso Arinos (1949, p. 1296; 1955, p. 5957), "a gesture of retaliation carried out by this Chamber, closed treacherously on November 10 [1937] by the dictator" – "one of the most unfortunate gestures in our constitution." Indeed, with such a device, the Constitutional Assembly tried to guarantee, in response to the 1937 Constitution and the threats of "the sword or the dictatorship" (Arinos, 1949, p. 1229), the strict separation among the legislative, executive, and judiciary, based on the assumption in Montesquieu's *Spirit Of Laws* that without such separation there would be no possible constitution (Saldanha, 1963).[3] This was what the constitutional reform commission assumed in its draft: "when inscribing the prohibition of Paragraph 2 in Art. 36, the 1946 constituent legislator undoubtedly wanted to emphasize the classic norm by which the powers, although harmonious, are independent" (Lima, Dantas, Medeiros Silva, *et al*, 1956, p. 21).

As a consequence of such a "Crisis," the legal debate expressed concern with the totalitarian threat. In one of his seminal works on the delegation of powers, Fagundes, analyzing the normative process, argued that "the approval of bills is delayed, while the facts succeed and multiply in the absence of efficient discipline [...]. Laws are approved late, are poorly drafted, contradictory, deprived of the systematization that is indispensable for a convenient application to the facts." At the extreme, the former minister continued, in the same vein as Nereu Ramos in 1956, this broad crisis, since it affected not only the National Congress but also all the republican branches, would equip opponents of free institutions with an excuse to convince the "masses" of the option for dictatorial forms of government (Fagundes, 1956, p. 13).

Themístocles Cavalcanti, a few years later, came to a similar conclusion regarding the normative process. The jurist argued that, until the war, in 1914, the legislative function "could still be exercised by a parliament constituted on the sole basis of vote selection." However, the dramatic evolution of social phenomena under industrial and technical production, with "the multiplication of purely technical problems, of political problems linked to the most complex economic factors," made the legislative function "inaccessible to the vast majority of members of Parliament" (1961, p. 13). Nonetheless, in his discussion, Cavalcanti underscored that the "problem is not just ours; it concerns all countries, which are verifying that it is essential to escape that excess separation among the various powers of the state, by organizing them properly." He took for examples the cases of the organization of a Parliamentary and Scientific Committee in England, in 1939, and, by the same token, the reformulations of parliamentary commissions, carried out in France with Articles 42 and 43 of the 1958 French Constitution; with Article 72 of the 1948 Italian Constitution; and with Articles 42, 45, and 52 of the 1949 German Constitution of Bonn (Cavalcanti, 1961, p. 13).

Indeed, the Brazilian legal debate came to find, in the Global North's discussion on the "Crisis of Parliaments," modes of conducting the issue of the "acceleration of the pace of history" with respect to the legislative task and the modernization effort in the country. On July 3 and 4, 1954, for instance, the French Political Science Association organized a roundtable in Paris, gathering political scientists and jurists, such as Georges Vedel and François Goguel, to discuss comparatively the parliamentary work in France, in Great Britain, in the United States, and in Switzerland. The French political scientist Goguel was responsible for the general *rapporteur* based on three fundamental issues: (1) the domain of law (the distinction between law and regulation); (2) the elaboration of law; and (3) the problems presented to parliamentary control. The curious aspect regarding those debates was that the 1946 French Constitution instituted Article 13, through which legislative delegation – or the expansion of regulatory power – was prohibited. As asserted by Marcel Prélot, one of the participants, "this was clearly seen by the constituents of 1946 who, to avoid any underhand transformation of the constitution and any attack on its democratic spirit, voted for the prohibition of Article 13" (Claude, 1954, p. 846).

In that same year, the Brazilian chapter of the International Political Science Association, headquartered at the FGV Institute of Public Law and Political Science (IDPCP), chaired by Themístocles Cavalcanti, published the study *Quatro Estudos* (*Four Studies*). Resembling the French Political Science Association's conclusions, the study advocated a normative role for specialized congressional committees, arguing that "there are any number of laws of a technical nature that require several rules that can only be drafted by specialists and that are deformed by a body as numerous as the National Congress" (Cavalcanti, 1954; 1951).[4] By the same token, one year later, in August 1955, extending until April 1956, Themístocles Cavalcanti presided over three round tables at the Institute of Public Law and Political Science concerning a constitutional review of the 1946 charter, which would involve the normative functions of the Brazilian Congress. Gathering the most important jurists of the country – Miguel Seabra Fagundes, João Mangabeira, Bilac Pinto, Victor Nunes Leal, Gustavo Capanema, Hermes Lima, Nestor Duarte, and Barbosa Lima Sobrinho; these discussions led to the suggestion of repealing Paragraph 2 of Article 36 – "it is forbidden for any of the branches to delegate duties" (Rocha, 2004, p. 175–178), thus allowing legislative delegation.

The common belief relied on the assumption that, concerning the normative function, the legislative branch should count on the broader support of the executive and of the internal congressional committees. The Ministry of Justice's Committee for Constitutional Reform, formed by almost the same jurists from the FGV roundtable, looked to the modernization of the U.S. Congress as one of the main supports for their conclusions with regard to the Brazilian case (Lima, Dantas, Medeiros Silva, *et al*, 1956).

Given the growing hypertrophy of the executive branch since World War I and the New Deal's policies, President Harry S. Truman sanctioned, in 1946, the Legislative Reorganization Act, the biggest restructuring of the U.S. Congress to date. Such a restructuring was carried out by a joint committee led by Senator Robert Lafollete, Jr. and House Representative Almer S. Monroney. The committee attempted to respond to the loss of the prestige of the legislative branch, particularly due to its growing inefficiency concerning modern social demands, a diagnosis that the Committee for Studies on Constitutional Reform in Brazil, ten years later, would also come to corroborate. One of the biggest targets of the U.S. reform was the modernization of the organization of the standing committee system. The method chosen was to reduce the number of less important or inactive committees, as well as unify those with related functions, in order to rationalize their activities. Moreover, the reform foresaw equipping the committees with qualified technical staff, documentation, and libraries, thus making them capable of producing draft bills and issuing opinions on projects before they are submitted to the plenary assembly (Galloway, 1951, p. 41–68).[5] In a study published by the journal of the Institute for Public Law and Political Science (IDPCP), the researcher Thereza Viana explained the organization of the U.S. Congress:

> [...] the type of advisory committee in the American Congress can be called a fan. The basic advisory bodies of each chamber of Congress are:

> in the House of Representatives, the Legislative Reference Service, which belongs to the Library of Congress, and the Legislative Drafting Service. The number of technicians that each committee can have is four, with the designation of "experts – staff assistants." Each parliamentarian has the right to hire technicians and assistants.
>
> (Viana, 1959, p. 68)

In Brazil, Article 40 of the 1946 Constitution stipulated the organization of the country's Congress in committees: dividing and systematizing congressional work, they constituted organs for rationalizing the normative production of the Senate and the Chamber of Deputies. The standing commissions were: I – Constitution and Justice; II – Diplomacy; III – Economics; IV – Education and Culture; V – Finance; VI – Social Legislation; VII – Budget and Financial Inspection; VIII – Writing; IX – Health; X – National Security; XI – Public Service; and XII – Transport, Communications, and Public Works (Ferreira, 1962; Viana, 1959). Taking the U.S. structure model (the "Congress of Committees") as a starting point, the preliminary reform project of 1956 foresaw the appreciation of the function of such committees. In this regard, accurate studies could not only perfect the work of Congress but also make it faster. To the jurists tasked with the studies, this could meet the requirements of a "modern legislation" capable of responding to the challenges imposed by the complex phenomena of a rapidly industrializing society (Lima, Dantas, Medeiros Silva, *et al*, 1956, p. 19).

Furthermore, in the preliminary draft, Brazilian jurists came to find in the "famous" Article 72 of the Italian Constitution of 1948 a work method for committees. It stipulated that either of the chambers in the Italian Legislative Power could decide in which cases the examination and approval of bills should be submitted to committees. Furthermore, the committees were able to approve a legislation directly, prescinding the need for discussion or a vote by the plenary (Sampaio, 1959, p. 12). In other words, the aforementioned legal institute organized the hypothesis of internal delegation, in which case the Senate and the Chamber of Deputies allowed its internal committees themselves to draft definitive bills (Lima, Dantas, Medeiros Silva, *et al*, 1956, p. 22). There would be, as a consequence, a more coherent and rapid production of laws concerning the efforts for modernization. Georges Langrod, a professor of public administrative law, was a great influence in this regard. In 1954, the FGV-IDPCP translated to Portuguese and published his famous comparative study *Réflexions sur la procédure législative en Europe Occidentale* (*The Legislative Process in Western Europe*). The book became a reference in Brazil (Ferreira, 1962; Fagundes, 1956) on the "Crisis of Parliaments" and on legislative drafting and delegation. Regarding the Italian Article 72, Langrod stated:

> The use of the process of transferring the power to adopt the text to the committees has, since 1948, been the current practice of Italian

> parliamentary chambers. Indeed, [....] between May 1948 and January 1, 1953, the comparative data are presented as follows: – In the Chamber of Deputies, out of 2,343 bills approved, 523 were adopted in plenary and 1,820 by the commissions. – In the Senate, out of 2,273 bills, 640 were adopted in plenary and 1,669 by the commissions.
>
> (Langrod, 1954, p. 103–104)

It was, furthermore, due to the need to comply with this modern legislation that the Committee for Studies on Constitutional Reform found a formula to overcome the problem of compromising the separation of powers – in order to ensure, at the same time, the instrumentalization of the executive, the conductor of the modernization process, and the preservation of the rule of law and of the individual as the fundamental political dimension of Western societies. The functionality of the legislative (in crisis) depended on a new relationship between the branches: a reinterpretation of Article 36 of the 1946 Constitution was proposed, by which the *independence* and *harmony* between the Legislative, Executive, and Judiciary were established. Indeed, "[...] **the possibility for the Legislative to authorize the Executive to draft** definitive bills **represents invaluable help** [for the effective harmony and independence of the branches], **since it combines** the government's experience and equipment **with the** specific and sovereign attributions of Congress" [emphasis in the original] (Langrod, 1954, p. 19; Lima, Dantas, Medeiros Silva, *et al*, 1956). In this same understanding, years later Themístocles Cavalcanti (1962) shared his conviction that the instrument of legislative delegation did not offend the principle of the separation of powers, as long as the legislative branch imposed a political line on it and oversaw its application.

It is worth noting that the International Commission of Jurists (ICJ) was working, throughout the 1950s and mid-1960s, precisely with broadening the rule of law concept, because the post-colonial nations and Latin America were eager to favor economic development under the baton of state intervention. In the first issue, in 1954, of its periodic publication *Bulletin*, the ICJ's editorial board clarified that the rule of law "fundamentals and this system of law are in danger." (ICJ, 1954, p. 4). The board discussed the increasing number of legally trained individuals, and how the number of laws promulgated attains unmanageable proportions. Nonetheless, the most threatening aspect of those years was that "more than ever law as a whole is menaced in its very foundations, from outside and within." The publication went further to affirm that the rule of law meant, as established in the Brazilian 1946 Constitution and expressed in Brazilian legal thinking, the "respect by the individual for the requirements of society and the State, respect by the State for the rights of the individual." (ICJ, 1954, p. 4). This involved a careful "balance" between the rights and duties of the individual and those of the state, along with their restriction, in: "a spirit of freedom and moderation." Only such an order could avoid the "systematic violation of the rights of the individual" by totalitarianism (ICJ, 1954, p. 4).

After its foundation in 1952, in Berlin, the International Commission of Jurists held the 1955 Athens Congress, the 1959 New Delhi Congress, and the 1961 Nigeria Congress. At the end of these meetings, the commission published legal resolutions (the *Act of Athens, the New Delhi Declaration* and the *Law of Lagos*) seeking to deepen the rule of law doctrine (ICJ, 1962a; ICJ, 1962b). Indeed, besides the independency of the judiciary, the ICJ tried to establish broader definitions of the concept of the rule of law. First and foremost, the concept would mean the acceptance of fundamental human values in the government and the legal system (Marsh, 1957, p. 6; Marsh, 1958). This definition, though somewhat generic, was quite opportune for encompassing different national realities and traditions under the same "umbrella" of legal principles.

In January 1961, at the Nigeria Congress, one of the committees, *Human Rights and Government Security – the Legislative, Executive, and Judiciary*,[6] addressed the problems concerning the delegation of powers to the executive branch. The practice of approving rules and regulations with legislative effect, as the committee argued, could result in a permanent state of emergency, which would thus be in detriment to the protection of fundamental rights, as provided by the natural law of human rights. A second committee, *Human Rights and Aspects of Criminal and Administrative Law*, also concerned with the executive's hypertrophy and the primacy of the rule of law, discussed the extent to which certain executive activities should be subject to review by the courts in order to keep it under scrutiny by the judiciary and the constitution (ICJ, 1961; Lalive, 1961).

It was, however, at the IV ICJ International Congress, held between December 11 and 15 1962, in the state of Rio de Janeiro, in the city of Petrópolis, that the issue of the separation of powers was better ordered. In this event, the ICJ turned to *Executive Action and the Rule of Law*. The debates were precisely on what the Brazilian legal elites had been trying to solve since the early 1950s: legislative delegation. How to allow expanded action by the executive while preserving the premise of the separation of powers, in particular the independence of the judiciary. Thus, the *Resolution of Rio de Janeiro*, an official document resulting from the debate organized by ICJ in Brazil, established that:

1. The complexity of modern society may necessitate the delegation of legislative power by the Legislative to the Executive, particularly where requirements of fair practice demand frequent changes or where the Legislative cannot reasonably be expected to deal with technical details.
2. The enactments by which such legislative powers are delegated should carefully define the extent, purpose, and where necessary duration of delegated legislation and should provide for the procedure by which it can be brought into effect.
3. Delegated legislation should always be fair and reasonable and should be drafted in clear form. In no circumstances should it deviate from

general principles of legislation or from the directions laid down by the Legislative.

4 To ensure that the Executive should loyally discharge its legislative mandate, the Legislative should entrust appropriate organs, such as standing committees, with the task of scrutinizing all delegated legislation and reporting to it at fixed intervals the results of their scrutiny.

5 Attention is called to the powers of the Legislative to exercise control through its right to appropriate public money. Such control can be strengthened by a high and independent official, like a Controller or Auditor-General, appointed by Parliament, who exercises control over expenditure of public money (ICJ, 1963, p. 28).

As previously mentioned, this was precisely the fundamental issue in the Brazilian legal debate. Embracing the delegation of powers, specifically by adopting the idea of "cooperation" among the branches, the constitutional reform promoted in the 1956 draft fundamentally aimed to ensure a legislative drafting process consentaneous to the legal solutions demanded by the social dynamics arising from modernization. In effect, in this renewal of the Legislative power a new organization was foreseen, particularly of its permanent committees, as in the U.S. Congress model, along with the introduction of the legal institutions of the delegation of powers, according to the model of Article 72 of the Italian Constitution. Also, deadlines were set for analyzing the bills sent by the executive to Congress. Therefore, the proposed amendment to Articles 67 and 68 of the 1946 Constitution foresaw deadlines for the analysis of projects sent, through the delegation of the normative function, by the President of the Republic to the President of the Senate. In addition, it also foresaw deadlines for review by one of the legislative chambers of a bill approved in the other. In both cases, after the stipulated period, having been analyzed or not, such projects would immediately gain the force of law (Lima, Dantas, Medeiros Silva, *et al*, 1956, p. 16–17).[7]

Nonetheless, despite what appeared to be a consensus among legal elites, including the dramatic character of the issue, the draft did not advance in Congress. Likewise, the *Preliminary Draft of the General Law of Legal Norms* – written by Haroldo Valladão, one of the exponents of private international law and comparative law in Brazil and a member of the The Hague Academy of International Law –, which also included the delegation of powers, also did not advance in Congress (Valladão, 1966). In the case of reforming the congressional committee, the role of the advisor was a controversial topic, since some believed that the advisor should be an "attaché" of committees and others were in favor of creating the advisory as its own body, with intrinsic authority and functions (Viana, 1959, p. 67).

Besides the aforementioned reasons, the central aspect of concern among Brazilian elites, particularly on the part of members of the National Congress, was the fear of an exaggerated personal and political power of the President of the Republic, or in other words, the centrality of the executive and the autarchies linked to it under the presidential regime. This position contrary to delegation was present in Congress and most prestigious Brazilian newspapers, such as the *Correio da Manhã*, and continued even after the 1964 coup (Pauperio, 1962; Nascimento Silva, 1965). On July 30, 1953, for example, the Rio newspaper printed a favorable comment to the position of Senator Ferreira de Souza, of the National Democratic Union party (UDN), against the Vargas government's attempt to establish state intervention power in the private sphere via the delegation of powers:

> The vote by Mr. Ferreira de Souza, speaking yesterday to the Senate Justice Committee about the state's power to intervene in private enterprises, will remain as one of the most brilliant lessons of the parliamentarian, who is also a specialist in commercial law and a professor of law. [....] The project in question, confusing [...] the power to legislate with the power to intervene, aims to submit every individual effort, responsible for the producing of national wealth, to the discretion of the Minister of Labor. [....] The power to legislate has always existed; the power to intervene, implying a legislative delegation to a holder of another power, namely, the Executive, as written in Art. 16 and 25 of the project, is the totalitarian novelty to destroy democracy in the country.[8]
>
> (*Correio da Manhã*, 1953, p. 4)

It was under this dilemma, then, that there arose the question of the most appropriate system of government for the country: if, as developed in this debate, the central problem of legislative elaboration was in the strict separation of the powers, Montesquieu's formula would have become an exclusive aspect of presidentialism. To some groups of Brazilian elites, in particular those linked to the knowledge of political scientists-jurists at the FGV-IDPCP, such as, for instance, Paulo Bonavides (1963), the remedy for the growing power of the Presidency of the Republic would be the adoption of a more appropriate political system in that accelerated time of modernization: parliamentarianism.

The parliamentary experience and the totalitarian threat: the "*ultimatum*" of the Brazilian crisis

The crisis generated by the resignation of Jânio Quadros in 1961, and the subsequent inauguration of the João Goulart administration led to the adoption in September 1961, by the National Congress, of Constitutional Amendment No. 4, which instituted the parliamentary system in Brazil. The measure, taken as an overcoming, in short, of the fears about the exacerbated powers of the Presidency, was not, however, consensual among legal intellectuals: it was the contingency solution to circumvent the problem of the succession of Quadros. João Goulart was connected to Getúlio Vargas (who committed suicide in 1954) and the left-wing Brazilian Labor Party

[Partido Trabalhista Brasileiro – PTB]. Indeed, jurists such as Milton Campos and Miguel Seabra Fagundes were not convinced that in a country "with a such a deficient political education as ours, this [parliamentary] regime, which requires, in its dynamics, seriously structured parties and a high-level political elite, may be more convenient than presidentialism" (Fagundes, 1962, p. 15; Campos, 1972). In any case, the issue that concerns this chapter is that the institution of parliamentarianism was followed by the revocation of Article 36, Paragraph 2 of the 1946 Constitution, including, by extension, legislative delegation among the branches. The regulation in Article 22 of the constitutional amendment, regarding delegation, would be carried out by a complementary law, dated June 17, 1962. The model of delegation adopted foresaw its control by Congress, insofar as both legislative chambers had to establish the delegation's content, object, and scope (Medeiros Silva, 1963). In other words, the model would be similar to that promoted in the 1956 draft, of *delegation-collaboration* and not *delegation-resignation*.

The form of government to be established in the country, however, came to be decided shortly afterward, in early 1963, through a national referendum. By the end of 1962, there was a clear inclination to presidentialism, which would mean the revocation of the constitutional amendment that instituted parliamentarianism. Given the defeat of parliamentarianism and, consequently, of the normative delegation among branches, some jurists defended the maintenance of delegation, despite the results of the referendum. Carlos Medeiros Silva, in a lecture at the Technical Council of the National Trade Confederation, in Rio de Janeiro, spoke to businessmen to advocate for the maintenance of the delegation's instrument, which was not antagonistic, as he argued, to the presidential system:

> The fact that the delegation of powers was admitted to the Additional Act, whose revocation has already been announced, with the plebiscite scheduled for January 6, 1963 [...], does not mean that its destiny is linked to the parliamentary regime. More frequently in this system of government, presidentialism does not exclude it [....]. The truth is that long before Amendment No. 4, the delegation of powers was already advocated among us, by public law scholars, as an indispensable measure for the improvement of the presidential regime [...]. My vote and that of the defenders of delegation is that it remains in our positive law, as an indispensable instrument for the functioning and improvement of institutions, whether a not yet consolidated parliamentarianism survives, or whether we turn to presidentialism.
>
> (Medeiros Silva, 1963, p. 8 and 15)

At the beginning of 1963, João Goulart's victory was achieved with the decision, in the national plebiscite, for the return of the presidential system of government. Constitutional Amendment No. 4 was automatically revoked and, with it, legislative delegation. The question of the separation of powers and delegation was immediately taken up again in the legal debate. Even at the beginning of 1963, the first issue of the IDPCP journal published the article *Separação de Poderes: reflexão sobre a permanência do problema* (*Separation of Powers: A Reflection on the Permanence of the Problem*), by jurist Nelson Nogueira Saldanha. One of the main specialists in the philosophy of law in the country, Saldanha highlighted, in addition to what was being said in the legal debate about the delegation of powers and the crisis in parliaments, that the aforementioned theory had been contradicted by the facts. He argued that the "separation of powers" had become an "interpenetration" of the powers, proper to those times when the effort for development was made through a cohesive national concert based on the central power of the Union.

Adding to the criticism of the strict formalistic interpretation of the separation of powers, besides Saldanha, jurists such as Miguel Reale (1959) and Paulo Dourado de Gusmão (1956) defended a re-evaluation of the philosophy of law, having in mind this somewhat "archaic conception" of the strictly legalistic tradition in Brazil, which was therefore overly attached to constitutional attributions and consequently to limiting social action. Reale and Dourado de Gusmão reproduce, as previously discussed, the diagnoses of disaggregation between positive law and modern reality. The political horizon of the field of law in Brazil was clearly presented by Miguel Seabra Fagundes (1960): Brazilian legal thinking was facing the country's tradition of written law, in which the contribution of jurisprudence to the unfolding of legal texts would be insignificant. Jurists such as Reale and Fagundes were arguing that the Brazilian legal tradition was opposed to the constant process of legitimizing legality, a practice that could be found in the Anglo-Saxon tradition of customary law. For Saldanha, there was a need to legitimize this new understanding of the separation of powers by which the concept of the rule of law could be revised fruitfully, assuring, however, the maintenance of its essence, since it would be "[...] a guarantee against totalitarianism" (Saldanha, 1963, p. 80).

Goulart's return to the Presidency, in early 1963, was followed by a conclave, at the University of São Paulo Law School and under the auspices of the newspapers *Correio da Manhã* and *Folha de S. Paulo*, to discuss and define a structural program of modernization for Brazil. The main reason was to produce a common understanding among political, intellectual, and legal elites regarding a new legal order and its legitimacy, one capable of maintaining the primacy of the rule of law, but in which the legislative branch would instead control the executive and make policy, in addition to being less normative. The aim of the Brazilian Congress for the Definition of Basic Reforms, as previously mentioned, was not only to oppose the program of basic reforms defined by the João Goulart administration (1961–1964), but also to enlist these elites into a cohesive political intervention agenda. For this purpose, it re-united and systematized the agendas of reforms debated at length in the country, especially during the 1950s, but that had not been evaluated or approved by the National Congress.

Facing Goulart's reform agenda, the elites understood that the problem concerning the difficulty with the National Congress had come to an unavoidable moment (Anais, 1963). In other words, as put by Paulo Bonavides (1963), the Brazilian crisis was imposing an *ultimatum* to the national contest regarding the country's modernization. The president of the Congress for the Definition of Basic Reforms, General Edmundo de Macedo Soares e Silva, advocated precisely such an understanding at the opening of the conclave:

> The national building must be renovated. The loads it must endure have increased over time. It is essential to reinforce structures, widen passages, improve environments, modernize architecture. It is a breathtaking work, requiring knowledge and experience, a healthy conception of needs, public spirit, loyalty to historical evolution, a secure vision, and confidence in the future.

Calling for an agreement among elites to profoundly modernize the country's institutional structures, Soares e Silva stressed that "[e]ach country must do its job. In Brazil, this is up to us: it is our duty and our privilege to suppress the mistakes of the past and prepare for a better and grandiose future" (Soares e Silva, 1963, p. 20–21).

The first of the five congressional committees was dedicated to the theme of *Constitutional, Political Party, and Electoral Reforms*, with the former Minister of Justice Antônio de Sampaio Dória as president, Mackenzie Law School professor Alfredo Cecílio Lopes as secretary, and the São Paulo judge Oswaldo Aranha Bandeira de Mello as rapporteur. The debates, from which formal resolutions were to be drafted and sent to the National Congress and disseminated to the public, were structured based on the presentation of theses on the various aspects of the modernization program. Although not resolving disagreements about the most appropriate form of government for Brazil, the debate within the scope of this Constitutional Reform Committee welcomed the legal instrument of the delegation of powers, as Carlos Medeiros Silva had intended.

Such was the case of Miguel Reale. Although presenting his "suggestions for constitutional reform regarding the regime," by which he advocated a plan of constitutional reforms given the increasing concentration of powers in the Presidency, Reale argued in favor of the delegation of powers. Indeed, after the result of the popular referendum, Reale, an advocate of parliamentarianism, made suggestions for the effective control of the executive and more consistent action by the legislative branch regarding the new dynamics of modernity. Among these suggestions, the jurist, despite asserting the chief executive's responsibility to freely appoint and dismiss the ministers of state, defended that Chamber of Deputies should have the power to dismiss a minister of state from his duties.

As other jurists who had been apprising the concept of the separation of powers, he supported this suggestion by arguing that "with this measure, there will be greater interplay between the policies of the President and the directives of the popular Chamber, establishing a system of control and limitation to presidential acts, preventing serious facts [....]" (1963, p. 2). Furthermore, approaching the 1956 preliminary draft of the constitutional reform prepared by the Committee for Studies on Constitutional Reform, especially the principle of internal delegation, in accordance with Article 72 of the Italian Constitution, and deepening the hypotheses of controlling the executive, the law professor defended the need to infuse elements of legislative technique into Congress. It did so, in particular, when proposing the modernization of the internal structure of the legislative branch, of its committees, stipulating, finally, that the projects approved by 2/3 of its members could not undergo alterations in the plenary, thus avoiding, by the set of such measures, the "legislative Babel" in which the country would find itself. Furthermore, even though favoring, through practical measures, the effective control of the Presidency's powers by the National Congress, Reale recognized the importance of legislative delegation, which would have demonstrated good results during its short period of use in Brazil (1963, p. 2–5).

In the same vein, another important contributor to the debate of the Constitutional Reform Committee, Professor José Horácio Teixeira Meirelles, indicated, with regard to the hypertrophy of the executive and its necessary control, the role to be performed by the judiciary. Meirelles underscored what would be the flawed system of constitutional control of laws in Brazil: a fundamental instrument to avoid what was referred to, by Miguel Reale, as a "legislative Babel" – the profusion of written laws without the appropriate techniques pertinent to the legal field (i.e., legislative inflation). The apparent imprecision in constitutional control would allow for the application of several legal instruments in contrast to the text of the Brazilian Constitution. Both Teixeira Meirelles and Reale recognized not only the control of presidential powers but also the increasingly reduced normative role of the National Congress, which the adoption of legislative delegation could importantly resolve. In this sense, its prohibition by the 1946 Constitution would have been a most serious error:

> [...] parliaments increasingly lose, in modern times, the character of law enforcement bodies, especially in the case of technical legislation [...] to become mere centers of political debate [...] setting **political guidelines**, or a **legislation of principles**. In the most perfected democracy in the world, which is now old England, the biggest and best part of the legislation is now delegated, that is, passed by the cabinet, and only reviewed or simply approved by the parliament.
>
> (Meirelles, 1963, p. 8)

At the end of the Brazilian Congress for the Definition of Basic Reforms, on the morning of January 22, 1963, the resolutions adopted in the debates of each of the five committees were held to a vote by the 250 delegates present at the meeting. These resolutions were subsequently sent to the National Congress for consideration. Regarding the legislative function, the Constitutional Reform Committee approved the following guidelines (which approached those foreseen by the preliminary draft of the committee of jurists appointed by Nereu Ramos in 1956):

> Legislative Action: 3 guidelines:
>
> a) – Competence of Congress without prejudice to the equal prerogative of the Executive, guaranteed to it the power of absolute veto of laws of the latter, within 30 days of their promulgation, or of the annulment, at any time, of those in force, by the majority of its members, preserving the right of any congressman or senator to initiate deliberation.
>
> b) – Recognition of Parliament's original legislative competence, with the admission of the delegation of prerogative in each specific case to the Executive, with the specification of the delegated powers.
>
> ...
>
> The 1st Committee recognizes the need, in certain cases, for delegation, as long as it takes effect by a law of Congress, with the specification of the matter and the subsequent control of Congress over the same legislation.
>
> (Terceira Sessão [Third Session], 1963, p. 14)

Due to these debates proposed by the Brazilian Congress for the Definition of Basic Reforms, the Institute for Research and Social Studies (IPES) think tank produced a series of studies presenting a program of 23 reforms. The aim was also to be a counterpoint to João Goulart's program and an agent of political and intellectual elites for a cohesive political intervention agenda. Officially formed in November 1962, under the aegis of the Alliance for Progress and the encyclical *Mater et Magistra*, the Institute was born as a think tank of elite groups in favor of a sophisticated and extensive program of reforms, propaganda, and a destabilization of the Goulart government. Indeed, the think tank was decisive not only for the success of the 1964 *coup d'état*, but also as a guide for the dictatorship's modernization agenda (Dreifuss, 1981). At the beginning of its activities, the IPES consolidated its position on such a program of reforms and modernization for the country, which the Brazilian Congress for the Definition of Basic Reforms had discussed at the beginning of 1963.

Presented, that year, to public opinion and the National Congress, the document *Basic Reforms: Positions of the IPES* included, among its proposals, a program of legislative reform and another one of political structure reform. The proposal for the legislative defended, in the spectrum of modernization of its organization, measures to renew the "internal organization and the functioning of the Legislative and, in particular, of its permanent committees and plenary sessions"; moreover, it advocated the institutionalization of devices to prevent changes, in the plenary sessions, of the work of specialized committees – changes that would cause the mutilation of bills of law and delay their processing. Thus, the fundamental measures for the Project of Legislative Reform by the IPES, which was in line with the 1956 draft and the resolutions of the Brazilian Congress for the Definition of Basic Reforms, were:

1 The limitation of the power of initiative of a certain category of projects, substitutes, and amendments;
2 The restructuring of the permanent committees with the strengthening of their attributions by the delegation of powers of the various parties to the representatives that integrate them;
3 Simplification of the processing of cases in the plenary through effective coordinating action by party leaders, whether in the discussion or the formulation of substitutes and amendments;
4 The creation of a broad documentation center for the legislative chambers capable of promptly and effectively attending to the consultations of members of Congress;
5 The establishment of a high-level technical advisory to ensure that representatives are fully and safely assisted in the analysis and resolution of problems of a geographical, statistical, legal, social, economic, administrative, technical, and scientific nature, on the issues covered by the bills (IPES, 1963, p. 20–21).

Regarding the reform of the political structure, which was focused on the reorganization of the state, it asserted that the respect for the rights to life, freedom, and the principles of human dignity was imperative. Additionally, the document advocated a doctrinal coherence and an adequate organicity to this state structuring. The central point was to assure the primacy of the individual's right over state power, establishing an anti-totalitarian framework to this modernization agenda that understood the need of the state apparatus to guarantee its fulfillment. Indeed, the IPES, which was engaged with the United States Cold War assumption on modernization and anti-totalitarianism (Dreifuss, 1981; Cancelli, 2017), relied on the agendas of the Congress for Cultural Freedom and the International Commission of Jurists concerning both issues. The IPES project, among other themes, foresaw:

1 The establishment of the most adequate delimitation of branches, the Legislative, the Executive, and the Judiciary;
2 The definition and explicit enumeration of the delegation of powers or legislative qualification of the executive branch, in the cases in which it becomes indispensable or in which it is advisable (IPES, 1963, p. 24).

This effort was a successful one. It was able to contain the João Goulart administration's agenda, which was furthermore facing difficulty with

Congress (Busseto, 2002), and it led to the formation of a common elite-block against Goulart. The legal structure set up in the first decade of the dictatorship brought, in essence, an arrangement that came to operate, partially, outside the country's legalistic tradition. The fundamental assumption was the imperative to modernize. However, because of the unwavering need for the leading role of the executive and the disruptive character of the development process, anti-totalitarianism offered a moral boundary to state intervention. The dictatorship's constitutional order was, then, founded with regard to this fundamental assumption, which can be seen with the Institutional Acts and, subsequently, with the 1967 Constitution and 1969 Amendment No. 1. The new legal order tried to structure – not as a disguise, as the literature argues, but as a political horizon and legitimacy among a wide range of Brazilian society – a revived rule of law concept. Authoritarianism came to be justified among elites – in Brazil and the Global North – as a secure (non-totalitarian) way to modernize.

1964 and after: executive hypertrophy and anti-totalitarianism

> The expression "independent and harmonious," in the Italian, German, and French constitutions, has disappeared. We are more or less attached to a republican fetishism at the end of the last century, in the Constitution of 91. There is, in fact, a separation of functions, each Power with its function. But the tendency – and this is the fundamental reason for the revolution – is to give supremacy to the Executive power, so that, respecting the role of each one, one can avoid the supervenience of future crises, of clashes between Powers.
>
> (Gama e Silva, 1982, p. 88)

Just over a week after the 1964 coup, on April 9, the "Supreme Command of the Revolution," formed by the leaders of the Army, General Arthur da Costa e Silva, of the Air Force, Lieutenant-Brigadier Francisco de Assis Correia de Mello, and of the Navy, Vice Admiral Augusto Hamann Rademaker Grunewald, promulgated Institutional Act Number 1 (AI-1). The legal instrument invested the "revolution" with constituent powers, offering, for the next two years, not only government guidelines, but the legal instruments to enforce them (Brasil, 1964). Shortly after deciding for the (indirect) presidential election to take place within two days, which would confirm General Castello Branco as president, AI-1 "resolved" the long political and legal debate concerning the strict separation of powers.

It did so to the extent that it opted for the resurgence of executive intervention and legislative drafting mechanisms and for the concentration of powers in the federal government to the detriment of states and municipalities (Brasil, 1961; Lopreato, 2002, p. 31–47).[9] It was the "integrated federalism" advocated by Haroldo Teixeira Valladão: a concerted national effort, under the aegis of the Union, in favor of development (Valladão 1974). Thus, alongside the regulation of the electoral process for presidential elections and the establishment of security mechanisms based on the assumptions of a so-called political compression, the Institutional Act, in Articles 3, 4, and 5, basically dealt with the normative function of the Presidency and, consequently, with a new order for the functions of the branches.

This was a fundamental aspect of the Institutional Act. Carlos Medeiros Silva,[10] the co-author of AI-1 alongside Francisco Campos, the organic legal intellectual of the Vargas regime, had been arguing since the early 1950s against the prohibition of the delegation of powers established in the 1946 Constitution. A few days after the coup, Medeiros Silva spoke at the Conference of the Technical Council of the National Trade Confederation (CNC). He evoked the 1952 article *O poder regulamentar no direito comparado* (*Regulatory Power in Comparative Law*) and the arguments that international intellectuals had been developing regarding the constitutional attributions of the executive branch in its search to solve the social issue. Medeiros Silva (1964a) also spoke to one of the most prestigious Brazilian newspapers, *O Globo,* on April 11 to clarify for a broader public those "fundamentals" of AI-1.

Indeed, Medeiros Silva defended such attributions based on the fundamental work of this debate, Georges Langrod's book on the legislative process in Western Europe. In the preface to the Portuguese translation of Langrod's book, Oswaldo Trigueiro, who would come to take a seat on the Supreme Court after the coup and a strong critique of the constitutional restriction on the delegation of powers, made a clear position in this regard:

> In Brazil, under the 1946 Constitution, the maladjustment of parliamentary life is of increasing evidence. The Brazilian political reality provides yet another example of the material impossibility in which the organs of the legislative branch find themselves: to satisfactorily fulfill the function that the constitution reserves for them. Congress has increased its productivity enormously, but it is unable to vote, within a reasonable time, on many necessary laws and to carry out, in terms of written law, the reforms required by the country's progress and by state interventionism in the social and economic domain.
>
> (Trigueiro, 1954, Preface)

Besides Langrod's book, Medeiros Silva found support in *La reforme du parliamentarisme*, written by René Capitant. In his 1934 book, the French jurist presented a solution to the malaise of the Western legal and political field: the complicated issue involving, on the one hand, the primacy of the rule of law and the defense of the individual, and, on the other, economic leadership and the "collective good." With respect to such a malaise, Capitant asserted that "to govern is no longer to act within the framework of existing laws; to govern is to direct the legislation itself; to govern, in a word, is to legislate" (Capitant, 1934, p. 11, cited in Medeiros Silva, 1964b, p. 9). With these substrates, Carlos Medeiros Silva defended AI-1:

> By changing the traditional legislative drafting process, the Institutional Act sought, during its validity, to remedy gaps in our legal system, with the purpose of accelerating its progress and allowing greater participation by the Executive in the making of laws. The Act did not re-establish legislative delegation in its various modalities, but gave the President of the Republic the initiative not only of constitutional amendments but also of ordinary legislation, without restrictions. It established an automatic procedure for projects originating from the Executive, subject to a special *quorum* and limited powers.
>
> (Medeiros Silva, 1964b, p. 11)

Thus, as René Capitant had prescribed, AI-1, as an instrument that legally legitimized the so-called revolution, gave the federal government the competence of a normative organ *par excellence* to the detriment, therefore, of the normative function of Congress. This was precisely what the AI-1 established when it stated that "the revolution does not seek to legitimize itself through Congress. In fact, the latter receives from this Institutional Act [...] its legitimation" (Brasil, 1964).

Medeiros Silva insisted that this was done according to the 1956 preliminary draft of the constitutional reform and with what an important part of the legal elites had been discussing throughout the 1950s: the premise of *collaboration* between branches, as established by Article 36 of the 1946 Constitution, which was maintained by AI-1. This was a fundamental assumption in this reorganization, since the preservation of the separation of powers constituted a fundamental distancing from totalitarian autarchies, demonstrating a difference between totalitarianism and democracy (or a temporary authoritarianism) that, as I have previously argued, U.S. power, through the ICJ and the CCF, was exploiting in the Cold War. Such an argument can be seen, for example, in the second edition of the seminal book *Totalitarian Dictatorship and Autocracy*. In the revised 1965 edition, Carl Friedrich and Zbigniew Brzezinski argued that the political order in Brazil after 1964 was a regime "instituted in order to ward off the threat of a possible takeover by a totalitarian movement" (Friedrich and Brzezinski, 1965, p. 8). Medeiros Silva would speak, once again, with *O Globo*'s newspaper in October, to explain the "non-dictatorial" reasons for the new legal order (Medeiros Silva, 1964c, p. 11).

By the same token, another jurist, Luiz Navarro de Britto, defended that the delegation instrument would not give the appearance of a dictatorship. Following modernization theory's general assumption that economic growth would lead to the development of democratic institutions, Britto advocated that, to avoid dictatorships, it was necessary to allow the executive branch to organize the country's economic forces, favoring a cohesive and coherent effort toward modernization (Britto, 1966). The Institutional Act had precisely put such an allowance into motion by normative means.

In effect, AI-1, in Articles 3, 4, and 5, respectively, established a deadline and a system for approving amendments sent by the Presidency to the National Congress, with the approval of the absolute majority of chamber members being enough; automatic processing in Congress for executive bills, highlighting that they would be approved by term (that is, even if they were not evaluated within 30 days of receipt); and, finally, the exclusive prerogative of the Presidency to initiate bills that create or increase budget expenditures.

Specifically, Article 3 established that the amendments sent by the executive should be considered jointly in a single session by the National Congress, their approval depending on an absolute majority vote in two sessions (the first to be held within 30 days of receipt of the project and the second, within 10 days). The processing of amendments from other sources (other than the Presidency) required a two-thirds vote to be approved. Article 4 established, in turn, automatic processing for the executive's bills of law, which would have a maximum period of 30 days for their appreciation as of their receipt by the Chamber of Deputies. The same would apply to the Senate. If such projects were not evaluated within that period, they would automatically gain legal force.

Furthermore, the aforementioned article stipulated that, in cases where the Presidency expressed urgency for the processing of projects, they should be considered, in a joint session of the National Congress, within a maximum of 30 days after the submission by the Executive. Finally, Article 5 made an exclusive competence of the Presidency of the Republic to initiate bills that would create or increase public expenditures, while not allowing the Legislative to approve budget amendments in order to increase the initially proposed expenditures by the Executive. In other words, in a more profound way than that of the committee nominated by Nereu Ramos with the 1956 preliminary draft of constitutional reform, the wording of the 1st Institutional Act's Article 5 made the budgetary issue an exclusive and de facto prerogative of the Presidency.[11]

According to Carlos Medeiros Silva, the first two articles represented the overcoming of the "dogma" of the separation of powers regarding the relationship between the executive and the legislative. In those times of "modern constitutionalism," these branches would find themselves interpenetrated by each other, interdependent on each other, and in a situation of collaboration with each other. The rule of law, in the democratic regime, would have become a simple "fiction of law," as demonstrated by the practice of the delegation of powers adopted in England, France, Italy, Germany, and the United States – models on which AI-1 could support itself (Medeiros Silva, 1964b; Brasil, 1964).

Specifically regarding the Presidency's prerogative for budgetary law initiatives, Article 5 worked in line with attempts, since the mid-1950s, by the federal government to achieve greater control of the state budget (a fiscal responsibility). Also in this respect, AI-1 used the U.S. model, adopted with the 1946 law of legislative reorganization that aimed, among its provisions, to guarantee effective fiscal control.[12] It can be inferred that the act, along with a new tax code and the rationalization of public expenditures, guaranteed instruments for the effectiveness of the state budget, constituting the bases of the Government Economic Action Program (PAEG) (Briso Neto, 2008; Penholato, 2017; Trubek, 1971). On May 22, 1964, using the prerogatives established by AI-1 (regarding the time limit for the evaluation of a bill by Congress), the Presidency of the Republic promoted two constitutional amendments on the budget issue, in particular, Constitutional Amendment No. 7, demonstrating the concern on the part of the Castello Branco administration with economic stabilization (IDPCP, 1965).[13]

Concerning the economic order, resuming the discussions of Nereu Ramos' 1956 committee, Castello Branco decreed Institutional Act Number 2 (AI-2) in October 1965, which stipulated the exclusive responsibility of the Presidency to introduce laws creating public positions, functions, or jobs and raising salaries or public expenditures. It also prohibited amendments that would increase the expenditures foreseen in the federal government budget. The São Paulo state attorney Paulo Celso Fortes recognized that, with the new law, the legislative role of Congress was mostly forbidden. Fortes argued that such measures, a defense against the legislative initiative to increase expenditure via amendments, represented the "foundation of the state's financial administration" (1966, p. 354).

Along the same lines, Act 2 allowed the chief of state to enact complementary acts as well as decree-laws on matters of national security. In addition, it provided that parliamentary recess could be the object of a complementary act by the Presidency and that, in this case, the head of state was authorized to legislate by decree-laws in all matters allowed by the constitution – an expedient that, as previously mentioned, Getúlio Vargas had used soon after the October coup and then with the 1937 Constitution, written by Francisco Campos (Rangel, 1966, p. 364).

During the authoritarian rule, the support for such a reorganization rested on a revised rule of law order. More precisely, it rested on the legal argument that the separation of powers was not due to the legislative action of parliament, but to the instruments of inspection and control that the branches should reciprocally exercise. In the rhetoric of a necessary organicity of the national modernization project under the aegis of a renewed executive, this arrangement appeared in terms of *collaboration* between them (Novelli, 1967). The new legal structure established by the acts and the constitutional amendments permitted, therefore, the expansion of the federal government power and responded to the accelerated rhythm of those times (Brasil, 1967). In other words, seeking development, the dictatorship invested in the task and role of correcting the "laissez-faire culture" in the country. Authoritarian rule was a way to secure state intervention – the elite's project since the 1930s – but avoid totalitarianism. These acts and amendments were producing a profound rearrangement of the Brazilian legal structure, destabilizing, however, the 1946 constitutional order. To return the country's constitutional cohesion and systematicity, the Castello Branco administration would soon organize a new charter, which would establish a new role for the National Congress (or the legislative elaboration) and the separation of powers.

In April of 1966, Castello Branco created, by decree, a commission of eminent jurists to produce a preliminary draft of the new constitution. The commission was formed by the liberal ex-minister of Justice, Miguel Seabra Fagundes; the Secretary-General of the Brazilian headquarters of the International Commission of Jurists, Levi Carneiro; the former minister of the Federal Supreme Court, Orosimbo Nonato; and by the president of the IDPCP and soon to become minister of the Supreme Court, Themístocles Cavalcanti, who was the commission's chairman (IDPCP, 1966). In that same year, the Institute of Brazilian Lawyers (IAB), one of the most prestigious Brazilian associations, appointed another commission, formed by Reginaldo Nunes, Otto Gil, Haroldo Valladão, Heráclito Fontoura Sobral Pinto, and Pontes de Miranda, to present a preliminary draft constitution (Gil, 1969; Nunes, 1967). Resulting from an intensive debate carried out throughout 1966, the new fundamental law of Brazil was enacted on January 24, 1967, largely under the mantle of Carlos Medeiros Silva – a jurist who, in July 1966, had resigned from the position of Minister of the Supreme Court to occupy, at the request of Castello Branco, the position of Minister of Justice and Interior Affairs and lead the effort for the new constitution. The central implication of the new constitutional text lay in what had sustained the legal debate in the country since the post-World War I period: the crisis of the rule of law and what would be Brazil's definitive entry into the 20th century's "modern social constitutionalism," overcoming the liberal formulas (Novelli, 1967; Cotrim Neto, 1968; RCP, 1967; Reis, 1968; Buzaid, 1971; 1974).

Thus, if the "constitutional fetish" of the 18th and above all 19th centuries had as its basic premise the defense of the individual – the individual as the foundational image of this post-absolutist era, assembling new concepts of society and government organization –, in the 20th century, jurists dealt with the "corruption" and "misery" of subjects who had ascended to public life in the form of the "masses" – the effect of an "exacerbated" liberalism – left to the fate of totalitarian seduction (Cotrim Neto, 1968; Bonavides, 1977). It was therefore in this post-World War I legal debate that the concept of the individual changed, gradually becoming conditioned to a broader view of social life and the common good: the "collective interest." In such a process one can find the weakening of civil law and the strengthening of public law; the passage from the autonomy of the individual's will regarding the uses of the property to the "social function" of the property; in sum, the transformation of an individual enterprise detached from broader social considerations in favor of one organized along with the "identity and indivisibility of the supreme national interests" and organized under the mantle of the federal government (Novelli, 1967, p. 11).[14]

In the time of Montesquieu, the strict separation of powers created to curb the power of the Ancien Régime's sovereigns could be relativized, given these national interests, based on an idea of (social) justice, or the common good. The curve of almost four decades since the first constitutional reform in Brazil, in 1926, by which the country became part of a broad effort in the West to respond to the constitutional crises that appeared in the post-World War I period came to find a resolution, albeit an authoritarian and violent one, with the Constitution of 1967. When elaborating on legislative production and delegation of powers and, therefore, formulating the functions of the National Congress, the legal legitimacy of the new charter was found in the function of instrumentalizing the state, particularly the executive, for modernization.

Since the parliament had become, as asserted by one jurist, "too political and not legislative, very concerned with the political survival of its members and a little careless about its legislative task," the constitution intended to discipline its action and give it a new conceptualization. The normative function was removed to a large extent from Congress and given to the Presidency: it was up to the Executive to catalyze economic growth in favor of modernity. This was the argument structured by Themístocles Cavalcanti: the restrictions on legislative function were meant to "discipline the behavior of Congress," specifically "a) by setting deadlines for the discussion and voting on draft initiatives of the President [....]; b) in the prohibition of amendments that increase expenditures; c) also in certain initiatives of the Executive; d) in the automatic approval of certain projects not voted within the preset deadlines" (1969, p. 23). Indeed, according to Article 60 of the 1967 Constitution:

> Art. 60 – It is the exclusive competence of the President of the Republic to initiate laws that:
>
> I provide for financial matters;
> II create public positions, functions, or jobs or increase salaries or public expenditures;
> III fix or modify the personnel of the armed forces;
> IV provide for the administration of the Federal District and Territories.
>
> Sole paragraph – Amendments that increase the planned expenses will not be allowed:
>
> a in projects originating from the exclusive competence of the President of the Republic;
> b in projects related to the organization of the administrative services of the Chamber of Deputies, the Federal Senate, and the Federal Courts (Brasil, 1967).

The "soul of the Constitution" – the legislative process – was thus, as suggested by the Castello Branco administration, and in the name of the continuity of the "revolution," largely handed over to the Executive (Novelli, 1967). With that, as asserted supportively by Flávio Novelli (1967, p. 10), the normative practice had been profoundly changed, becoming "faster and more efficient, avoiding sterile formalisms and thus curbing abuses and political vices that were exercised through them."

Regarding the legislative process, the 1967 Constitution, which had accepted the principles stipulated in Institutional Acts 1 and 2, specifically, Articles 3 and 4 of AI-1 and Article 5, of AI-2 (Reis, 1968), transformed, in the initiative by the Presidency, the constitutional amendment projects, thus simplifying their processing (Articles 50 to 52). Furthermore, the Constitution ensured: a privileged position in the normative hierarchy to complementary laws (Article 53); special processing, when requested, of the bill sent by the Head of State to Congress (Article 54); the introduction of legislative delegation to congressional committees and to the President (Articles 5 to 57); and the use of the decree, by the Head of State, with the force of law, in matters of national security and public finances (Article 58) (Gill, 1969; RCP, 1967; Novelli, 1967).

The new charter, however, was born under protest from the jurists participating in this debate, insofar as they saw the constitution as legitimizing a dictatorship or, furthermore, as an expression of unavoidable inaccuracies, given the limited time in which Institutional Act Number 4, which determined the systematic guidelines for its vote by the National Congress. Indeed, the text called, in extraordinary fashion, for the National Congress to discuss, vote, and deliberate, between December 12, 1966 and January 24, 1967, the project presented by the Castello Branco administration (Brasil, 1966). It was noted that the approved text, apparently inspired by the French Constitution of 1958, which had given ample normative mechanisms to the Presidency, at the time occupied by Charles de Gaulle, ended up turning, after discussion and approval by Congress, into something eclectic: a compromise between the constitutional mechanisms of individual rights and guarantees and the normative powers invested in the executive branch, such as in the French model.

One of the aspects that spurred this criticism was the instrument of decree-laws (Article 58), which, it was argued, definitively emptied the power of the country's Legislative, insofar as the Executive could legislate without Congress. Such criticism came, for example, from the Public Law Institute at Faculty of Law of the University of São Paulo (USP), particularly from Celso Antônio Bandeira de Melo and Geraldo Ataliba Nogueira. Otto Gil, specifically analyzing the decree-laws, recognized that, although he disagreed with the aforementioned criticisms by USP professors, "the practice of decree-laws, in a country where the Legislative is not strengthened before public opinion [...] clears the way for the Executive dictatorship" (1969, p. 20).

The new constitution would have been born, thus, under the sign of "reform," such was the official rush for its approval. This criticism becomes common sense among legal elites, including Reginaldo Nunes, a hard-hitting critic of the 1967 Constitution, who belonged to the Institute of Brazilian Lawyers' commission responsible for drafting it (Nunes, 1967). Indeed, it would not take long for a constitutional reform to happen. Two years later, President General Artur da Costa e Silva appointed a "high level" committee – formed by himself and Vice President Pedro Aleixo; Ministers Rondon Pacheco, Luiz Antônio Gama e Silva, Hélio Brandão, and Carlos Medeiros Silva; Supreme Court Minister Themístocles Cavalcanti; and Miguel Reale – to reform the 1967 Constitution (Comissão Alto Nível, 1982a; 1982b; 1982c). Completed between July 14 and July 17, 1969, the work of this commission culminated in Constitutional Amendment No. 1, ratified on October 17 of that year, which fundamentally expanded the powers, including the normative ones, of the Chief Executive and enshrined the aforementioned reform of the public administration, promulgated by Decree-Law 200/67. In practical terms, the 1969 constitutional amendment extended the possibilities in which the Presidency could resort to a decree-law: in addition to national security and public finances, tax rules were included, along with the creation of public positions and salary fixing. Moreover, it was clarified that, in case of rejection by the National Congress of a decree-law, the previous acts would not be nullified (Cretella Jr., 1984, p. 18–19).

The official rush regarding the approval of the 1967 Constitution was due, at least in part, to the fact that the Institutional Acts imposed a new domain on the legal system and thus functioned above the constitution. This was a central concern for the dictatorship. Based on anti-totalitarianism and the legitimacy of economic development, the authoritarian rule had to manage, as I will argue, the degree of political "compression" in the country, and with it, the political alliance among liberals and conservatives. It was in this regard that the 1967 Constitution, and after it, the 1969 amendment returned the legal order to the constitutional domain, nullifying, respectively, Institutional Acts 1, 2, and 3, regarding the 1946 Constitution, and Institutional Acts 5 to 17, concerning the 1967 Constitution. The Institutional Acts were the legal basis for the "revolutionary" conception of authoritarian rule; they were *extraordinary* and *temporary* in their essence. This was precisely what the political scientist and jurist Candido Mendes de Almeida, one of the most prestigious figures in the Brazilian "political transition," illustrates when, referring to the Legislative power after the 1964 coup: the Constitution of 1967 "absorbed previous political reforms and subsequently suffered the impact of new technocratic demands embodied in Constitutional Amendment No. 1, of October 17, 1969" (Mendes, 1975, p. 124).

In 1974, Candido Mendes, in a discussion on the Legislative and development that was related to "political decompression," recognized the "special sensibility of Brazilian technocracy" to a legal framework always "in the making." In other words, he referred to the strategies regarding the

Institutional Acts, their extraordinary and temporary character. Indeed, for Mendes, as instruments to correct the political behavior of Congress, AI-1 to AI-4 were "resistant," in a first stage, "to the model designed by the Executive." Meanwhile, AI-5 to AI-17, in particular AI-5, which decidedly "hardened" the regime, were characterized by the "need for institutional corrections." Finally, by the mid-1970s, the elites were leading a discussion on "political transition" and the role to be played in it by the Legislative, assuming that the branch had become "over-conditioned by such readjustments," representing "not only a cooperation, but also a real hyper adaptability to the demands that the Executive address to it and expects from it" (Mendes, 1974, p. 125).

Indeed, as defended by Luiz Antônio da Gama e Silva, whose words open this section of the chapter, the "revolution" maintained the primacy for which it had been mobilized: the prominence of the executive in favor of a secure modernization agenda that would include Brazil in the social constitutionalism of the 20th century. Nonetheless, opposition begins to form against the direction of the "revolution," specifically regarding its normative policy (Nascimento Silva, 1965). "Legislative inflation" not only uncomfortably resembled totalitarian autocracies, as asserted by Brzezinski and Friedrich in their seminal book, but also expressed the moral lack, in the dictatorship's agenda, of a political dimension "made by and for Men." (1965, p. 5). Between the late 1960s and early 1970s, legal thinking in Brazil, relying on ideas and institutions directly promoted by U.S. actors, began an effort to imagine a political organization based on such a humanistic dimension.

Notes

1 Legislative work was suspended for nine years – until January 31, 1946.

2 The rule of law emerged as an attempt to ensure what the German authors who founded it called Gesetzmäßigkeit ("legality"): the conformity of government acts with the prescriptions of the law. By the early 20th century, German public law specialists were redefining the rule of law concept as a rationalized order of administrative law: in favor of subjective rights and private citizenship rights, the exercise of administration should be subject to predetermined legal and judicial standards, configuring what would be a "state of administrative justice" (Dallari, 1973).

3 The 1937 Constitution, unlike the previous constitutions and that of 1946, did not prohibit "legislative delegation." Furthermore, the charter made the expression "decree-law" official, allowing the president to issue laws over all matters within the Union's legislative competence, while Congress was in recess (which was the case throughout the Estado Novo, until 1945). Vargas thus circumvented the doctrinal principle, which was fundamentally liberal, whereby the impediment to delegation was a consequence of the principle of the separation of powers (Rocha, 2004; Sampaio, 1959).

4 On February 17, 1955, Cavalcanti published an article, in one of the major Brazilian newspapers, trying to sensitize public opinion to the need for the delegation of powers (Cavalcanti, 1955, p. 3).

5 It is worth noting that, in 1970, a new Legislative Reorganization Act was passed under the chairmanship of Richard Nixon.

6 The committee was formed by the following lawyers: T. M. Franck (Canada); J. Pouabou (Congo); G. Burdeau (France); E. R. M. Carlton, Y. Coulibali and L. Yapobi (Ivory Coast); S. N. Waruhiu (Kenya); P. A. George (Liberia); R. Rakotobe, A. Razafimahefa and G. Razafintsambaina (Madagascar); M. Bengaly (Mali); B. T. Gardner (Northern Rhodesia); J. M. Greenfield (Southern Rhodesia); J. S. R. Cole (Tanganyika, today Tanzania); and D. S. Bakkabulindi (Uganda).

7 It is worth noting that, by the late 1950s, a Technical Assistance Office had been constituted both in the state of São Paulo and in the Northern and Northeastern states. The offices followed a similar process as that in the United States. See Viana (1959).

8 A similar position was expressed in the article "*Clandestina e Fraudulenta Emissão de Papel-Moeda sem Autorização Expressa do Congresso* [*Clandestine and Fraudulent Issue of Currency Paper without Express Authorization from the Congress*]," published by the same newspaper in 1959: *Correio da Manhã* (1959, p. 1).

9 It was a defining position on the greater autonomy for states and municipalities, as established by the 1946 Constitution. Constitutional Amendment No. 5, of November 1961, which gave new wording to Articles 15, 19, and 29 of the constitution, instituted, among other issues, a new income distribution in favor of municipalities, with which it sought to recover losses in the distribution of tax resources during the J. Kubistchek administration. However, in November of that year, the Senate approved a new draft bill that sought, in turn, to strengthen states. At the same time, the Council of Ministers, during the term of the parliamentary system, referred to Congress a project of Tax Reform with the objective of raising the Union's revenues. This debate, which had dragged on throughout the 1950s, would have a new arrangement during the authoritarian rule, as I have argued, which was favorable to the Union. In this regard, see Brasil (1961); Lopreato (2002).

10 Medeiros was appointed to the Federal Supreme Court in 1965. However, in 1966, the jurist left his position at the court to become Minister of Justice and Interior Affairs in the Castello Branco administration. Medeiros was the editor-in-chief of *Revista Forense* and general director of FGV's *Revista de Administração Pública*, two major Brazilian law journals. A profile of Medeiros Silva can be found in Machado (2016).

11 It should be noted that, in the preliminary draft of constitutional reform, with which Medeiros Silva collaborated, the initiative of laws that create jobs in existing services and raise salaries of the armed forces should be the exclusive responsibility of the Presidency. However, the draft emphasized that, when there was an indication of the source of revenue that would support it, Congress could amend the law to the Union's budget. Finally, it maintained the budgetary issue as a normative competence of the Legislative, although it imposed procedural restrictions to it (Lima, Dantas, Medeiros Silva, *et al*, 1956; Brasil, 1964; Medeiros Silva, 1964b).

12 Such precepts were stipulated in Sections 133 and 139 of the aforementioned U.S. law of 1946.

13 More specifically, Constitutional Amendment No. 7 allowed the Presidency, from 1964 on, to collect taxes without prior budgetary authorization.

14 According to Novelli (1967, p. 11), it is through this cohesion that the idea of a federative pact in Brazil is reformulated. The Castelo Branco administration,

in order to favor the Federal Government aimed at correcting the "numerous abuses and errors that flourished in the shadow of an irrational and precarious municipalism."

Bibliography

Anais Do Congresso Brasileiro Para Definição Das Reformas De Base. (1963). Vol. I. Edição Preliminar Mimeografada.
Arinos, A. (1949). *Diário Do Congresso Nacional*. 24 de fevereiro.
______ (1955). *Diário Do Congresso Nacional*. 1.° de julho.
Bonavides, P. (1963). "A crise brasileira lança um 'ultimatum'," *Rev. do Inst. de Direito Púb. e Ciência Política*, Rio de Janeiro – FGV, Vol. VI, No. 3.
______ (1977). "O poder legislativo no moderno Estado social," *Revista Forense*, Rio de Janeiro, Vol. 257, Ano 73, Jan-Fev-Mar.
BRASIL. (1930a). Decreto No. 19.393, de 11 de novembro de 1930. Rio de Janeiro.
BRASIL. (1930b). Decreto No. 19.469, de 6 de dezembro de 1930. Rio de Janeiro.
BRASIL. (1961). Emenda Constitucional n° 5, de 21 de novembro de 1961. Brasília.
BRASIL. (1964). Ato Institucional n° 1, de 9 de abril de 1964. Brasília.
BRASIL. (1966). Ato Institucional N° 4, de 7 de dezembro de 1966. Brasília.
BRASIL. (1967). Constituição da República Federativa do Brasil de 1967. Brasília.
Briso Neto, J. L. P. (2008). *O conservadorismo em construção: o IPES e as reformas financeiras da Ditadura Militar (1961–1966)*. Dissertação de Mestrado. Campinas: Unicamp.
Britto, L. N. (1966). "Legislação e Poder Executivo," *Rev. Dir. Públ. e Ciência Política* – Rio de Janeiro – FGV, Vol. IX. No. 1 – Jan./Mar.
Busetto, A. (2002). *A democracia cristã no Brasil: princípios e práticas*. São Paulo: Editora UNESP.
Buzaid, A. (1971). *A renovação da ordem jurídica positiva*. Conferência proferida na Escola Superior de Guerra no dia 1.° de Junho de 1971. Brasília: Ministério da Justiça.
______ (1974). *O Ministério da Justiça. (Relatório de 1969 a 1974)*. Brasília: Departamento de Imprensa Nacional.
Campos, F. (1938). "Diretrizes constitucionais do novo Estado Brasileiro," *Revista Forense*, Rio de Janeiro, Vol. LXXIII, No. 415, jan.
______ (2001). *O Estado Nacional – sua estrutura, seu conteúdo ideológico*. (Coleção Biblioteca Básica Brasileira) Brasília: Senado Federal, Conselho Editorial.
Campos, M. (1972). *Testemunhos e ensinamentos*. Rio de Janeiro: Livraria José Olympio Editora.
Cancelli, E. (1994). *O mundo da violência: a polícia da Era Vargas*. 02. ed. Brasília: Editora Universidade de Brasília.
______ (2017). *O Brasil em Guerra Fria Cultural: o pós-guerra em releitura*. São Paulo: Intermeios.
Capitant, R. (1934). *La reforme du parlamentarisme*. Imprenta: Paris, Recueil Sirey. Cited in Medeiros Silva, C. 1964b. "O Ato Institucional e a Elaboração Legislativa," Revista dos Tribunais, São Paulo, Ano 53, Vol. 347, Setembro.
Cavalcanti, T. (1951). "O Estado e a Ordem Econômica – Problemas de Técnica Legislativa," *Revista de Direito Administrativo*, Rio de Janeiro – FGV, Vol. 25.
______(1954). *Quatro estudos*. Rio de Janeiro: Instituto de Direito Público e Ciência Política (IDPCP-FGV).

______(1955). “O Sistema Eleitoral deveria ser legislativo,” *Correio da Manhã*, Rio de Janeiro, cad. 1, 17 de fevereiro de 1955.

______ (1961) “A crise constitucional de nosso tempo”. *Rev. Dir. Públ. e Ciência Política*, Rio de Janeiro – FGV, Vol. IV, No. 3, setembro/dezembro.

______(1962). “Separação de Poderes e delegação legislativa,” *Rev. Dir. Públ. e Ciência Política*, Rio de Janeiro – FGV, Vol. V, No. 9, setembro/dezembro.

Claude, J. (1954). “Compte rendu de la Table Ronde sur le travail parlementaire,” *Revue française de science politique*, 4e année, n°4, p. 843–868. https://doi.org/10.3406/rfsp.1954.452680

Comissão De ‘Alto Nível’. (1982a). Estudo para a Reforma da Constituição de 1967. Vol. I, Presidência da República, Arquivo Brasília.

Comissão De ‘Alto Nível’. (1982b). Estudo para a Reforma da Constituição de 1967. Vol. II, Presidência da República, Arquivo Brasília.

Comissão De ‘Alto Nível’. (1982c). Estudo para a Reforma da Constituição de 1967. Vol. III, Presidência da República, Arquivo Brasília.

Congresso Nacional de Direito Judiciário. (1936). *Revista Forense*, Rio de Janeiro, Vol. LXVII, No. 398, pp. 809–810, ago. Cited in Silveira, M. M. 2016. “Direito, Ciência Social: o lugar dos juristas nos debates do Brasil dos anos 1930 e 1940,” *Estudos Históricos*, Rio de Janeiro – FGV, Vol. 29, No. 58, pp. 441–460, maio-agosto.

Correio da Manhã. (1953). “*Poder de Intervir*,” *Correio da Manhã*, June 30, 1953, Rio de Janeiro, Caderno 1, No. 18.511. Ano LIII.

______(1959). “Clandestina e Fraudulenta Emissão de Papel-Moeda sem Autorização Expressa do Congresso,” *Correio da Manhã*, April 5, 1959, Rio de Janeiro, Caderno 2, No. 20.252, Ano LVIII.

Cotrim Neto, A. B. (1968).“A Crise do Estado de Direito e a Nova Constituição do Brasil,” *Revista Forense*, Rio de Janeiro, Vol. 224, Ano 64, Out-Nov-Dez.

Cretella Jr., J. (1984). “O decreto-lei no direito brasileiro,” *Revista Forense*, Rio de Janeiro, Vol. 285, Ano 80, Jan-Fev-Mar.

Dallari, D. de A. (1973). Elementos de Teoria Geral do Estado. 2.ª Edição. São Paulo: Saraiva.

Dreifuss, R. A. (1981). *1964: A conquista do Estado: ação política, poder e golpe de classe*. Petrópolis: Vozes, 3 ed.

Fagundes, M. S. (1956). “Reformas essenciais ao aperfeiçoamento das instituições políticas brasileiras,” *Revista Forense*, Rio de Janeiro, Vol. 163, Ano 53, janeiro-fevereiro.

______ (1960) “Treze anos de prática da Constituição”. *Revista Forense*, Rio de Janeiro, Vol. 187. Ano 57, janeiro-fevereiro.

______ (1962). “O parlamentarismo no Ato Adicional,” *Revista Forense*, Rio de Janeiro, Vol. 200, Ano 59, Out-Nov-Dez.

Ferreira, P. (1962). “As comissões parlamentares,” *Revista Forense*, Rio de Janeiro, Janeiro-Fevereiro-Março.

Fortes, P. C. (1966). “Atividade legislativa do Poder Executivo”. *Revista de Direito Administrativo*, Rio de Janeiro – FGV, Vol. 84.

Friedrich, C. J. and Brzezinski, Z. (1965). *Totalitarian Dictatorship and Autocracy*. 2nd ed. Cambridge, Massachusetts: Harvard University Press.

Galloway, G. B. (1951).“The Operation of the Legislative Reorganization Act of 1946,” *The American Political Science Review*, Vol. 45, No. 1, March.

Gama e Silva, L. A. (1982a). *COMISSÃO DE ‘ALTO NÍVEL’. Estudo para a Reforma da Constituição de 1967*, Vol. I, Presidência da República, Arquivo Brasília.

Gil, O. (1969). "Os decretos-leis na Constituição de 1967," *Revista Forense,* Rio de Janeiro, Vol. 225, Ano 65, jan-fev-mar.

Gusmão, P. D. (1956). "Direito como cultura," *Revista Forense,* Rio de Janeiro, março-abril.

ICJ. (1954). "For the Rule of Law," *Bulletin of the International Commission of Jurists,* No. 1. ICJ: The Hague.

______ (1961). INTERNATIONAL COMMISSION OF JURISTS. *African Conference on the Rule of Law: A Report on the Proceedings of the Conference,* Lagos, Nigeria, January 3–7.

______ (1962a). INTERNATIONAL CONGRESS OF JURISTS. *Working Paper on Executive Action and the Rule of Law* (Rio de Janeiro, Petropolis, Brazil – December 11–15, 1962). International Commission of Jurists: Geneva, Switzerland.

______ (1962b). INTERNATIONAL CONGRESS OF JURISTS. *Executive Action and the Rule of Law: A Report on the Proceedings of the International Congress of Jurists,* Rio de Janeiro, Brazil, 1962. Geneva, Switzerland.

______ (1963). CONGRESSO INTERNACIONAL DE JURISTAS. RESOLUÇÃO DO RIO. *Rev. Dir. Públ. e Ciência Política,* Rio de Janeiro, Vol. VI, No. 1, janeiro/abril.

IDPCP.FGV. (1965). "EMENDAS CONSTITUCIONAIS," *Rev. Dir. Públ. e Ciência Política,* Rio de Janeiro – FGV, Vol. VIII, No.2, Maio/Abril, 1965..

______ (1966). "Anteprojeto Da Constituição Dos Estados Unidos Do Brasil," *Revista do Inst. De Direito Púb. e Ciência Política,* Rio de Janeiro, FGV, Vol. IX, No.4, out/dez.

IPÊS – Instituto de Pesquisa e Estudos Sociais. 1963. *Reformas de Base: posição do IPÊS,* Rio de Janeiro.

Lalive, J. F. (1961). "From Delhi to Lagos" (Editorial), *Journal of the International Commission of Jurists,* Vol. III, No. 1, Spring.

Lamy Filho, A. (1970). "A Reforma da Lei das Sociedades Anônimas," *Revista Forense,* Rio de Janeiro, Jul-Set.

Langrod, G. (1954). *O Processo Legislativo na Europa Ocidental.* Rio de Janeiro: IDPCP-FGV.

Leal, V. N. (1945). "Lei e regulamento," *Revista de Direito Administrativo,* Rio de Janeiro, Vol. 1, No. 1, pp. 371–396.

Lima, H, Dantas, S.T., Medeiros Silva, C. *et al.* (1956). "Elaboração Legislativa (Anteprojeto de Emenda Constitucional)," *Revista Forense,* Rio de Janeiro, Vol. 167, Ano 53, setembro-outubro.

Lopreato, F. L. C. (2002). *O colapso das finanças estaduais e a crise da federação.* São Paulo: Editora Unesp – Unicamp.

Machado, R. (2016). "Juristas de exceção." In Monteleone, J., Amorim, F., Machado, R. *et al.* (Eds). *À espera da verdade: empresários, juristas e elite transnacional – histórias de civis que fizeram a ditadura militar.* São Paulo: Alameda.

Marsh, N. S. (1957). "Editorial: Domestic jurisdiction and International Concern," *Journal of the International Commission of Jurists,* Vol. 1, N. 1, autumn.

______(1958). "Editorial: The Rule of Law: Form and Substance," *Journal of the International Commission of Jurists,* Vol. 1, No. 2, Spring-Summer.

Medeiros Silva, C. (1952). "O poder regulamentar no direito comparado," *Revista de Direito Administrativo,* Rio de Janeiro – FGV, Vol. 30.

______(1953). "As Atribuições Constitucionais do Poder Executivo," Revista de Direito Administrativo, Rio de Janeiro – FGV, Vol. 31.

______(1963). "A Legislação Delegada," Revista de Direito Administrativo, Rio de Janeiro – FGV, Vol. 71.

______(1964a). "Observações Sobre o Ato Institucional," *Revista de Direito Administrativo*, Rio de Janeiro – FGV, Vol. 76.

______(1964b). "O Ato Institucional e a Elaboração Legislativa," *Revista dos Tribunais,* São Paulo, Ano 53, Vol. 347, Setembro.

______(1964c). "Seis meses de aplicação do ato institucional," *Revista de Direito Administrativo*, Rio de Janeiro – FGV, Vol. 78.

Mendes, C. (1974). "O Congresso Brasileiro pós-64: um legislativo para a tecnocracia?" In Mendes, C (Org.). *O legislativo e a tecnocracia.* Rio de Janeiro: Imago Editora/ Conjunto Universitário Candido Mendes.

______ (1975). "O Congresso Brasileiro pós-64: um legislativo para a tecnocracia?". Mendes, C (Org.) *O legislativo e a tecnocracia.* Rio de Janeiro: Imago Editora/ Conjunto Universitário Candido Mendes.

Meirelles, J. H. T. (1963). "Reformas Constitucional, Político-partidária e eleitoral" (tese), *Anais Do Congresso Brasileiro Para Definição Das Reformas De Base Vol.* I. Edição Preliminar Mimeografada.

Mota Filho, C. (1960). "O poder e as transformações do Estado," *Revista Forense,* Rio de Janeiro, Ano 57, Vol. 191, setembro-outubro.

Mumford, L. (1955). *Technics and Civilization.* London: Routledge & Kegan Paul.

Nascimento Silva, L. G. 1965. "Delegação de Poderes," *Revista de Direito Administrativo*, Rio de Janeiro – FGV, Vol. 81.

Novelli, F. B. (1967). "A relatividade do Conceito de Constituição e a Constituição de 1967," *Revista Forense,* Rio de Janeiro, Vol. 218, Ano 63, abr-mai-jun.

Nunes, R. (1967). "Considerações gerais sobre a legislação revolucionária," *Revista dos Tribunais,* São Paulo, Ano 56, Vol. 386, dezembro.

Pauperio, A. M. (1962). "Delegação de poderes," *Revista Brasileira de Estudos Políticos*, Minas Gerais.

Penholato, D. (2017). *José Garrido Torres nas Sombras do Poder: Um Economista na Construção do Projeto de Modernização de 1964.* Dissertação de Mestrado. FFLCH, Universidade de São Paulo.

Pinheiro, N. (1923). "Bibliographia" (discurso, de 26 de janeiro de 1922, em comemoração à publicação da obra "Systema de Sciencia Positiva do Direito,", de Pontes de Miranda, de 1922), Revista de Direito Público e de Administração Federal, Estadual e Municipal., Rio de Janeiro., Anno III, Vol., No. 1.

Rangel, L. C. B. (1966). "Delegação Legislativa," *Revista de Direito Administrativo*, Rio de Janeiro – FGV, Vol. 84.

RCP. (1967). "O Projeto e a Constituição Do Brasil," *Revista de Ciência Política*, Rio de Janeiro – FGV, Vol. 1, No. 1.

Reale, M. (1959). "A Filosofia do Direito e as Formas de Conhecimento Jurídico," *Revista dos Tribunais*, São Paulo.

______ (1963). "Sugestões para a reforma constitucional no tocante ao regime" (tese). *Anais Do Congresso Brasileiro Para Definição Das Reformas De Base* Vol. I. Edição Preliminar Mimeografada.

Reis, H. (1968). "O Poder Legislativo na atual Constituição," *Revista de Direito Administrativo*, Rio de Janeiro – FGV, Vol. 94.

Rocha, J. P. C. V. (2004). A capacidade normativa de Conjuntura no Direito Econômico: o Déficit Democrático da *Regulação Financeira*. Tese de Doutorado. Faculdade de Direito da Universidade de São Paulo.

Saldanha, N. N. (1963). "Separação de Poderes: reflexão sobre a permanência do problema," *Rer. Dir. Públ. e Ciência Política,* Rio de Janeiro – FGV, Vol. VI, No. 1, janeiro/abril.

Sampaio, N. de S. (1959). "Delegação legislativa e reforma constitucional," *Revista Forense,* Rio de Janeiro, Novembro-Dezembro.

Soares e Silva, E. de M. (1963). "Discurso inaugural." *Anais Do Congresso Brasileiro Para Definição Das Reformas De Base,* Vol. I. Edição Preliminar Mimeografada.

Souza, J. S. de S. (1893). *Principios Geraes de Direito Publico e Constitucional.* Rio de Janeiro. Casa Editora: Empreza d'A Provincia.

Teixeira, M. (2018). "Making a Brazilian New Deal: Oliveira Vianna and the Transnational Sources of Brazil's Corporatist Experiment," *Journal of Latin American Studies,* Vol. 50, No. 3, pp. 613–641. http://doi:10.1017/S0022216X17001602

Terceira Sessão. (1963). *Anais Do Congresso Brasileiro Para Definição Das Reformas De Base,* Vol. I. Edição Preliminar Mimeografada.

Trigueiro, O. (1954). "Prefácio." In Langrod, G. (Ed.). *O Processo Legislativo na Europa Ocidental.* Rio de Janeiro: IDPCP-FGV.

______(1959). "A crise legislativa e o regime presidencial," *Revista Brasileira de Estudos Políticos,* Minas Gerais, No. 7.

Trubek, D. (1971). "Law, Planning, and the Development of the Brazilian Capital Market: a Study of Law in Economic Change." *Yale Law School Studies in Law and Modernization.* No. 3, April.

Valladão, H. (1966). "Problemas jurídicos da cooperação internacional no campo do desenvolvimento econômico e social," *Revista dos Tribunais,* São Paulo, Ano 55, Vol. 364, fevereiro.

______ (1974). "A influência das estruturas federalistas sobre a fonte legislativa do Direito – um federalismo integrado," *Revisa dos Tribunais,* São Paulo, Ano 63, Vol. 460, fevereiro.

Vargas, G. (1935). *Discursos, mensagens e manifestos* (1930–1934). Rio de Janeiro: Imprensa Nacional.

Viana, T. de J. (1959). "A elaboração legislativa e o assessor," *Revista do Inst. De Direito Púb. e Ciência Política,* Rio de Janeiro – FGV, Vol. 2, No.1, jan-jun.

4 The executive and legal education

The "role of lawyers in a changing society"

The age of industry, cities and the "socializing and interventionist state, in which the colossal throng of the masses echoes," (Mota Filho, 1965, p. 48) imposed a profound renewal of social discipline. As a privileged *locus* of human development, education became one of the preferred fronts in which this transformation should be produced. Legal education was no different, involving particularly the "need" for a broader approach to social phenomena. In legal thinking it concerns a history of facing the country's culture of "bacharelismo," that is, a professional behavior more connected to literary life and political disputes among elites than to the specificities of the law as a field of knowledge (Adorno, 1998, chapter 4). Such culture would have led to a legal technique that "applies and does not formulate the law" and defends "the established formulas, the immutability of structures, solidarity with the created systems" (Melo Franco, 1965, p. 48). The criticism of such culture was born in the 1920s, gaining force after 1930 with an emerging state bureaucracy formed of engineers, military and, especially after the war, economists who since the country's independence questioned the centrality of lawyers ("law bachelors") in the making of the national state (Gomes, 1994, p. 5).

Legal education's reorganization took place shortly after the October 1930 takeover by Getúlio Vargas. In the months following the coup, Vargas created a specific ministry for education and culture, naming jurist Francisco Campos and designing an educational reform. The reform, inserted into the broader agenda of renewal of the national order, reached higher education in the form of decrees 19.851, on the "Statute of Brazilian Universities," and 19.852, which provided for the reorganization of the University of Rio de Janeiro, both of April 11, 1931.

A part of this project was to bring the legal profession closer to the expansion of public authority; the decrees reorganized the curriculum of law schools by replacing the chair of philosophy of law with introduction to the science of law as a propaedeutic discipline structuring the other ramifications of the law. Taken as a whole, chairs considered purely doctrinal or cultural, that is, of improvement or high culture, were excluded, giving priority to disciplines that would allow a more adequate (technical) professional training. Campos' project foresaw the division of legal education into two: one with a five-year bachelor's

DOI: 10.4324/9781003123941-5

degree and the other with two years of doctoral specialization. From the first, aimed at training legal practitioners, disciplines such as Roman law and private international law were excluded. The doctorate, intended for the training of future law professors, where high-culture disciplines had their place of purpose, was organized around three major divisions: (a) private law; (b) constitutional public law; (c) criminal law and criminological sciences (Brasil, 1931). In sum, "the educational reform was implemented in an attempt to adapt national education to the needs resulting from industrialization and urbanization, introducing to legal education the study of economic fundamentals with 'reflective and methodological autonomy'" (Bastos, 1998, p. 338).

Campos redefined the curricular structure of law courses in the country, proposing to invert civil law's primacy. Supported by the premises of the laissez-faire order, civil law tradition, based on the European heritage in Brazil, was the very foundation of the country's "bachelor culture." Given the re-foundational character of Vargas' project, Campos tried to further administrative law and public economic law's assumptions in this curricular reform. The classic molds of civil law could not offer solutions to the social needs demanded in modern times. In Brazil, as observed by Oliveira Vianna, one of the collaborators of the draft of labor laws in the 1930s, there was a misunderstanding regarding public law. This was caused, according to him, by a "strictly forensic activity of most of our legislators" and an inexistence "of real public law specialist in our country, versed not only in constitutional law technique, but in public law, in political science, in general and national history." Going further, Vianna argued that the legal field in Brazil was composed almost solely of civil, commercial, and procedural law specialists, or great lawyers – not having the "mentality of true public law specialist; without a spirit dedicated to the observation of the realities of the life of societies, to the study of economic and political structures and their immense reflections on the constitutional superstructure of the state" (Vianna, 1938, p. 28; 1999).

The techno-scientific approach to political life was a fundamental aspect of this aggregation process around the state. It was, moreover, the time when a scientific technicality penetrated into ideas about public life, informing the "objective" ways in which social relations should be thought and organized, thus overcoming the "class struggle," the "passions of ideologies." There was, indeed, a profound process of *socialization of law*, an approximation, by *the charm of science and the seduction of objectivity* (Bresciani, 2005, p. 319), with nascent sociology by which a rigorous normative formulation, consistent with modern phenomena, should be produced (Silveira, 2016). This corresponded to an executive power that increasingly began to intervene in public order, reverberating in the expansion of the legal provisions of public law (Saldanha, 1963; Campos, 2001). In a speech at the University of Bahia, Francisco Campos elucidated this scientific approach, arguing that "the world today lives under the sign of the economic, as it once lived under the sign of the religious and the political." This required an educational system "of a technical and professional nature," allowing an "intense scientific and practical preparation of a body of technicians and experts destined to guide legislative measures and government interventions" to drive the economy in an organized and rationalized way (Abreu, 2001, p. 1).

Campos' reform was accompanied by a restructuring of higher education in Brazil during the 1930s. Elites were needed to conduct the national renewal, as proposed by Vargas. Indeed, as Campos explained, his project of educational reform sought to technically equip the country's professional elites and to provide a favorable environment for the creation of a national culture, specifically through research, investigation, and science (1931). The project, however, did not evolve as intended by the jurist. In September 1940, Vargas introduced new legislation, the Decree-Law 2.639, which folded the discipline of *constitutional public law* into *constitutional law* and *general theory of state*, the latter devoted to the study of the state in all aspects, including its origin, organization, functioning, and purposes. Here, once again, the Vargas administration sought to face the predominantly private character of legal education, opening it up to the formation of new professional cadres versed in the expanded competencies of public authority. The objective was also to allow the teaching of constitutional law by jurists connected to the authoritarian regime and capable of transmitting their knowledge regarding state intervention beyond the Vargas period (Gomes, 1961, p. 462). In other words, the aim was to accompany the repositioning of the state as a center for formulating economic policies, including planning techniques, offering qualified knowledge and human resources for a modernized operation of public administration (Dallari, 1973; Brasil, 1940).

The reforms under Vargas, however, did not re-establish what was identified as the deep division between education, lawyer training, and the reality of the legal system in the country. The doctorate, for instance, did not produce anything relevant. The legal education reform remained almost the same as the previous 1930s organization (Venâncio Filho, 1977). In sum, legal education remained detached from the evolution of the Brazilian legal order: the unavoidable march toward state developmental competencies capable of engendering renewed forms of political and social cohesion. This diagnosis, reproduced throughout the period between the early 1930s and the mid-1970s, nevertheless did not produce a consensual solution. In 1976, José Nabantino Ramos, professor of law at the University of São Paulo, put it very clearly: "if the law is that – the discipline of social life by the law – it is obvious that its teaching must not be restricted to the law only, but must also cover the aspects of life that it commands, and the reason for the solutions adopted by the state: fact, value, and norms" (Ramos, 1976, p. 254).

Modernization theories and legal education: "bacharelismo" and the "social reality"

> This concern with the destiny – near and distant – of things and ideas, this fear of compromises with ephemeral values, is certainly one of the

> dramatic and, at the same time, fruitful aspects of the modern spirit. Every culture aspires to last. It can even be said that culture is nothing but an effort to overcome the contingencies of time and to establish an order that survives the incessant march of history, that dominates and absorbs the new of events [....]. Labor laws, tax laws, laws that express the transition from the free to the directed economy, the new public law, this world in gestation that is administrative law, everything overwhelms and asks the jurist, who is in the world today as the geographer must have been at the time of the discoveries.
>
> (Dantas, 2001, p. 10 and 18)

On December 12, 1945, the graduates of the National Law School gathered at the Municipal Theater in downtown Rio de Janeiro for their graduation ceremony: for them and a large audience that appeared at the Municipal, the class honoree, San Tiago Dantas, addressed a speech in which he summarized the above "renewal of law" of 1941. He argued that the decline of the law in those times – and not only in Brazil but in "all countries" – was a consequence of the inadequacy of the legal culture itself. Jurists had not taken "an advanced position in revising dogmatic concepts and adjusting science to new legislative realities and the higher demands of social reform." Dantas, who would become a totem in legal education reform in the 1960s, believed furthermore in a "change of base" of the legal order, a "shift from the center of social equilibrium, from 'property' to 'work'." It was the task of the development of public law, whose inadequacy had led to an arbitrary role of public authority in the country: "or we find, within the reality of each people and the spiritual and material conditions of our time, the form of government that realizes and preserves 'essential democracy,' or we will see the nations return to the shadow of Caesarism, which the masses, in times of crisis, consider more capable of quickly resolving their problems" (Dantas, 2001, p. 28).

Dantas resorted to a necessary balance, fundamental to an entire post-World War II class of intellectuals, between state power and private enterprise. In particular, he stressed the need for developing public law and administrative law premises regarding state intervention in the economic order. In a sense, Dantas, exemplarily, followed the general assumptions of the educational reform proposed by Campos in the 1930s. However, as his writings show, the evolution (and objection to) of state intervention since the 1930s led legal thought to articulate state intervention under the beacon of anti-totalitarianism: the "shadow of Caesarism" was a great threat, whose seductive appeal not even the anti-communist character of the Brazilian media could avoid when Sputnik sailed the sky to the world's amazement (Cattai, 2019; Schickler and Caughey, 2011).

Dantas' speech emphasized the mismatch between the educational system and economic and social realities, a condition aggravated, in particular, in the teaching of law. To Dantas and the country's elites, the legal profession lost space to this economic and administrative knowledge, given that the training offered in law schools was not adequate to the demands of economic development and the rapid evolution of social phenomena, especially concerning economic life (Dantas, 2001; Wald, 1969; Lamy Filho, 1976; Nascimento Silva, 1970; Trubek, 1966). Unlike what was seen with social sciences, where there was an expansion of higher education and rapid absorption by the state apparatus and public and private companies, law education did not follow the industrial growth experienced by the country since the re-democratization (Dezalay and Garth, 2002).

At the outset of the Cold War, public law however still had important disciplinary support from political science. U.S. power had a fundamental role, with an important number of studies brought to Brazil, as well as the strengthening of university ties between both countries (Dallari, 1973). The development of public law concerning the institutional functioning and exercise of state power and governance arrangements, as defended by Dantas, was indeed strengthened. This link gained systematization, starting in February 1948, with the elaboration of a project with the United Nations Educational, Scientific and Cultural Organization (UNESCO) and led by Princeton Professor William Ebenstein, aimed at creating a common international research agenda for a new political science (Salvadori, 1950, p. 2).

This effort paved the way for the foundation, in September 1949, of the International Political Science Association (IPSA), from which this agenda was centered and unfolded through its headquarters worldwide. The move was from ideas per se, as previously developed in political science, to the "political facts," involving research concerned with "social control," especially the expansion of state functions and intervention in the public domain. This international agenda for political science was thus aimed at (1) study of "social control"; (2) organization and evolution of power (analysis of political institutions); (3) study of "political forces" – pressure groups, especially economic ones; (4) study of the relationships between institutionalized power organizations; (5) study of "political doctrines"; and (6) issues of conceptualization, object, and methodologies in political science (Leal, 1959).

According to Victor Nunes Leal (1959), who took a seat on the Federal Supreme Court, public law's articulation with political science was welcomed in Brazil and in the Latin American Center for Research in Social Sciences (UNESCO), the Army's School of Command and General Staff, the Superior School of War (ESG), and the Higher Institute of Brazilian Studies (ISEB). One of the privileged forums for this agenda was the *Revista Brasileira de Estudos Políticos* [Brazilian Journal of Political Studies], from Minas Gerais and led by Orlando de Carvalho. Most influential, however, was the Getúlio Vargas Foundation's Institute of Public Law and Political Science (IDPCP), founded in Rio de Janeiro in 1952. IDPCP was created to replace the FGV's Nucleus of Public Law, responsible for publishing, under the leadership of Carlos Medeiros Silva, the important *Revista de Administração Pública* [Public

Administration Journal]. The Nucleus was initiated, in 1947, by Themístocles Cavalcanti, one of the founders of the Getúlio Vargas Foundation, whose associates included the permanent members Medeiros Silva and Olavo Bilac Pinto, and, as members, Caio Tácito, Seabra Fagundes, and Djacyr Menezes (D'arajuo, 1999, p. 106). In sum, the Nucleus was part of the original Vargas agenda – and especially the Administrative Department of the Public Service in 1938 (Bittencourt, 1947) – to train technical and intellectual elites to work within public administration.

IDPCP was therefore a renewal of those efforts but one that was nonetheless linked in its birth to the Global North's social sciences development and U.S. anti-totalitarian Cold War assumptions. Indeed, the institute based its work precisely on the International Political Science Association's research program, becoming part of the IPSA's Council. Themístocles Cavalcanti assumed the institute's leadership, an apparently natural move since he belonged to the IPSA's Executive Committee. The Institute of Public Law and Political Science subsequently dedicated itself to the formation of elites capable of carrying out the country's institutional objectives. According to its president, the institute inserted itself in the orientation that had allowed the creation of specialized schools in administration and economics throughout the 1950s. Focused on political science – the science of the state and its power – in its connection with public law, IDPCP assumed a character that was complementary to the social sciences, operating as a teaching and research center capable of correcting the political institutions (Cavalcanti, 1955).

This would take place through the formalization of legal rules "most appropriate to the reality" of the country. IDPCP works emphasized: (1) analysis of parliamentary technique; the legislative drafting process in Brazil and abroad; (2) analysis of electoral systems, their operation; (3) improving the administrative structure, its control mechanisms, and bodies; (4) analysis of financial policy; and (5) analysis of the organization and nature of the public company (Cavalcanti, 1958). It is worth mentioning that in this work IDPCP was followed by the Superior School of War, especially in regards to legislative delegation. Under the leadership of Golbery do Couto e Silva, Emílio Maurell Filho, and Cordeiro de Farias, the military was, indeed, shaping national security as a direct development of government capacities and state-led economic growth (Amado, 2021). Contrary to the consensus in the literature regarding the absence of a clear project by the dictatorship, these were central themes in the post-World War II national debate. These movements underpinned the modernization carried out under the mantle of Government Economic Action Program after the 1964 coup, with legislative delegation, electoral reform, Decree-Law 200, reform of the economic order and capital market law, to name some of the more salient examples.

Despite the sophistication of IDPCP's work, the institute was not devoted to the basic and broad training of lawyers. It did not respond to the wider malaise, present in legal thinking, concerning the inadequacies and significant gaps between teaching, the practice of law, and the new realities imposed for this post-war world. This criticism was centered on what would be an "excess of theory," preventing an empirical approach to legal phenomena and the development of technical knowledge capable of bringing legal practice closer to that "world of constant transformation." Many criticize the very foundation of Brazilian tradition since the Empire (1822–1889): the Portuguese and the Napoleonic Code's (French Civil Code of 1804) heritage, specially developed in the São Paulo and Olinda Law Schools, the most influential law schools in the country. From Portugal, the local legal culture inherited the view that the law is "reduced" to the code that materializes it, instituting a rigid legal order ("aspiring to eternity," as expressed by Lamy Filho) and emanating from the legislative authority. In other words, as argued by the Portuguese jurisconsult, João Mário Júlio de Almeida Costa, "the identification of legalism with legality has led to the denial of the importance of *custom* as a source of law. ... Likewise, it implied the subordination of the role of jurisprudence and doctrine... to the detriment of popular and scientific lives" (Costa, 2018, p. 437). From France, in particular from the School of Exegesis, Brazilian tradition developed the view that law manifests a sovereign will whose interpretation relies on the deductive-formal method, a strict or internal exegesis of the law, thereby preventing legal innovations (Cury, 2001). Both influences developed into the culture of "bacharelismo," the positivist and formalist legal tradition in Brazil.

The teaching of law in the United States appealed to legal elites precisely because it was opposed to that theoretical approach, focusing on "pragmatism." They recalled the systematization carried out in the last quarter of the 19th century by Christopher Columbus Langdell, dean of Harvard Law School, of the *case system* method. Based on the student's analytical and critical capacities, such a method prescribes that the student should be inserted into a discussion environment fed by a concrete legal case whose critical analyses would lead to a legal principle. Ergo, it constitutes the reverse of the *classic method*, common to legal education in Brazil, which starts with the legal principle, "framing" into it the specific case (Gomes, 1961; Almeida, 1947, p. 125–159).

The case system model was not, however, a novelty to Latin American legal traditions. It can be traced back to the interwar period, at the very least, in particular with the American Institute of International Law receiving a special welcome in Brazil from Ruy Barbosa (Scarfi, 2018). Founded in 1912 and maintained by the Carnegie Endowment for International Peace, the institute produced a codification of public international law and private international law, gathering legal elites across the American continent under U.S. leadership (Scarfi, 2017, p. 175; Valladão, 1966). The institute defended, especially by James B. Scott, the projection of U.S. traditions to legal forms on the continent, including the case system. Responsible for regrouping legal, diplomatic, and political elites in the name of the constitution, development, and codification of international law in the region, the institute promoted the U.S. constitutional model, the organization of its Supreme Court of

Justice, the Anglo-Saxon legal approach to normative work and the case study method as the foundations of America's legal institutions and practices (Scarfi, 2017, p. 107).

Nonetheless, even considering the U.S. influence in Latin America, the same issues regarding legal education persisted. After World War II, professors, students, and lawyers in Brazil were voicing the "urgent need" for reform to make it possible to face the challenges of the modern world and the technical and practical issues facing the legal profession. In the mid-1950s, responding to a demand from the federal government, the Brazilian Bar Association produced proposals for reforming legal education, including the creation of disciplines such as financial law and a de-emphasis on "theoretical study" (Vannucchi, 2018, p. 597). As expressed by the director of the law school at the University of Bahia, Orlando Gomes, the question was whether legal courses should return to the training of "lawyers" or "technicians" (Gomes, 1961). Those who advocated a more "realistic," "technical," and less "cultural" legal practice could, thus, rely on the U.S. teaching method.

The strongest diagnosis of the situation of legal education in Brazil in its relations with this wider "crisis" came from Francisco Clementino de San Tiago Dantas. Pursuing a perceptible intellectual elaboration since at least the 1941 speech calling for a "renovation," in his 1955 inaugural class at the National Law School the jurist resumed his reflections on legal education and the Brazilian crisis. The speech had international repercussions (Tacito, 1971, p. 233). The jurist's words formulated, in moral-normative terms, a diagnosis of the Brazilian crisis: the gradual loss of the specific capacity of the ruling class to solve problems and to produce instruments of control of society and nature. The university was the privileged space for such transformation. It should offer a way for elites to reverse the stagnation and growing rupture, impeding the development of techniques of control and strengthening of the bonds between the elites and the directed groups. On the contrary, according to Dantas (1955), universities no longer produced anything other than a body that was sealed and detached from the reality that surrounded it. The urgent need to reverse this situation was as much or more evident in the field of legal education.

As mentioned in Chapter 1, Dantas maintained his concern with the increasing loss of importance of the law practice to other, "less ethical" and "more efficient" techniques, such as administration and economics. Sustaining a critical posture toward the normative production of this technocracy (echoing an early criticism of legislative inflation), he argued that it would be rare for the administrator not to believe in the usefulness of dictating rules, not having to pass through debate with the legislative branch. Indeed, it had become viable for the technocracy to act according to administrative technique but to the detriment of legal norms. Finally, he called for a reorganization of the teaching of law in Brazil to re-establish the supremacy of the legal culture and confidence in law as a technique for social discipline. At this point in his argument, he turned to proposing a program for law schools. His fundamental assumption was the need to reform, advocating the case system method, which would make possible, ultimately, the national modernization under the aegis of the democratic norm.

> The new didactic [....] would take the predominant form of the "case system," which is not, as many think, strictly dependent on the Anglo-American "praxis" of judicial precedents. The primary objective of the teacher [....] is not the elegant 50-minute conference on a topic in the program, but the analysis of a controversy selected to highlight the issues contained therein and its good ordering to find a satisfactory solution; the study of reasoning in each of its adventures; the preparation of the solution, with the consultation not only of positive sources but also of literary sources and repertoires of judges. And, finally, the criticism of the solution given, with the comparison of the alternatives. [....] The true legal education, the one that will train jurists for the task of social life, must repeat this fundamental scheme, putting the student not in the face of a body of norms, from which a systematic classification is raised, as another natural history, but in the face of controversies, conflicts of interest in search of a solution. Education focused on legal reasoning itself, placing its emphasis on examining and resolving specific disputes, and not on the expository study of institutions, brings the jurist back to the social fact that generates the law, places his spirit at the root of the problem so that the norm should provide the solution.
>
> (Dantas, 1955, p. 453)

Along with this teaching method and, maintaining the same reformist assumptions, there was a more systematic discussion about a "necessary" readjustment of the so-called minimum curriculum, which had concentrated the first initiatives with Francisco Campos. The 1946 Constitution maintained as the exclusive competence of the federal government the role of legislating on the guidelines of education. The minister of education, Clemente Mariani, appointed in 1947 a commission to elaborate a project to modernize the country's entire educational system, including the law schools. As happened with Mariani's initiative, Aliomar Baleeiro's project[1] of 1951 and the one developed by the commission[2] created by Juscelino Kubistchek's minister of education, Clóvis Salgado, none of these projects were completed or approved by Congress. Despite the great repercussion of Dantas' speech in 1955, a decisive mobilization was not achieved (Venâncio Filho, 1977; Arruda, 1958).

By the late 1950s, Congress discussed the final aspects regarding the Law responsible to structure the guidelines of national education. The law was sanctioned by the Goulart administration as Law 4.024, on December 20, 1961. The norm created the Federal Council of Education which became responsible for developing educational policies, especially in the field of higher education. The council established the minimum curriculum for the teaching of law (and for all other bachelor's courses) which, however, did not, as intended, represent a renewal (Cury, 2001). Indicating flexibility and, through it, adapting the legal profession to the different regional realities of the country (Valladão, 1963, p. 8), the Federal Council – after opening a large inquiry along with law schools' congregations – took as a guide for legal education the minimum duration of five years and a minimum curriculum, structured into 14 disciplines:

> 1.) Introduction to the science of law; 2.) Civil law; 3.) Commercial law; 4.) Civil judicial law (with forensic practice); 5.) Private international law; 6.) Constitutional law (including notions of state theory); 7.) Public international law; 8.) Administrative law; 9.) Labor law; 10.) Criminal law; 11.) Criminal judicial law (with forensic practice); 12.) Financial law and finance; 13.) Political economy; 14.) Forensic medicine.

Difficulties arose from the absence of agreement between the diverse proposals suggested at the time of the work of the Federal Council, such as those presented by Arnold Wald, San Tiago Dantas, and C. J. de Assis Ribeiro (Valladão, 1963). According to Alberto Venâncio Filho (1977, p. 318), in extensive work on legal education in the country, the minimum curriculum – replacing the rigid and uniform "single curriculum" –, to be a reference for the elaboration of a "full curriculum" in each law school, became in fact the "maximum." Furthermore, the disciplines not covered by this new curriculum, such as general theory of the state and Roman law, were in fact maintained in schools by "force of tradition." Discussions on reform of the compulsory disciplines in law schools evidenced the centrality that the theme of economics had come to occupy, resuming Francisco Campos' diagnosis, despite the different political purposes. Indeed, in the 1961 Federal Council's project, the minimum curriculum stipulated the autonomy of the chair of financial law, given the "current developments of the legal profession, providing assistance to companies and providing guidance with financial regulations and tax charges"; and the establishment of a chair in political economy, "indispensable" since the "economic is necessarily intertwined with the legal and the social" (Venâncio Filho, 1977, p. 318).

In any case, despite the great diffusion of reformist energy and the criticism of the "excess of theory," the clash between two tendencies seems to have imposed difficulties on the issue of whether law schools should train "jurists" or "technicians." In other words, 30 years after Campos' initiative, the "bachelor culture" still centered the discussions concerning the reform and the U.S. case system method catalyzed the alternatives to it. In 1961, analyzing legal education in Brazil, the jurist Orlando Gomes stated that there was not a consensus regarding legal education reform. To Gomes, the transplantation of the case system method to Brazil was not a successful initiative in the country, the experience showing, indeed, the impropriety of the pure replication of such a method in countries where the law tradition was codified or condensed into systematized formulas. Accordingly, "the prevailing average thinking today," Gomes said, "is not to superimpose practical teaching to theoretical, but rather to intertwine them, putting an end to the exaggerated theoretical approach that characterizes the teaching of law" (1961, p. 461). The question was, precisely *how* to intertwine practice and theory.

Law and development: from formalism to the instrumentalization of legal practice

The "inadequacy" of the legal field in Latin America and the Third World would become a Cold War issue. The U.S. political structure – the aforementioned "integral state" (Huo and Parmar, 2019) – developed a program for the reform of legal education in the Global South. The main reason was not only modernization of the order of rule of law, as the International Commission of Jurists in its noblesse oblige had been articulating since the early 1950s. The program of reform was aware of the loss of prestige of the legal profession through the development process under the aegis of the modernization theory assumptions, particularly in Latin America. Here, once again, one can find the U.S. pursuit of a network of elites, "a coterie of indigenous experts who internalize certain norms and who are destined to assume leadership positions in their respective societies," moving their nations through the path of development "in a way to guarantee political stability, economic growth, and minimally, a policy of benevolent neutrality toward the Western bloc" (Berman, 1983, p. 14). The three main U.S. philanthropic foundations (Ford, Rockefeller, and Carnegie), the international aid agencies linked to the Department of State, the law schools in major U.S. Universities (such as Yale, Harvard, Michigan, and New York), and the legal elites at the American Bar Association (ABA) and the American Society of International Law (ASIL) joined the effort. Such a program, especially organized by the Ford Foundation, was named the *Law and Development Movement*.

From 1954 onwards, the model of law and development turned to countries that became independent in Africa and Asia, specifically in training programs for local legal elites. Those programs were dedicated to legal education, to influencing the institutional life and political order of these countries in line with the rule of law premises. The political organization in developing countries became, indeed, a major issue in Cold War disputes between Washington and Moscow. Both began to dedicate a set of actions aimed at the creation of political, intellectual, and technical elites to formalize and conduct nation-building agendas (Bu, 1999; 2003). After becoming the most active U.S. philanthropic institution in the 1950s, following the understanding of the country's foreign policy in the Cold War (Parmar, 2012; Chaves, 2018), in 1954 the Ford Foundation invested approximately $7.5 million in U.S. law schools. Harvard, Columbia, Michigan, Stanford, Berkeley, Yale, and Chicago law schools assembled to develop an international law curriculum for the training of foreign lawyers and to promote research and specialization in international law and comparative law. Deepening this strategy, Ford dedicated another

$3 million for the establishment of exchanges and "cooperative programs" between United States and foreign Bar Associations and Asian and European law schools. The purpose of these programs was to promote the U.S. legal model in those regions and West Germany, favoring a social change in how Western values are perceived (Krishnan, 2004; 2012).[3]

These efforts elucidate the common concern between the Ford Foundation and the Department of State regarding the projection of legal forms based on the principles of equality and guarantees in the area of criminal law (due process) and individual rights. In their eagerness for *primacy* in global affairs (Wertheim, 2020), the U.S. foreign policy elites focused their energies on countries such as India, Ethiopia, Nigeria, Turkey, and Pakistan, centering on comparative law. The comparative approach would be widely accepted as a modernizing resource in national legal systems, as noted by the Brazilian jurist Haroldo Valladão (1970), allowing "improvements" to legal practices throughout the world. Indeed, as fitting to the U.S. assumptions regarding the Global South, the comparative approach reproduced a certain "set of beliefs, anxieties, prejudices, and values" (Latham, 1998, p. 206) and would very well serve the purposes of modernization theory in the region. In other words, the comparative method established, in practical terms, the *modern* (Global North) and the *archaic* (South) and the (procedural) path of going from one to the other. It is worth noting that in 1946 the National Committee on Comparative Law was founded in Brazil. This organization was affiliated with the International Committee on Comparative Law and, later, the International Association of Legal Sciences, based at the former University of Brazil. Valladão[4] became the National Committee's president, and Arnold Wald its secretary. Under such an understanding the disciplines of comparative private law, comparative public law, and comparative criminal law were created in the doctorate course of the National Law School and, later, comparative procedural law and comparative labor law (Valladão, 1971).

Besides these initiatives, one can find the same approach to the training of legal elites at the Hague Academy of International Law, where Valladão taught. During the 1950s, Ford, Rockefeller, and Carnegie Foundations organized a modernization program for the Academy, seeking to redefine its teaching method and curricular structure. In addition to the role of the United Nations, the Academy's courses were mainly dedicated to three major themes: international public law, international organizations, and private international law. The courses of study focused on the jurisprudence of international courts, human rights, and national sovereignty; the relations between and among nation states, and universal and regional organizations, such as the Council of Europe and the League of Arab States. There were courses such as René Cassin's "The Universal Declaration and Implementation of Human Rights" (1951); Haroldo Valladão's "Private International Law of American States" (1952); Angelo Piero Sereni's "International Economic Institutions and the Municipal Law of the States" (1959); and Ricardo

Joaquin Alfaro's "The Rights and Duties of States" (1959) (Dupuy, 1973; Scott-Smith, 2007).

In sum, the U.S. "integral state" sought to counter Soviet influence at the U.N., particularly its support for anti-colonial and anti-racist struggles in the third world (Pruden, 1997, p. 108) and to enlist the state-building agenda in those countries within the framework of the Western legal system. In the words of Secretary of State John Foster Dulles, the United States was trying to secure an "orderly evolution" from colonial status to that of a free nation (Scott-Smith, 2007, p. 512).[5]

As part of this Cold War effort and counting on the support of the Rockefeller and Ford Foundations as well as the State Department and the Peace Corps, U.S. universities created Staffing of African Institutions for Legal Education and Research (SAILER). Founded in 1962 and devoted to Africa, where in 1960 alone 17 countries became independent, the program's purpose was to offer financial support to African law schools, focusing on academic exchange between the United States and African countries. As was the case, for example, in the Ford program for cities in India, such as Calcutta, Mumbai, New Delhi, Varanasi, and Chennai, the reform was intended to establish the U.S. legal education model in African universities (Krishnan, 2004; 2012). SAILER, however, was constituted as a program focused not on the inseparable combination of teaching and research – according to the U.S. higher education model – but centered on teaching alone. It was especially based on the premises of rule of law, favoring "legal certainty" and, thus, political stability and order (Krishnan, 2012). Indeed, the assumption of legal assistance to these regions was not based on the intellectual exploration of the legal development problems but defended strict rule of law foundations.

By the second half of the 1960s the U.S. foreign policy establishment found it necessary to remove "legal formalism" from the development path. An instrumental (more "creative" and "constructive") approach to law would lead to economic growth and favor the modernization process. Such a position regarding law practice was welcomed by those in the Brazilian legal field such as San Tiago Dantas, José M. Rodrigues (1953, p. 48), and Cesarino Júnior (1953, p. 149) who had criticized the culture of "bacharelismo." However, this creative and constructive approach was also criticized because it relied on the legislative police developed by technocratic elites in their quest for economic growth, specifically those trained in economics and administration. In other words, legal security and the legal order were threatened by technocratic instrumentalization of the law, given that it could not consider the fundamentals of the legal discipline. It is worth recalling that Brazil was under military rule. In sum, it was understood that Brazil could sustain such instrumentalization because the authoritarian regime was based on "security" premises, avoiding the disruptive character of economic growth and consequently the threat of totalitarianism (Cancelli, 2017).

This transformed U.S. legal assistance was grounded on the systematizing of U.S. aid to Latin America with the creation of the United States Agency for International Development (USAID) and the launching of the Alliance for Progress program by the administration of John F. Kennedy (1961–1963) in the early 1960s. Reacting to the Cuban Revolution and framed by the development view, the Alliance schematized a deterministic model of economic growth in which the "poor countries" would pass through progressive stages of development until they converged on industrial capitalism of the "central countries" (Krever, 2011). On a concrete basis, and in general terms, the Alliance for Progress, officially launched in 1961, systematized U.S. aid to Latin America, providing for an annual increase of 2.5% in *per capita* income, land reform, income distribution, and a commitment (as opposed to the local "oligarchies") to the establishment of democratic governments in the region, further privileging capital investment policies of a mixed economy and associating state intervention with private enterprise (Trubek, 1966; Darnton, 2012). However, under the Johnson administration (1963–1969) and the Mann Doctrine for Latin America, those principles became more conservative, as described by the former Kennedy and then Johnson' administration special assistant, Arthur Schlesinger Jr., giving their support to dictatorships and the suppression of freedoms in the region (Schlesinger, 1970; Allcock, 2014, p. 1017; Cancelli, 2017, p. 107–109). Recalling the development of aid policies in Brazil, one of the USAID's staff member in the country, David M. Trubek, said that they "were offering any alternative to communism and that included the ability to have greater and faster economic growth." To this end, they intended to train lawyers, showing that Latin America "did not need to go in that [communist] direction" (Falcão, Lacerda, and Rangel, 2012, p. 9).

Regarding the developmental projects for Brazil, Trubek (who arrived in the country shortly before the 1964 coup) and other USAID officials reported the "legal bottlenecks" in the Brazilian intervention process. Moreover, Brazil's lawyers were unprepared for the financial system, specifically the aspects related to the capital market. USAID officials furthermore did not consider Brazilian lawyers to be an important part of the development of regulatory legislation aimed at economic growth. Such legislative work was better settled by technocrats, economists, and administrators endorsed by the Castelo Branco administration with the decree-law instrument. Indeed, until 1970 the dictatorship approved about 10,000 new laws, following the government's economic action program and its broad program of structural modernization. This included tax and banking reforms, new wage and housing policies, and the institution of monetary correction. Initially, Castelo Branco's measures, with Roberto Campos and Otávio Bulhões at the head of the ministries of finance and planning, respectively, tried a gradualist plan of economic stabilization in the short term, with contractionary fiscal and monetary policies to combat inflation. On another front, a tax law codification intended to transform a miscellany of revenue devices into what would be an instrument of economic development, insofar as it would allow an increase in the state resources and new financial systems of housing, banking, and capital market, paving the way for economic growth via private capital (Trubek, 1971).

In July 1965, at a seminar on "legal problems of international cooperation," Trubek presented the paper *Practical Problems of the International Cooperation Program in the Field of Development*, focusing on the role of laws and lawyers in the execution of the program. He stressed the practical problems in the Alliance for Progress's program: "problems of national law that have to be solved or overcome before the development of a sector of the national economy. Although they are problems with the internal laws of the developing country, they are also problems for international cooperation institutions, because these institutions cannot achieve the common goal, which is development…" (Trubek, 1966, p. 368).

If there was reason in the Alliance's goals of "providing the qualified personnel required by the rapidly developing societies," namely in the areas of science, engineering, and economics, Trubek reasoned, advanced legal training was also needed. Trubek argued that the legal profession should take a leading role in regulatory efforts and, thus, manage economic development coherently and securely (Trubek, 1966). Trubek's analysis represented a common diagnosis made by USAID personnel in Brazil. They believed that the best preparation of Brazilian lawyers, particularly with graduate studies, could make the international financial assistance more effective in their arbitration of the loan agreements with international agencies (Gardner, 1978, p. 62; Trubek, 1971).

The Center for Studies and Research in the Teaching of Law: facing the culture of "bacharelismo"

Shortly after the 1965 seminar, Trubek sent a proposal for the creation of an institute in "law and economic development" to Peter Bell at the Ford Foundation's office in Rio de Janeiro. The lawyer had in mind the Foundation's interest in programs aimed at legal reform. Through research and an advanced training program, the main objective of the institute was to diagnose the practical legal problems involving Brazilian development. Furthermore, it envisaged working as a catalyst for the "necessary" modernization of legal education in the country. The proposal emphasized that the research program should have a practical direction, capable of dealing with the legal problems of development and preparing regulatory projects regarding the economic agenda underway since the 1964 coup. He also stressed the possibility of offering consulting services to state agencies. The Advanced Training Program, which includes a doctoral course of study, was designed to develop a specialization in fields such as foreign investment, international business transactions, import-export law, regulation of real estate values, housing, and legal aspects of economic integration (Trubek, 1966). For both programs, Trubek indicated the need for dedicated full-time teachers.[6]

Since at least the second half of 1965, USAID, especially through David Trubek, had been in contact with Ford Foundation staff in Rio and the foundation's New York headquarters representative in the country,

Stacey Widdicombe. The Rio office and the Office of Latin America and the Caribbean, headed by Harry Wilhelm, were interested in the same development program for Brazilian legal institutions that involved staff of the U.S. Agency for International Development at the time. Peter Bell and Ivan Almeida, legal counsel for Ford's Rio office, could not define an original project, while Trubek was eager to launch his plan.[7]

Bell and Almeida had been collecting information about the law schools in Minas Gerais and Ceará and did not make the same diagnosis about the possibilities of introducing the institute to Brazilian universities. Both were inclined to deepen discussions in this regard. At that point, they wanted to start conversations with Roberto Lyra Filho, a professor at the University of Brasilia (UnB), who could, in their opinion, help to fine-tune the proposal to create the program. Ford Foundation employees harbored a certain hope that the institute could be created at UnB since its structure resembled that of U.S. universities and the curricular organization of its law school would favor it.[8] Nonetheless, they recognized that the student convulsions experienced there after the 1964 coup made any prospect in this regard uncertain (Motta, 2014).[9]

These proposals for the creation of the new institute were in close dialogue with the broader agenda for the modernization of the educational system in Brazil, discussed with U.S. international aid officials since the 1950s. After the 1964 coup, these ideas gained momentum, counting on the support of Ford and, above all, USAID. In 1965, the Ministry of Education and Culture had signed cooperation agreements with the agency, which provided for book translations, restructuration of educational programs, planning for university reform, and changes in elementary levels of education. Concerning higher education, in particular, U.S. officials favored ideas of administrative centralization; the professionalization of management; structuring of research and teaching in departments; the creation of development agencies; investment in university campuses; autonomy in relation to the public authority; and diversification of sources of funds (Motta, 2014).

However, law schools were especially unresponsive to these changes, inclining instead to maintain their isolation from university campuses, including with legal instruments. Such resistance complicated the reforming program as imagined by USAID and Ford Foundation personnel. Trubek believed this involved an "anti-United States" sentiment within some of the Brazilian universities.[10] Trubek was eager to put the program into action, believing that its further development would lead to the reorganization of legal education and practice as a whole. Moreover, the institute would make it possible to systematize legislative efforts and consequently favor the country's economic development. In November 1965, USAID's legal advisor had already met with Luiz Simões Lopes, president of the Getúlio Vargas Foundation, Mário Henrique Simonsen, director of the graduate school of economics at Getúlio Vargas, and Caio Tácito, vice-president director of the law school of the State University of Guanabara (UEG), member of the

IDPCP of FGV and legal adviser of Rio-Light Company. He awaited Ford's position on the institute's financing plan, to be created under the custody of the Getúlio Vargas Foundation.[11] Lopes, Simonsen, and Tácito, all linked to FGV and very receptive to the idea of creating the institute, according to Trubek, suggested the young lawyer Alberto Venâncio Filho and José Luiz Bulhões Pedreira to be included in the project. The first was at the time writing a study on public economic law under the auspices of the Ford Foundation.[12] The second had been one of the most important corporate lawyers, through whom passed a large part of the decisions related to the modernization of the country's economic institutions since the 1950s (Garth and Dezalay, 2002, p. 97; Gatto, Faro and, Almeida, 2009).[13]

Following these understandings, in 1966 the project was adjusted in discussions between a group of Brazilian teachers, led by Tácito,[14] Trubek, Henry Steiner, a Harvard professor and Ford consultant for legal reform in Brazil, and employees of Ford's office in Rio. They decided to establish a legal studies center that would not directly confront the status quo of Brazilian law schools, constituting rather as an instrument from which, little by little, reform would reach other institutions. On a more immediate level, the center could offer the legal training required, as Trubek argued at the seminar on international cooperation, due to for the country's rapid economic growth.

On April 15, 1966, the Council of the State University of Guanabara approved Resolution No. 284/66, which created the *Center for Studies and Research in the Teaching of Law* (CEPED). It established Caio Tácito as its director, allowing him to apply for grants from private organizations. Operating as a flexible and experimental institution, the declared objective of the center linked was to favor the improvement of the teaching of law and the conduct of research and studies in the area. Favored by such autonomy, the center was to be linked to the Getúlio Vargas Foundation, specifically to its graduate program in economics directed by Mário Henrique Simonsen. The building was located at Praia de Botafogo, in Rio de Janeiro.

The financial plan was adopted according to Trubek's suggestion and following a similar strategy developed by the law and development programs in Africa and Asia. USAID granted approximately $100,000 USD to cover local expenses with the program, including the payroll for teachers and researchers, administrative services, acquisition of library material, and awarding five scholarships; Ford, in turn, awarded a subsidy of just over $485,000 USD, guaranteeing the purchase of material for the library and the payment of scholarships at U.S. universities and visiting professors for long and short term to CEPED.[15]

Although the financial plan demonstrates the level of agreement between both organizations, some differences in the strategy for developing the center remained. USAID personnel, as Trubek had indicated in 1965, believed there was an "urgent" need to *instrumentalize* Brazilian development, advocating the specialized training of lawyers in the public and private sectors. Ford's view, according to the July 1966 internal report, followed a different line:

> Law schools in Brazil are traditionally the schools of the governing elite. 19th-century law academies were considered "the anterooms of Parliament." But legal education in Brazil has not kept up with the changes in Brazilian society: in the 20th century, lawyers' contribution to development has been, at best, marginal. The law is seen as an instrument of the status quo rather than an instrument of development, and the advocate is not sought after by reform administrators. To a large extent, the important and recent legislation in Brazil – for example, Agrarian Reform, Banking Reform, Tax Reform, and the Capital Market Law – was drafted by economists and is not fully understood by lawyers.
>
> Legal education in Brazil is oriented towards strict, black, and white knowledge of the law. The professor teaches his classes in an elegant yet abstract style, from the old Portuguese universities where Brazilians studied law until their independence. Lawyers typically view the teaching profession in law schools as the crowning achievement of a prestige they have earned in public and private offices. Students, who also have work outside universities, hurriedly and absently attend classes. At the end of the school year, they prepare for the final exams by memorizing poorly compiled summaries of the read authors. Law graduates are considered cultured by virtue of having attended law schools, but just over twenty percent of them do not even practice law.
>
> In short, legal education in Brazil has become separated (…) from the current social reality. **Before the law can be transformed into an instrument for development, legal education will need to be placed in a social context, and law schools will have to change in content, approach, and structure. It would be a mistake to underestimate the power of one of the oldest, largest, most prestigious, most traditional, and most elusive Brazilian educational institutions in the face of the radical reform effort. The new effort represents a modest start towards improving legal education in Brazil.**
>
> (…) As an initial commitment, (…) [the Institute] should conduct a course for law professors and lawyers working in the private and public investment sector in Brazil and international economic relations. The course will introduce new research and teaching techniques for Brazilian legal education, such as the Socratic Method and the Case Study. Attempts will be made to interweave law and economics.[16] (Emphasis added)

Thus, for the Ford Foundation, the Brazilian tradition of formalism, expressed in the exposition of content, in the passivity of students and the inexistent relationship with the practice of concrete cases, was only suitable for the reproduction of a social category encased in the state and unable to sustain and clarify the legislative activism that accompanied the developmental process under Castelo Branco. Before the law became an instrument of development, it was necessary to modify the teaching system, which, according to the prognosis presented, would be done through the introduction of the Socratic method and case studies. In other words, Ford's assumption was to reproduce in Brazil the U.S. approach to "realism": the "pragmatic," "imaginative," and "creative" responses to the challenges imposed by the new social reality. Ford's personnel, however, understood that the reformist foray into one of the most traditional Brazilian institutions would be the greatest challenge for the center. Therefore, unlike USAID, they described it as a modest initial effort, insufficient per se. At its birth, CEPED would be an experiment, a manifestation of intentions rather than a finished project, with clear outlines in view of the challenge it proposed to face.

Even so, U.S. assumptions regarding legal modernization in the country tried to redefine the relationship between lawyers and the state, to which end it was necessary to transform the culture of "bacharelismo." This was a critique presented in Brazilian legal thought since the 1920s and 1930s. In fact, more broadly, there was an attempt in Brazil, under modernization theory assumptions, to move away from everything that seemed "less technical." As wisely expressed by the sociologist Maria Sylvia de Carvalho Franco in an interview in the early 1980s, "there was a determined effort to transform the social sciences in Brazil into positive knowledge, disregarding its humanistic aspects." Brazilian intellectuals were critical of the culture of "bacharelismo," viewing it as "rhetorical, superficial, bombastic, and bureaucratic" (1981, p. 167).

CEPED was founded as a complementary training institution for lawyers, offering specialization courses in the economic area that aimed to instrumentalize the developmental agenda through the regulatory action of the law. The focus was not on organizing a broad strategy for reforming the teaching method – which was the initial inclination of USAID personnel. With the center institutionally created and resources at their disposal, United States and Brazilian jurists began to discuss the courses to be offered the following year, 1967. Between the beginning of October and November 1966 the main group of Brazilian lawyers involved with CEPED since its creation (Caio Tácito, Alfredo Lamy Filho, Arnold Wald, Amílcar de Arruda Falcão, Carlos Leoni R. Siqueira, Carlos A. da Siqueira Lobo, Cláudio Vianna de Lima, and Alberto Venâncio Filho) traveled to the United States. They took part in seminars, classes, and debates with the directors and professors of the law schools at Harvard, Yale, Columbia, Stanford, New York, and California (Berkeley and Los Angeles). The visit was intended to put this Brazilian legal elite in touch with U.S. teaching techniques and to perfect a teaching program to be developed in Brazil.[17]

Tácio, Lamy Filho, and the others were introduced not only to the case study method, but to the very foundation of the teaching-research structure and its connection with the problems faced by public and private agencies. In this regard, they would be able to understand the connection between universities, the private sector, civil organizations, and state organs in their organic articulation to solve issues regarding social life and economic development. In other words, it should indicate that, in modern times, legal practice was not only dedicated to sponsoring cases before the courts but also to consulting individuals, companies, and the state itself (Barreto Filho, 1970, p. 384).[18] A couple of years later, Arnold Wald claimed that in the United States he witnessed a "cross-fertilization" process. Technology had established the company as the "fundamental cell" of modern life, demanding planning and research for organized management. In Wald's words, a "greater contact between the company, the university, and the state started to occur, as a phenomenon of reciprocal influences…" (1969, p. 436).

Even before the Brazilian lawyers' trip to the United States, Alfredo Lamy Filho outlined in a discussion memorandum the emphasis to be given to the course and its methodological orientation. A persistent advocate of the changing patterns of the making of the legal norm and thus critical of the "positivist" character of the Brazilian tradition, Lamy Filho argued that the courses had not only to transmit the knowledge of positive law, but should be guided by the principle that, under the progression of modernization, there was a constant "changing reality, that there is a permanent … law renewal process." Furthermore, the lawyer made the case that CEPED should not constitute itself just as "a laboratory for experimenting with new teaching techniques" but had to be "the center of research and dissemination of a new understanding of law," capable of bringing "substantial collaboration to the modeling of a developing society" (Lamy Filho (1966), p. 5, cited in Venâncio Filho, 1977, p. 326).

In March of 1967, with the presence, among others, of the University of Guanabara dean, Haroldo L. da Cunha, the president of FGV, Simões Lopes, Ford Foundation representative Stacey Widdicombe, USAID legal advisors Peter Hornbostel and Jack Heller, and the director of Brazilian Cia Progresso, Marcílio Marques Moreira, CEPED launched its first course on "corporate lawyers." Other participants were UEG's Álvaro Cumplido de Sant'Anna; and the director of the Institute for Economic, Political, and Social Studies at UEG, João Lyra Filho. The objective was to prepare lawyers for tasks related to the development and application of the new economic and financial legislation in the country. The curriculum was structured on the case study methodology on two fronts: the problems facing large companies and those of that smaller companies face. Focusing on these fronts, the students were separated into two groups, one led by Arnold Wald and the other by Alfredo Lamy Filho. Although separate, it was expected that they would keep in constant contact, since the discussions should aim at solving the listed problems, based on a dialogue between law and the disciplines of social sciences, especially economics.

To this end, the course focused on the general aspects of corporate law in Brazil. It is worth mentioning that the emphasis was on the Decree-Law 2627, introduced by Vargas on September 26, 1940. By the time of the CEPED's discussion, commercial law specialists such as Lamy Filho and Arnold Wald were proposing a new corporate law.[19] Furthermore, the course emphasized concepts and practices of accounting and economics, corporate law, tax law, constitutional law, administrative law, capital markets law, the relationship with foreign investors, and issues related to land development and civil construction in particular for small companies. The large company case study, in turn, tried to simulate joint Brazilian and foreign group efforts in the development of a business in the mining sector. The students were encouraged to act in the best interest of such a company.

> In carrying out this project, the class was divided into groups tasked with sponsoring the various interests that were associated. The beginning of the year started with the pre-contract debate and after the end of the deal with the examination of several possible alternatives. Finally, the course ended with a test, usually, a company balance sheet, previously distributed, for the students' examination and on which, at the time, questions of corporate, tax, and administrative law, economics, and accounting were asked.
>
> (Venâncio Filho, 1977, p. 327)

In that first year, 17 lawyers from important public entities (National Development Bank, National Housing Bank, Central Bank, Banco do Brasil, Eletrobrás, Furnas, and Agrarian Reform Institute) and 13 private entities (Rio Light, Indústria e Comércio de Ore, Cia Soutex de Roupas, Cia de Cimento Portland Barroso, and Banco de Desenvolvimento e Investimento Brascan) were trained. In 1967, a total of 46 lawyers were trained in CEPED courses. By the end of the CEPED experience in the early 1970s, approximately 220 lawyers took part in this legal training on corporate law. Thirteen of them attended graduate school at Harvard, Yale, Berkeley, and Michigan.[20] In that first year, the Brazilian lawyers at CEPED sought to respond to the weaknesses of the research program and the difficulties in putting forward the reform with other institutions, as Lamy Filho had indicated in his memorandum.

In the second week of August, the center hosted an urban law seminar, with the collaboration of the Rio de Janeiro Secretariat for Public Works and financial assistance from Ford, FGV, and the National Housing Bank. Trubek, who was at the time at Yale researching legal problems and urban development, Henry Steiner and professors George Lefcoe (University of South Carolina) and Kenneth L. Karst (UCLA) took part in the event. The seminar objective was to study the housing and urban problems in Rio and other Brazilian states and their relations with the country's legal organization in these areas. The seminar accompanied the Brazilian modernization agenda after the 1964 coup, especially the creation of the National Housing Bank. CEPED intended to contribute to such an agenda. The event moreover tried to demonstrate the types of links that the center could establish with Brazilian state agencies, showing its usefulness in solving government and development problems. Such services, as Arnold Wald argued (1969), would reproduce the "cross-fertilization" that exists in the United States between individuals, companies, public and private agencies, and universities.[21]

By the same token, also in August, Arnold Wald led a joint effort by the Institute of Brazilian Lawyers and CEPED to discuss legal education. The seminar was attended by professors from the law schools of Rio de Janeiro, São Paulo, Pernambuco, Minas Gerais, and Rio Grande do Sul. Funded by USAID, the seminar had as its theme the teaching practices in Brazil and abroad, characteristics of the curriculum, the methods, and criteria for diploma, in addition to the internship in forensic practice. The experience of UnB was discussed, as well as that of the new Center for Studies and Research in the Teaching of Law, emphasizing the challenges of reformulating teaching methods.[22]

The achievements of CEPED in 1967 were perceived enthusiastically by USAID and Ford Foundation officials, especially concerning the use of U.S. curriculum and teaching methodologies: the previous delivery of didactic material to students and the pedagogy through active debate were highlighted as the most notable advances. Indeed, Keith Rosenn,[23] a law professor at Ohio University hired by the Ford Foundation to monitor and suggest improvements to classroom work, noted that "… both students and teachers at CEPED have been impressed by the enormous pedagogical benefit of teaching law with discussions in the room, using previously distributed material."[24] Going further, Henry Steiner acknowledged that there was also an innovation in the treatment of problems previously unfamiliar to university education. This was especially true, according to Steiner, for the problems related to the "inadequate structure" of commercial or corporate law in Brazil and the complex, poorly written and vaguely understood torrent of regulatory laws that had been introduced in the country since the "1964 revolution."[25]

USAID and Ford expected that the scholarship recipients sent to U.S. universities would employ the North's expertise at CEPED. In the academic year of 1966–1967, Ford's agreement with the Institute of International Education ensured the development of studies at Harvard by two students, Joaquim de Arruda Falcão Neto and Gabriel de Araújo Lacerda. With a financial supplement from the Fulbright program, Ford also secured a fellowship for Sérgio Francisco Aguiar Tostes to study at New York University. At the end of the first course for corporate lawyers in 1967, by the same agreement, Rubens Paulo Cury de Almeida Torres, Paulo Fernandes de Sá, Gustavo M. de Mello, Hugo Ibeas, Luiz Eduardo de Gama e Silva, and Jorge Hilário Gouvêia Vieira were also sent to universities in the United States. Fellows were seen as potential agents for spreading U.S. methods in Brazilian law schools.[26]

However, amid the praiseworthy comments about the center's "move forward," some analyses indicated the lack of more structural changes in legal practice. Such critical assessment of CEPED's program and impact took shape particularly in the reports produced by Trubek and Steiner after their visit to Brazil for the August 1967 seminars. Henry Steiner, in conversation with Caio Tácito, director of CEPED, said that the curricular proposals pointed to specialized training in "business planning," but they neglected discussions regarding the country's law practice. In other words, it was not favoring the formulation of proposals for state legislative and administrative reform and, thus, not contributing to an intellectual horizon in search of the most adequate methods for the country's modernization. Steiner advocated a more balanced curriculum, in which the very content work of the disciplines related to "business planning" should include discussions on these more structural issues of Brazilian life.[27] By that time, the Ford Foundation was developing agreements with the National Bank for Economic Development, NYU, and FGV to train specialized "human resources" capable of managing the country's new economic order. This also took place with the courses offered by the IPES to train executives between 1967 and 1970 (Assis, 2001, p. 51).

In sum, they argued that there was no reason to divide CEPED between research and teaching programs. Through corporate law, or, more precisely, through the relationship between law and development, CEPED aimed to formulate sophisticated solutions to the problems of Brazilian development and the "open society" that it would engender, comprising a process to integrate the public and private sectors.[28] However, this inclination of the U.S. grantors, teachers, and consultants to modify the teaching program had not progressed. That is because the Brazilian participants, especially the director of the center, Caio Tácito, resisted the proposal to reform. According to U.S. participants, Brazilians did not want to confront the educational traditions of the law schools. Tácito, besides expecting to secure a high position in the judiciary, noted that there was great pressure from the "market" for lawyers who could work creatively and effectively with corporate interests, a new elite that CEPED was eager to train.[29] Moreover, Brazilian participants did not want to challenge the centralization framework in which the relationship between the state and society was organized by the dictatorship.

In a memo from Peter Bell dated May 2, 1967, he discusses the initiatives in social sciences research and training in Rio de Janeiro, such as the CEPED project, and Candido Mendes' proposal to integrate them with other Latin Americans efforts in the field. Bell argued that the Global North initiatives, since the early 1960s, for renewing the general assumptions on modernization (previously focused on economics, administration, and the technocracy), with the infusion of the "social" dimension, faced resistance, for instance, from *General Theory of State* professors Themístocles Cavalcanti and Euticilio Leal (Amorim, 2021, p. 71).[30] It is worth noting that the centrality of the *General Theory* discipline in curricular structure was on the major transformations intended in legal reforms of the post-World War II period.

In light of the growing criticism of its legal program,[31] Ford's office in Rio began to evaluate some possibilities for developing the research program. One of these possibilities was the Institute of Urban Law. Created with resources from the National Housing Bank, the institute could rely on the expertise of CEPED professors Arnold Wald and Cláudio Vianna Lima, besides Luiz Gonzaga do Nascimento Silva, legal advisor to Roberto Campos at the National Development Bank. Another possibility discussed was to take the research program to FGV's Brazilian Institute of Economics, with which former scholarship holders Joaquim Falcão and Jorge Hilário Gouvêia were having conversations. Finally, Ford officers considered joining the negotiations that Brazilian professors such as Wald, led by Harlan Blake from Columbia University, were having with John Howard of the International Legal Center[32] to institute a legal reform program in a Brazilian university.

Yet the most promising initiative was that being carried out at Cândido Mendes University, where in 1969 Ford sponsored the creation of the University Research Institute of Rio de Janeiro (IUPERJ) together with the Pontifical Catholic University of Rio de Janeiro (PUC-Rio). The proposal for legal reform at PUC-Rio, which had CEDEPC Professor Lamy Filho on its staff, was able to take advantage of the restructuring that the institution was undergoing since 1966. Indeed, greater centralization and subsequent decrease in the powers and autonomy of the various schools led to the elimination of schools and institutes and the introduction of the center-departments structure (Penholato, 2017). In effect, PUC's law school, drawing on the university modernization of Castelo Branco and Costa e Silva administrations, became a department within a large Center for Social Sciences (Cunha, 2007, p. 198–199), relying to a great extent on the CEPED model.

The law school at PUC-Rio was organized into areas of concentration. The first was corporate law, whose purpose was to train lawyers in economic expertise and focused on companies and the remodeling of the public sector. The second concentration was aimed at law and development, whose objective was to train researchers in the legal field oriented toward the integration between law and social sciences and toward the reform of legal education.[33] As at the beginning of CEPED's work, the PUC program was able to develop initiatives with state agencies. Coordinated by Jorge Hilário Gouvêia Vieira and Alberto Venâncio Filho, it developed a partnership with the Ministry of Mines and Energy through which the university offered between 1971 and 1972 a full-time course of study for the specialization of lawyers to work at the ministry. In May 1972, CEPED signed a cooperation agreement with PUC, which was developing its Masters in Legal Sciences degree program. Under the agreement, the Center would reserve 15 vacancies for master's degree students in its corporate lawyers course of study.[34]

The initiatives that U.S. participants proposed to CEPED remained centered on the training of a legal elite focused on the new laws, regulations, and codes of the country's economic order, involving in particular corporate law. The center, in sum, continued exclusively as an elite training institution. Close, therefore, to initiatives such as the training courses in economics offered under the agreement between BNDE, Ford, New York University, and FGV in the capital markets area and the courses offered by IPES aiming to train an elite of business executives (Souza, 1981, p. 33–34; Assis, 2001, p. 51). Those elites would be able to carry on a new order of economic development, one in which the capital market played a central role (Penholato, 2017, p. 88–90). Indeed, it is precisely in this field that the most evident legacy of the "law and development movement" in Brazil can be found: the support and development of the business or corporate law firm. They became fundamental agents for the internationalization of the economies of Latin American countries, a process that, since the 1950s, indicated the modernization of the capitalist order in the region (Dreifuss, 1987).

Having used only $144,000 of the $485,000 USD available, CEPED ended its activities in 1973 – largely because Ford sponsors conditioned the continuity of the program on an effort to reform legal education. In the early 1970s, the Médici administration (1969–1974) returned to the debate on the minimum curriculum in universities. On November 16, 1971, under the direction of Newton Sucupira, the Department of University Affairs of the Ministry of Education and Culture formed through Ordinance No. 235 a commission to review the minimum curriculum of law schools. Formed by Caio Tácito (then director of CEPED), Alfredo Lamy Filho (PUC-Rio and professor at CEPED), Emílio Maya Gischkow (UFRGS), José Carlos Moreira Alves (USP), Daniel Coelho de Sousa (UFPA), and Lourival Vilanova (UFPE), the commission proposed greater flexibility and varieties of curricula to "enable the student to collaborate effectively in the process of social transformation, and contribute to the reformulation of legal education with the student's participation both in the practical process and in the curricular option" (Venâncio Filho, 1977, p. 333).

Notably, the justification for the commission's project was based on a dissatisfaction that had appeared in the legal education seminar organized by USAID in 1967 and that had dragged on in the legal debate since the immediate post-World War II period. Commenting on the project, Caio Tacito recognized the crisis of the leading role played historically by law schools in the foundation of Brazilian political institutions – a crisis that was common to all countries with the civil law tradition. Given the flexibility, Tacito exhorted law schools to take responsibility in overcoming such a crisis, arguing that the solution proposed was an act of faith in their capacities to reform legal education – "they must, and necessarily, be held responsible and recognize the merit of the results that the curriculum change will achieve" (Tacito, 1972, p. 23).

Embracing the curricular flexibility that had arisen since the debates of the early 1960s, the Federal Council on Education approved a new minimum curriculum, maintaining non-professional propaedeutic and eight professional disciplines, but expanded those optional disciplines to eight, of which two should be mandatory. Among the mandatory disciplines were: (1) constitutional law; (2) administrative law; (3) civil law; (4) commercial law; (5) criminal law; (6) labor law; (7) civil procedural law; and (8) criminal procedural law. Among the optional disciplines were: (1) private international law; (2) public international law; (3) science of finance and financial law (tax and fiscal); (4) navigation law (maritime and aeronautical); (5) Roman law; (6) social security law; (7) forensic medicine; and (8) agrarian law.

In a recent interview, Trubek said that FGV's São Paulo law school, one of the major legal institutions in Brazil, was the fulfillment of CEPED's "dream" of teaching reform once it embraced its methods and structure (full-time dedicated professors).[35] Furthermore, "law and development" – the legal phenomenon in its societal context – survived in Brazil and the United States as a sub-field in legal education, for instance at FGV and Harvard.[36]

Between late December 1971 and the first half of January 1972, James Gardner, a lawyer who at the time was working at the Ford Foundation office in Chile, wrote to foundation employees in Brazil to discuss legal assistance in the region. He clarified that the appropriation for the legal reform program in Chile, also under reformulation, pointed to a new definition, a new focus in the Foundation's legal programs: from *law and development* to *law and social change*. Gardner was advocating a more systematic approach to the social sciences, as indicated before him by the social sciences consultant for Ford's Latin America and Caribbean Office, Kalman Silvert,[37] and by the Candido Mendes proposal. Gardner did not hide his enthusiasm for "law in action," seeing no reason to insist on the modernization of law schools and their teaching methods.[38] In short, Gardner expressed the renewed gospel regarding the modernization process: development could not prosper as a morally empty project. A human dimension should a priori constitute any political reason, including that of philanthropy.

Indeed, this was becoming a trend among Ford Foundation's officials. Steven Quarles, discussing the future of CEPED after a meeting with Tacito in June 1969, argued that Ford's officials and observers depreciate the center's curriculum. They did not understand, according to Quarles, why a legal reform was launched in corporate law, economics and finance, taxation, and government regulation of business. To them, the "new law" focus should be to assist "the more severe social problems in such areas as urban planning, health care, poverty, etc. – areas which are less richly endowed with financial and human resources than the corporations and the large-institutionalized economy."[39]

Years later, in July 1977, Raymundo Faoro, then president of the Brazilian Bar Association, was one of the most vocal advocates of the rule of law precepts and legal "formalism." In his view, the legal practice should be secured in the strict interpretation of the written law, guaranteeing security to the national legal order. Faoro opposed the legal modeling introduced in the country with CEPED[40] in its technocratic approach that had inflated national legislation: the "instrumentalism" of the law, the training of technical advocacy operating in the name of developmentalism. The jurist argued that by downgrading the lawyer to a technician, transforming the profession into a technocratic assumption, they forget that the very foundation of legal practice is always devoted to legitimate legal order. Gardner reproduced Faoro's words:

> In place of the rationality of law, they impose system-breaking decision-making, taken by new actors who know everything except how to translate the English hurriedly learned in their semestral courses. They legislate, administrate, plan, contract, and negotiate, free from the formalism of law and juridical procedures. As a group not held accountable, either to the people or to the hierarchy, they develop their own esoteric language… with promises and charms that only fool the actors, they evidence all the sensitivity of those who want to see the world through technocratic lenses. The lawyer, accustomed to reasoning on the basis of enduring legal propositions, will be the most able critic of this package surprises.
>
> (Gardner, 1978, p. 117)

In a sense, such a criticism and the desire to recover the fundamentals of the legal practice and legal order were put against the technical role in motion since the 1930s. Indeed, by the late 1960s, elites facing the exhaustion of political authority of Social State assumptions were preparing the means for local and transnational political renewal. A new institutional modernization would take place based on human rights and neoliberalism, remaking the relation between the state and the individual.

Following such transformations, USAID and Ford would revise their agendas. Legal assistance transitioned from "law and development," at least in its technical facet, to "law and social change," that is, to programs focused on "social justice and human rights" and the "assault on poverty."[41] The empowerment and mobilization of civil society through human rights – an interdependence and decentralization process (Kelly, 2018; Offner, 2019) – would become the new tendency in the democratization effort. And yet this tendency would be developed by the elites from "within," assuring stability and avoiding political ruptures.

Notes

1 The commission was formed by Pereira Lira, Braz de Souza Arruda, Arnoldo Medeiros da Fonseca, later replaced by Hélio Tornaghi, José Olympio de Castro Filho, and Joaquim Amazonas. The Commission's work has not been completed. See Arruda (1958).

2 The bill advocated the creation of a three-year political science course of study at law schools, furthermore providing for the split into two years of political economy instruction and the creation of a government law and municipal finance course of study. The Baleeiro Project was resisted, in particular by Martins Rodrigues and Djacir Menezes, and ended up not advancing in congress. See Venâncio Filho (1977).

3 In 1962, the "Law Books USA" program was also developed, aimed at the export of U.S. law books: "Lawyers in these new nations must know and have the very feel of the American concept of law if peace through law is to be achieved" (Kuchel, 1964, p. 1163).

4 Haroldo Valladão was responsible for the Preliminary Draft of the General Law for the Application of Legal Norms, which intended to reform the law enacted by Vargas, with the Decree-Law n. 4657/1942. The law, after several changes throughout the 1950s and 1960s, apparently due to an adaptation of national law to the country's development process and its relationship with the international economic order, ended up being reformed only in 2010. The General Law for the Application of Legal Norms, as a reflection on the legal system itself, guides how the interpretation of national law operates (the elaboration of norms, their validity in time and space), resolving conflicts of interpretation, and providing for understandings of domestic and international law. In other words, the Introduction Law works as a kind of leveling or homogenization instrument in the reading and interpretation of positive national law. See the Decree-Law of 1942 (Brasil, 1942). See also Valladão (1960; 1971).

5 Such understanding can be also found, for instance, in the 1962 annual message from the president of the American Bar Association, John C. Satterfiel (1962, p. 922): "In this day when new nations are rising in ancient lands and the people of all nations are examining the fundamental relationship of man to man and man to government, the legal profession of the United States has a greater opportunity and a graver responsibility than has rested upon the members of any profession in the history of the world."

6 "Proposal for an Advanced Institute of Law and Economic Development." From David Trubek to Peter Bell. October 29, 1965, in *Ford Foundation records*. Grants S-Thel (FA732G). Folder: State University of Rio de Janeiro (06600386). Date: 1966 July 19–1971 July 18. Reel 3114. Rockefeller Archive Center (RAC).

7 Peter Bell attributed the lack of time to the difficulty of defining a project. Letter from David Trubek to Harry Wilhelm. October 1, 1965; and "Law Projects" (Inter-Office Memorandum). From Peter Bell to Stacey Widdicombe. November 12, 1965, in *Ford Foundation records*. Grants S-Thel (FA732G). Folder: State University of Rio de Janeiro (06600386). Date: 1966 July 19–1971 July 18. Reel 3114. RAC.

8 The law course program at UnB focused in the first two years on social science subjects and, in the fifth year, it had more specialized subjects than most law schools in the country. See "Law Projects" (Inter-Office Memorandum). From Peter Bell to Stacey Widdicombe. November 12, 1965, in *Ford Foundation Records*. Grants S-Thel (FA732G). Folder: State University of Rio de Janeiro (06600386). Date: 1966 July 19–1971 July 18. Reel 3114. RAC.

9 UnB was founded in 1962 as a modern university. Its connections with figures on the left, such as Darcy Ribeiro and Oscar Niemayer, made it a special target of repression.

10 See "Law Projects" (Inter-Office Memorandum). From Peter Bell to Stacey Widdicombe. February 3, 1966, in *Ford Foundation Records*. Grants S-Thel (FA732G). Folder: State University of Rio de Janeiro (06600386). Date: 1966 July 19–1971 July 18. Reel 3114. RAC. On the situation of universities, especially in view of the University Reform, see (Motta, 2014).

11 Trubek indicated that USAID would be responsible for the costs in cruzeiros (all operations on Brazilian soil), and the Ford Foundation for the costs in dollars, which meant paying for the visiting professors to come to the institute. See "Law Projects" (Inter-Office Memorandum). From Peter Bell to Stacey Widdicombe. November 12, 1965, in *Ford Foundation Records*. Grants S-Thel (FA732G).

Folder: State University of Rio de Janeiro (06600386). Date: 1966 July 19–1971 July 18. Reel 3114. RAC.

12 That book was published in 1968 with the title *The State's Intervention in the Economic Domain*.

13 Bulhões Pedreira was a member, along with Roberto Campos, of the Joint Brazil-U.S. Commission for Economic Development, created in the early 1950s and which also involved the World Bank. This Commission played a central role in organizing Brazil's economic development policies after World War II, with the creation, for example, of the National Bank for Economic Development and many of the country's main state-owned companies, such as Petrobrás and Eletrobrás.

14 The group of Brazilians involved Lamy Filho, Arnold Wald, Luiz Fernando da S. Pinto, Amílcar Falcão, Carlos Leoni Siqueira, Carlos A. da Silveira Lobo, Augusto J. Lemos, Gabriel Lacerda, Venâncio, and Simonsen.

15 The Ford allocation provided that, of the total amount, 2 million and 100 thousand dollars would be with the Foundation itself for direct distribution to visiting professors and speakers from the U.S.; 133 thousand would stay with UEG to acquire books for the library of the new center; and 1 million and 340 thousand went to the Institute of International Education (IIE), responsible for administering graduate scholarships for the "cepedistas" in the United States. See "Program Action No. 66–386." July 19, 1966, in *Ford Foundation Records*. Grants S-Thel (FA732G). Folder: State University of Rio de Janeiro (06600386). Date: 1966 July 19–1971 July 18. Reel 3114. RAC. Regarding IIE, see Berman (1983, p. 129–131).

16 The Ford Foundation. Request for Grant Action, "Development of a Center for Legal Studies" (July 23, 1966), in *Ford Foundation Reports Information*. RAC *Apud* Gardner (1978, p. 314).

17 Report 1st year of CEPED Activities. From Caio Tácito to João Lyra Filho. September 28, 1967, in *Ford Foundation Records*. Grants S-Thel (FA732G). Folder: State University of Rio de Janeiro (06600386). Date: 1966 July 19–1971 July 18. Reel 3114. RAC.

18 This understanding of a necessary link between the university and economic life, in particular the private company and how it related to education, was the topic of debate at the "Education Forum" organized by IPES in 1968. One of the themes was dedicated to the "link between university and company." Responsible for this theme, Professor Teophilo de Azeredo Santos defended that "… this problem between university / company can only be solved in an appropriate way, as long as there is a change in the teaching method. Brazilian universities, as a rule, with few and honorable exceptions, are unprepared for professional training that satisfies technological advances, the achievements of science and also the more advanced university practices. The truth … is that Brazilian universities are still steeped in teaching that is typically medieval, academic, Coimbra based, rhetoric [….]" (Santos, 1968, p. 2, cited in Souza, 1981, appendices).

19 This would take place with new legislation in 1976, at the request of Minister Mario H. Simonsen. Bill No. 6.404, written by José L. Bulhões Pedreira and Lamy Filho, aimed to strengthen private companies through the capitalization of resources in the capital market (Gatto, Faro, and Almeida, 2009, p. 17–18).

20 "Report on Trip to Center for Studies and Research in the Teaching of Law and Description of CEPED's Development and Prospects." From: Henry Steiner.

Memorandum to Ford Foundation (Copy to USAID). Confidential. September 1967, p. 3; and Report on the 1st Year of CEPED's activities. From Caio Tácito to João Lyra Filho. September 28, 1967, in *Ford Foundation Records*. Grants S-Thel (FA732G). Folder: State University of Rio de Janeiro (06600386). Date: 1966 July 19–1971 July 18. Reel 3114. RAC. The corporate lawyers course of study was offered a total of six times, until 1972, when the agreements with the Ford Foundation entered into the finalization process.

21 The seminar's theme was organized into five categories: (1) administrative system of urban and housing planning; (2) financing of housing and urbanism plans; (3) financial policy in urban development; (4) eradication and recovery of favelas; and 5.) Guanabara industrial development. The regime's housing program was created through the BNH and the National Housing System, with which the construction of houses was intended. This was linked to the new (tightening) wage policy, with the end of job stability and the creation of the Employment Time Guarantee Fund (FGTS), whose resources served as the basis for housing policy developed by the civil construction sector. See Melo (2013).

22 Letter from Caio Tacito to Trubek. June 28, 1967; and Letter of Tacitus to Charles A. Frankenhoff. June 20, 1976, in *Ford Foundation Records*. Grants S-Thel (FA732G). Folder: State University of Rio de Janeiro (06600386). Date: 1966 July 19–1971 July 18. Reel 3114. RAC. "There was a general feeling of interest in change, although in many cases this desire was combined with an interest in maintaining the status quo" (Venâncio Filho, 1977, p. 330).

23 Rosenn and Henry Steiner were hired by the Ford Foundation as visiting professors and consultants. Steiner had been providing advice since before the creation of CEPED. See Programa do Curso de Advogado de Empresa. 1967, in *Ford Foundation Records*. Grants S-Thel (FA732G). Folder: State University of Rio de Janeiro (06600386). Date: 1966 July 19–1971 July 18. Reel 3114. RAC.

24 Keith Rosenn, "Random Thoughts on Present and Future Operations of CEPED," at 2 (April 14, 1967). Ford Foundation Reports Information, RAC.

25 "Report on Trip to Center for Studies and Research in Law Education and Description of CEPED's Development and Prospects." From Henry J. Steiner to Ford Foundation (copy to USAID). Confidential. September 1967, in *Ford Foundation Records*. Grants S-Thel (FA732G). Folder: State University of Rio de Janeiro (06600386). Date: 1966 July 19–1971 July 18. Reel 3114. RAC.

26 Letter from Caio Tacito to William Carmichael. Rio de Janeiro, April 11, 1969, in *Ford Foundation Records*. Grants S-Thel (FA732G). Folder: State University of Rio de Janeiro (06600386). Date: 1966 July 19–1971 July 18. Reel 3114. RAC.

27 See "Report on Trip to Center for Studies and Research in the Teaching of Law (CEPED) and Description of CEPED's Development and Prospects" From: Henry Steiner. Memorandum to: Ford Foundation (Copy to USAID). Confidential. September, 1967, in *Ford Foundation Records*. Grants S-Thel (FA732G). Folder: State University of Rio de Janeiro (06600386). Date: 1966 July 19–1971 July 18. Reel 3114. RAC.

28 "Report on Trip to Center for Studies and Research in Law Education and Description of CEPED's Development and Prospect." Op. Cit.; and David Trubek's letter to Stacey Widdicombe. September 14, 1967, in Ford Foundation records. Grants S-Thel (FA732G). Folder: State University of Rio de Janeiro (06600386). Date: 1966 July 19–1971 July 18. Reel 3114. RAC. On the Trubek report, see also: Letter from Stacey Widdicombe to David Trubek. September

27, 1967; and David Trubek's letter to Peter Bell. September 27, 1967, in *Ford Foundation Records*. Grants S-Thel (FA732G). Folder: State University of Rio de Janeiro (06600386). Date: 1966 July 19–1971 July 18. Reel 3114. RAC.

29 "Report on Trip to Center for Studies and Research in the Teaching of Law (CEPED) and Description of CEPED's Development and Prospects" From: Henry Steiner. Memorandum to: Ford Foundation (Copy to USAID). Confidential. September, 1967, in Ford Foundation records. Grants S-Thel (FA732G). Folder: State University of Rio de Janeiro (06600386). Date: 1966 July 19–1971 July 18. Reel 3114. RAC; and Henry Steiner's letter to David Trubek. August 23, 1968, in *Ford Foundation Records*. Grants S-Thel (FA732G). Folder: State University of Rio de Janeiro (06600386). Date: 1966 July 19–1971 July 18. Reel 3114. RAC. In an interview, David Trubek reaffirms the impression that the U.S. participants wished that, from CEPED, the teaching structure of the Brazilian law schools would be modified, while the Brazilians were satisfied with the corporate law training, non-existent in the country at the time. David Trubek interview with Júlio Barnez P. Cattai and Felipe Amorim, on October 12, 2017.

30 Peter Bell to Stacey Widdicombe, Inter-Office Memorandum, "Brazilian Society for Instruction: Social Science Research and Training (L66–566)"; May 2, 1967, in *Ford Foundation Records*. Grant files (PA67–492). Reel 5351, RAC.

31 In 1971, a negative assessment of the Foundation's efforts with legal reform in Latin America arrived at the FF's New York office. The assessment was that attempts at reform were based on the American legal model, foreign to the reality of the countries in the region. See McClymont and Golub 2000.

32 The International Legal Center was founded with funds from the Ford Foundation in 1965 with the aim of systematizing the legal assistance efforts of U.S. organizations for the third world and Latin America.

33 The Socratic method and case study are also used, the class material was distributed in advance and a growing number of full-time teachers were hired. At PUC-Rio, nine former CEPED students came to work. See Gardner (1978).

34 "Term of Agreement between the Pontifical Catholic University of Rio de Janeiro and the Center for Studies and Research in Law Education," *Ford Foundation Records*. Grants S-Thel (FA732G). Folder: State University of Rio de Janeiro (06600386). Date: 1966 July 19–1971 July 18. Reel 3114. RAC.

35 David Trubek interview with Júlio Barnez P. Cattai and Felipe Amorim on October 12, 2017. CEPED participants, such as J. Falcão and G. Lacerda, now active at FGV, corroborate Trubek's analysis. See Falcão, Lacerda, and Rangel (2012).

36 See, for instance: Henry Steiner Memorandum to participants in meeting on February 7 on law and development, in Alex Inkeles Papers. Box 466. Folder: Meeting on Law and Development Movement, 2/7/1970 (Steiner). Hoover Institution Archives. The documents from the Hoover Institution were kindly granted by Felipe Amorim.

37 Silvert was the first president of the Latin American Studies Association (LASA). After his death in 1976, LASA created an award named after him, the Kalman Silvert Award, offered to senior researchers in Latin American studies and delivered at its international conventions. Silvert had indicated, in his criticisms of the reports produced by Henry Steiner on CEPED that, when analyzing the Research Program, he did not address, even once, the role to be played by the social sciences.

38 "University of the State of Guanabara, Legal Education (PA66–386)." (Inter-Office Memorandum). From James Gardner to Stanley Nicholson and Peter Reichard. Date: January 11, 1972; and "Chile Law Program (PA67–273A). From James Gardner to William Carmichael. December 27, 1971, in *Ford Foundation Records*. Grants S-Thel (FA732G). Folder: State University of Rio de Janeiro (06600386). Date: 1966 July 19–1971 July 18. Reel 3114. RAC. Gardner was part of a trend inside Ford which was opposed to the agenda around business law, aiming to improve the education of law through a series of "activist" strategies, including human rights and public interest law. See Dezalay and Garth (2002).

39 Steven P. Quarles. "The Future of CEPED, Meeting with Dr. Caio Tácito, June 2, 1969." June 11, 1969, in *Ford Foundation Records*. Grants S-Thel (FA732G). Folder: State University of Rio de Janeiro (06600386). Date: 1966 July 19–1971 July 18. Reel 3114. RAC.

40 David Trubek reports that Faoro has become one of the leading voices to criticize CEPED. See David Trubek interview for Júlio Barnez P. Cattai and Felipe Amorim, on October 12, 2017.

41 See David Heaps, "Draft Report on Human Rights." August, 1975, p. 4, in *Ford Foundation Records* (FA739). Catalogued Reports. Box 254, Report 5643. RAC; and Human Rights and Intellectual Freedom (Information Paper). November 1975, in *Ford Foundation Records* (FA739). Catalogued Reports. Box 3. Shepard Forman Human Rights. RAC.

Bibliography

Abreu, A. A. *et al.* (Eds). (2001). *Dicionário histórico-biográfico brasileiro pós-1930*. Rio de Janeiro: FGV.

Adorno, S. (1998). *Os aprendizes do poder: o bacharelismo liberal na política brasileira*. Rio de Janeiro, São Paulo: Editora Paz e Terra.

Allcock, T. T. (2014). "Becoming "Mr. Latin America": Thomas C. Mann Reconsidered," *Diplomatic History*, Vol. 38, Issue 5, November. https://doi.org/10.1093/dh/dht116

Almeida Júnior, A. (1947). "A propósito do ensino de direito nos Estados Unidos," *Revista da Faculdade de Direito da Universidade de São Paulo*, Vol. 42.

Amado, Thiago. (2021). *A Escola Superior de Guerra (ESG) e a Guerra Fria (1949–1964): uma análise a partir do Curso Superior de Guerra*. Report (FAPESP). São Paulo.

Amorim, F. C. (2021). *The Birth of a Discipline": o convênio Ford-Iuperj e a modernização da ciência política no Brasil (1967–1973)*. Dissertação (Mestrado). História Social, Universidade de São Paulo, São Paulo.

Arruda, B. S. (1958). "Reforma do Ensino Jurídico," *Revista da Faculdade de Direito da Universidade de São Paulo*, São Paulo, Vol. 53.

Assis, D. (2001). *Propaganda e cinema a serviço do Golpe (1962–1964)*. Rio de Janeiro: Muad/FAPERJ.

Barreto Filho, O. (1970). "Novos Métodos de Ensino do Direito – a experiência norte-americana," *Revista Forense*, São Paulo, Ano 66, Vol. 229, janeiro-fevereiro, março.

Bastos, A. W. (1998). *O Ensino Jurídico no Brasil*. Rio de Janeiro: Editora Lumen Juris.

Berman, E. H. (1983). *The Influence of the Carnegie, Ford, and Rockefeller Foundations on American Foreign Policy: The Ideology of Philanthropy*. Albany: State University of New York Press.

Bittencourt, C. A. L. (1947). "O D.A.S.P. como imperativo democrático e técnico," *Revista de Direito Administrativo*, Rio de Janeiro – FGV, Vol. 7.
BRASIL. (1931). Decreto No 19.852, de 11 de Abril de 1931. Rio de Janeiro, 1931.
______ (1940). Decreto-Lei No 2.639, de 27 de setembro de 1940. Rio de Janeiro, 1940.
______ (1942). Decreto-Lei No 4.657, de 4 de setembro de 1942. Rio de Janeiro, 1942.
Bresciani, M. S. M. (2005). *O charme da ciência e a sedução da objetividade. Oliveira Vianna entre intérpretes do Brasil*. São Paulo: UNESP.
Bu, L. (1999) "Education Exchange and Cultural Diplomacy in the Cold War,". *Journal of American Studies*, 33
Campos, F. (1931). "Exposição de Motivos aos Decretos 19.851 e 19.852, ambos de 11 de abril de 1931," *Revista Forense*, São Paulo, Vol. 331, No. LXI.
______ (2001). *O Estado Nacional – sua estrutura, seu conteúdo ideológico*. (Coleção Biblioteca Básica Brasileira) Brasília: Senado Federal, Conselho Editorial.
Cancelli, E. (2017). O Brasil em Guerra Fria Cultural: o pós-guerra em releitura. São Paulo: Intermeios.
Cattai, J. (2019). *Guerra Fria e Propaganda: a U.S. Information Agency no Brasil*. Curitiba: Appris.
Cavalcanti, T. (1955). *Introdução à Ciência Política*. Rio de Janeiro: Instituto de Direito Público e Ciência Política (IDPCP-FGV).
______ (1958). "O Instituto de Direito Público e Ciência Política: por que e para que foi criado?" *ReV. do Inst. de Direito Púb. e Ciência Política*, Rio de Janeiro – FGV, Vol. 1, No. 1.
Cesarino Júnior, A. F. (1953). *Anais do I Congresso Nacional de Ensino Jurídico*. Fortaleza.
Chaves, W. (2018). *A questão negra: a Fundação Ford e a Guerra Fria (1950–1970)*. Curitiba: Prismas.
Costa, M. J. A. (2018). *História do Direito Português*. Reimpressão da 5.ª Edição Revista e Actualizada de 2012. Coimbra: Livraria Almedina.
Cunha, L. A. (2007). *A universidade reformada: o Golpe de 1964 e a modernização do ensino superior*. 2.ª Edição. São Paulo: Editora Unesp.
Cury, V. A. R. (2001). *O ensino do Direito: raízes histórico-ideológicas e novas diretrizes*. Tese de doutorado em Educação. Campinas, Universidade Estadual de Campinas.
Dallari, D. de A. (1973). *Elementos de Teoria Geral do Estado*. 2.ª Edição. São Paulo: Saraiva.
Dantas, S. T. (1955). "A educação e a Crise Brasileira" (aula inaugural dos cursos da Faculdade Nacional de Direito, 1955), *Revista dos Tribunais*, São Paulo.
______ (2001). *Palavras de um Professor*. 2.ª Edição. Rio de Janeiro: Forense.
D'araujo, M. C. (Org). (1999). *Fundação Getúlio Vargas: Concretização de um ideal*. Rio de Janeiro: Editora FGV.
Darnton, C. (2012). "Asymmetry and Agenda-Setting in U.S.-Latin American relations: rethinking the origins of the Alliance for Progress," *Journal of Cold War Studies*, Vol. 14, No. 4, Fall. www.doi:10.2307/26924150
Dezalay, Y. and Garth, B. G. (2002). *Global Prescriptions: The Production, Exportation, and Importation of a New Legal Orthodoxy*. Ann Arbor: University of Michigan Press.
D.J. (1951). (British Institute of International and Comparative Law). "The Inter-American Council of Jurists," *The International Law Quarterly*, Vol. 4, No. 4. October, pp. 521–525.

Dreifuss, R. A. (1981). 1964: A conquista do Estado: ação política, poder e golpe de classe. Petrópolis: Vozes, 3 ed.

Dupuy, R. J. (Ed.). (1973). *The Hague Academy of International Law: Jubilee Book 1923–1973*. Leiden: Sijthoff.

Falcão, J., Lacerda, G., and Rangel, T. (Eds). (2012). *Aventura e Legado no ensino jurídico*. Rio de Janeiro: FGV Direito Rio.

Franco, M. S. C. (1981). "Entrevista," *Revista Trans/Form/Ação*, Vol. 4, pp. 5–14. http://dx.doi.org/10.1590/S0101-31732011000300007

Gardner, J. (1978). *Legal Imperialism: American Lawyers and Foreign Aid in Latin America.* Madison: The University of Wisconsin Press.

Garth, B. G. (2000). "James Willard Hurst as Entrepreneur for the Field of Law and Social Science," *Law and History Review*, Vol. 18, No. 1, Spring. https://doi.org/10.2307/744348

Gatto, C., Faro, L, and Almeida, R. (2009). *José Luiz Bulhões Pedreira: invenção do estado moderno brasileiro*. Rio de Janeiro: Insight Engenharia de Comunicação.

Gomes, Â. C. (Ed.). (1994). *Engenheiros e economistas: novas elites burocráticas*. Rio de Janeiro: Editora Fundação Getúlio Vargas.

Gomes, O. (1961). "O municipalismo e a reforma do Estado." *Revista Forense*, São Paulo, Ano 58, Vol. 195, julho-agosto-setembro.

Huo, S. and Parmar, I. (2019). "'A new type of great power relationship'? Gramsci, Kautsky and the role of the Ford Foundation's transformational elite knowledge networks in China," *Review of International Political Economy*, June. http://doi:10.1080/09692290.2019.1625427

Kelly, P. (2018). *Sovereign Emergencies: Latin America and the Making of Global Human Rights Politics*. Cambridge: Cambridge University Press.

Krever, T. (2011). "The Legal Turn in Late Development Theory: The Rule of Law and the World Bank's Development Model," *Harvard International Law Journal*, Vol. 52, N. 1, Winter.

Krishnan, J. K. (2004). "Professor Kingsfeld Goes to Delhi: American Academics, the Ford Foundation, and the Development of Legal Education in India," *Articles by Maurer Faculty*, Paper 345.

______ (2012). "Academic SAILERS: The Ford Foundation and the Efforts to Shape Legal Education in Africa, 1957–1977," *American Journal of Legal History*, Vol. 52, Issue 3, July, pp. 261–324. https://doi.org/10.1093/ajlh/52.3.261

Kuchel, Thomas H. (1964). "Lawbooks USA: messenger of World Peace through Law," *American Bar Association Journal*, Vol. 58.

Lamy Filho, A. (1966) "Considerações sobre o CEPED, o método de ensino e o programa a adotar," cited in 0000000 Filho, A. (1997). *Das Arcadas ao Bacharelismo: 150 anos de Ensino Jurídico no Brasil*. São Paulo: Editora Perspectiva.

______ (1976). "Pressupostos e objetivos da reforma da lei de sociedades por ações," *Revista Forense*, Ano 72, Vol. 255, Julho-Agosto-Setembro.

Latham, M. E. (2000). *Modernization as Ideology: American Social Science and 'Nation Building' in the Kenney Era.* Chapel Hill and London: The University of North Carolina Press.

Leal, V. N. (1959). "Ciência Política," *Rev. do Inst. de Direito Púb. e Ciência Política*, Rio de Janeiro – FGV, Vol. II, No.1.

McClymont, M. E. and Golub, S. (Eds). (2000). *Many Roads to Justice: The Law-related Work of Ford Foundation Grantees around the world.* The Ford Foundation.

Melo, W. F. (2013). "A ditadura, a questão da moradia e a modernização excludente: Roberto Campos em defesa do Sistema Financeiro da Habitação," *Verinotio revista on-line*, No. 17. Ano IX, abr.

Mota Filho, C. M. (1965). "A Reforma Eleitoral," *Arquivos do Ministério da Justiça e Negócios Interiores*, Brasília, Ano XXIII, No. 94, junho.

Motta, R. P. S. (2014). *As universidades e o regime militar: cultura política brasileira e modernização autoritária*. Rio de Janeiro: Zahar Editora.

Nascimento Silva, L. G. (1970). "O papel do jurista em um mundo em transformação," *Revista Forense*, Rio de Janeiro, Ano 67, abr-mai-jun.

Offner, A. C. (2019). *Sorting Out the Mixed Economy: The Rise and Fall of Welfare and Developmental States in the Americas*. New Jersey: Princeton University Press.

Parmar, I. (2012). *Foundations of the American Century: The Ford, Carnegie, and Rockefeller Foundations in the Rise of American Power*. New York: Columbia University Press.

Penholato, D. (2017). José Garrido Torres nas Sombras do Poder: Um Economista na Construção do Projeto de Modernização de 1964. Dissertação (Mestrado) – FFLCH, Universidade de São Paulo, São Paulo.

Pruden, C. (1998). *Conditional Partners. Eisenhower, the United Nations, and the Search for a Permanent Peace*. Lousiana State University Press.

Ramos, J. N. (1976). "O ensino do Direito," *Revista dos Tribunais*, São Paulo, Ano 65, Vol. 490, agosto.

Rodrigues, J. M. (1953). "O ensino jurídico no Brasil," *Revista da Faculdade de Direito da Universidade do Paraná*, Ano I, No. 1.

Saldanha, N. N. (1963). "Separação de Poderes: reflexão sobre a permanência do problema," *Rer. Dir. Públ. e Ciência Política*, – Rio de Janeiro – FGV., Vol. VI, No. 1, janeiro/abril.

Salvadori, M. (1950). "Introdução," *UNESCO. La Science Politique Contemporaine: contribution à la recherche, la méthode et l'enseignement*. UNESCO, Publication No. 427, le 27 décembre.

Santos, T. A. (1968). "Vinculação Universidade-Empresa," *Conferência Fórum de Educação do Instituto de Pesquisa e Estudos Sociais* – IPES/Guanabara, outubro, cited in Souza, M. I. S. (1981). *Os empresários e a educação: o IPES e a política educacional após 1964*. Petrópolis: Editora Vozes.

Satterfield, J. C. (1962). "Law and Lawyers in a Changing World: The President's Annual Address," *American Bar Association Journal*, Vol. 49.

Scarfi, J. P. (2017). *The Hidden History of International Law in the Americas: Empire and Legal Networks*. New York: Oxford University Press.

______ (2018). "Globalizing the Latin American legal field: continental and regional approaches to the international legal order in Latin America," *Rev. bras. polít. Int*, Brasília, Vol 61, No. 2. http://dx.doi.org/10.1590/0034-7329201800205

Schickler, E. and Caughey, D. (2011). "Public Opinion, Organized Labor, and the Limits of New Deal Liberalism, 1936–1945," *Studies in American Political Development*, Vol. 25. October, pp. 162–189. http://doi:10.1017/S0898588X11000101

Schlesinger, Jr. A. M. (1970). "The Lowering Hemisphere," *The Atlantic Monthly*, Vol. 225, No. 1, January.

Scott-Smith, G. (2007). "Attempting to Secure an 'Orderly Evolution': American Foundations, The Hague Academy of International Law and the Third World," *Journal of American Studies*, Vol. 41, No. 3, pp. 509–532. http://10.1017/S0021875807003970

Silveira, M. M. 2016. "Direito, Ciência Social: o lugar dos juristas nos debates do Brasil dos anos 1930 e 1940," *Estudos Históricos*, Rio de Janeiro – FGV, Vol.. 29, No. 58, pp. 441–460, maio-agosto.
Souza, M. I. S. (1981). *Os empresários e a educação: o IPES e a política educacional após 1964*. Petrópolis: Editora Vozes.
Tácito, C. (1971). "O Desafio no Ensino do Direito," *Revista Forense*, São Paulo. Ano 67, Vol. 233, março.
______ (1972). *Currículo Mínimo do Curso de Direito. Texto e Histórico*. Rio de Janeiro: Universidade do Estado da Guanabara.
Trubek, D. M. (1966). "Problemas Práticos do Programa de Cooperação Internacional no Campo do Desenvolvimento," *Revista dos Tribunais*, São Paulo, Ano 55, Vol. 373, novembro.
______ (1971). "Law, Planning, and the Development of the Brazilian Capital Market: a Study of Law in Economic Change." *Yale Law School Studies in Law and Modernization*, No. 3, April.
Valladão, H. (1960). "A Lei de Introdução ao Código Civil e sua reforma," *Revista dos Tribunais*, Vol. 292, fev.
______ (1963). "O currículo mínimo e a duração dos cursos de direito," *Revista dos Tribunais*, São Paulo, Ano 52, Vol. 332, junho.
______(1966). "Problemas Jurídicos da cooperação internacional no campo do desenvolvimento econômico e social," *Revista dos Tribunais*, São Paulo, Ano 55, Vol. 364, fevereiro.
______(1970). *Direito Internacional Privado*. 2. ed. Rio de Janeiro: Livraria Freitas Bastos.
______(1971). "O Estudo e o Ensino do Direito Comparado no Brasil: séculos XIX e XX," *Revista de Informação Legislativa*. Senado Federal – diretoria de informação legislativa, Brasília, Ano VIII, No. 30, abril-junho.
Vannucchi, M. A. (2018). "Estado, capitalsimo e profissão: metamorfoses da advocacia nas décadas de 1940 e 1960," *História Unisinos,* Vol. 22, No. 4, pp. 192–603, novembro/dezembro. https://doi.org/10.4013/htu.2018.224.07
Venâncio Filho, A. (1977). *Das Arcadas ao Bacharelismo: 150 anos de Ensino Jurídico no Brasil.* São Paulo: Editora Perspectiva.
Vianna, O. (1938). *Problemas de Direito Corporativo*. Rio de Janeiro: José Olympio.
______(1999). *Instituições políticas brasileiras*. Brasília: Conselho Editorial do Senado Federal.
Wald, A. (1969). "O advogado e a Sociedade Industrial," *Revista de Direito Público*, São Paulo. (USP), junho.
Wertheim, S. (2020). *Tomorrow, the World: The Birth of U.S. Global Supremacy*. Cambridge, MA: The Belknap Press of Harvard University Press.

5 The decline of the Social State and the rise of neoliberalism

U.S. power and the Brazilian transition to the global order

By the late 1960s, a new crisis had arrived. It was a moral one and concerned assumptions about the constitution of the Social State that, despite considering the reorganization process that took place in the aftermath of World War II, had dominated legal thinking since the 1930s. The crisis led to a growing contestation of the state's technocratic dominance of political life, which indicated the moral failure or the non-humanistic character of such a consensus. The modernization process discussed in the previous chapters had thus come to a close by the end of the 1960s and early 1970s. Insisting on those questions would make no sense to the elites in the 1970s, even because, facing the decline in legitimacy, they were seeking a new vocabulary for ideas. A new political engagement took place: a *transition* process capable of consolidating the industrial and institutional modernization process and paving the way for an interdependent international order. Elites sought to define the moral substance that should inform political life, reacting to the profound and generalized crisis regarding the previous assumptions about the Social State that were prevalent in the period.

Throughout the 1970s, elites in Brazil devoted themselves to the institutional adjustment of the modernization program that the dictatorship had set in motion since 1964. Most importantly, the period was fundamentally dominated by discussions about the "political opening" – the *abertura* – process: which of the various social groups that appeared as a result of the modernization process in the country's political life should be integrated into palace politics, when should they be included, and how much power should they be granted?

Following the trail of such a discourse, this chapter supports the hypothesis that the political opening (also called "decompression" or "transition to democracy") agenda in Brazil – its framework, strategies, alliances, and scope – was deeply connected to the increasing exhaustion with the technocratic politics developed in the Global North. It shows the making of a new political establishment. In this sense, it was the structure of legal (and political) thinking developed between the 1930s and the 1970s, as discussed in the previous chapters, that came to find itself in crisis by the mid-1960s. Thus, despite divergences between the Global South and the Global North, elites

DOI: 10.4324/9781003123941-6

sought to renew the global order and the legitimacy of local government, a process that underpinned the transition to the era of human rights and neoliberalism. In the beginning, though, as a response to the waning consensus on the technocratic state, elites were echoing calls for humanitarianism as the proper moral dimension for the technological and globalized era. More precisely, the construction among elites of this new political consensus was departing from growing opposition to the state's function in economic development and social life, thus intensifying cross-border exchanges and the rise of interdependence.

By the early 20th century, when laissez-faire liberalism showed its "pernicious" and "individualistic" character and social misery became a moral issue, the elites started to aggregate instruments and concepts, specifically through scientific knowledge. Assuming that individual enterprise operates imperfectly, legal thinking aggregated instruments and concepts to emulate a macro-approach to the social reality, making it possible to fulfill a new moral standard: the collective interest. Jurists and political figures in Brazil paved the way for constituting a unique locus of authority, the Social State, an institutional complex capable of establishing such a correlation between individual enterprise and collective interest. In the 1970s, elites, while not precisely seeking a return to laissez-faire, were criticizing this intellectual construct: the state as *the* legitimate organizer of social life, capable of educating and conducting the political behavior of the masses, thus embracing the "acceleration of the pace of history" into a new governance. A modern individual dimension, one that would overcome the culture of the laissez-faire, could arise if the state bureaucracy were not in the way. Or, more precisely, the liberty "should be produced and defended" by the state, to which end it was necessary to reorganize and reallocate its instruments of intervention (Safatle, 2020, p. 24; Slobodian, 2018). The "politics of decentralization" would soon capture the political imagination (Offner, 2019; Moyn, 2018; Kelly, 2018), opening the transition to the human rights and neoliberal era (Brown, 2005; Whyte, 2019).

This chapter does not evolve to the late 1970s and the 1980s, which would need further research. Yet, as argued, it shows how the passage from authoritarian rule to democracy in Brazil was directly informed by growing opposition to the technocratic state, including by the elites' absorption of human rights as a transnational resource against the most radical right-wing sectors linked to the dictatorship. In a way, authoritarian rule would have been identified with the institutional foundations of the Social State since the 1930s. Legal elites in the country were active in the broad political and intellectual criticism of the technocracy and took an important part in the renewed research agenda of social scientists in the 1960s, particularly regarding the regime's promotion of political changes from within, avoiding "extremisms" from the right and the left. The transition sought to reconcile the "coalition between liberals and right-wing groups that supported the dictatorship" in 1964 (Cancelli, 2020, p. 3), allowing Brazilian elites and institutions to follow the transformation of the international order taking place in the period. The former centrality of the state in seeking to correct individual behavior as a way to achieve social justice would be directly challenged and transformed.

U.S. foreign policy, Latin American dictatorships, and the quest for a new morality

In the late 1960s, Arnold Wald wrote an article in a prestigious Brazilian Law Journal arguing that legal thought at the time found itself between the techno-structure promoted by John K. Galbraith, which was exempt of a moral foundation and based on the rule of greater profitability, and a more comprehensive humane development, advocated by the philosopher Raymond Aron, which was guided not only by economic but also and likewise by moral and legal premises. For Wald, there was a need to recover a virtue, a humanitarian morality, that re-centralized humankind as the measure of all things (Wald, 1969).

Wald was expressing a growing international awareness regarding the political establishment. Among other intellectuals, the historian Arnold Toynbee, who was acknowledged by Brazilian elites, was supporting the role a new virtue should play in political life. Known in Brazil since the publication of *A Study of History*,[1] the British historian was appearing alongside with Gunnar Myrdal, François Perroux, and Bertrand Russell, as part of the Ford Foundation's preoccupation with the development, discussed later, of its new research agenda in Brazil by the mid-1960s. In 1966, they visited the Candido Mendes Law School[2] in Rio de Janeiro, helping, according to Peter Bell, to "create widespread publicity and generat[ing] considerable debate" regarding Brazilian development.[3]

A few years later, in 1971, the British historian published *Surviving the Future*,[4] a rewritten discussion with Japanese Kei Wakaizumi. In the book, Toynbee argues that, at one point, there would be a slowdown in technology and a spiritual ascent. The technology could, Toynbee said, offer humanity material power, which could be used for good or evil, but not as a direction for political action. Thus, echoing a concern common to Brazilian legal thought, the historian believed that the technocrat government was amoral. For him, technological resources must be directed by virtue of love, wisdom, and spirit: virtue as the only safe (and superior) guide to human achievement (Toynbee, 1971).

Wald's attacks on Galbraith, one of the most important representatives of the Democratic Party's Americans for Democratic Action and a well-known member of the Congress for Cultural Freedom (Powers, 1998; Ehrman, 1993), were deeply connected to the Global North's gradual turn against the bulwarks of post-war liberalism. Indeed, this was a protest directed at the heart of U.S. liberal consensus (Ehrman, 1993; Borstelmann, 2012), including the U.S. presence in international affairs. The protest included a challenge, by scholars and intellectuals, to foreign policy as a "collusion of dependent development, authoritarianism, and, often, U.S. foreign policy" (Guilhot, 2005, p. 134). In practice, development literature could not after all avoid poverty or famine. Local distributive justice was neglected, as Kalman Silvert argued regarding the University of Guanabara-FGV's Center for Studies and Research in the Teaching of Law (CEPED). Moreover, development literature ended up supporting dictatorships, the suppression of freedoms, and torture as a political tool in the Global South.

In sum, the failure of a distributive justice on a local level was part of a broad criticism of modernization theories, particularly that engendered by dependency and unequal exchange theories (Guilhot, 2005, p. 129; Dezalay and Garth, 2002). The Global South began to propose a reform to an international order based on the premise of the Global North's economic exploitation of the Global South (Toye and Toye, 2003). Along with the erosion of the Bretton Woods system and the OPEC's oil crisis, the post-II World War liberal international system was being contested (Gilman, 2015; Sargent, 2015). Indeed, liberal assumptions regarding growth, affluence, and stability, which were common ground to Keynesian macroeconomics, theories of modernization, and the foundations of post-industrial society were deteriorating. The government, as a unique source of authority and the only political structure capable of rationally giving meaning to social life, was being defied (Forrester, 2019, p. 172–173). The future became uncertain as the sense of crises became the norm: in short, the bases of political thought in the 20th century, the set of shared assumptions, went into a profound decline. This was not, thus, only a crisis of the post-II World War liberal consensus but also one related to the state as an institutional complex capable of achieving social justice and born out of the laissez-faire crisis of the early 20th century.

This was of particular importance to the leading role of the United States in world affairs, while the country itself was facing political turmoil. Directly influenced by the demoralization in Vietnam, institutions seemed to decline in the face of a series of economic and political crises that took place in the period (Borstelmann, 2012). Even the most important institution devoted to discussing the U.S. foreign policy, the Council on Foreign Relations, broke with the unfolding of Vietnam (Mello, 2022). The rise of transnational humanitarianism, the awareness of the human condition worldwide, in particular regarding the Biafra War of 1967–70 and the South Asian crisis of 1971, underpinned the transformation of palace politics locally and internationally.

Prominently, at an institutional level, the doctrine of sovereign inviolability came under pressure, as transnational activists demanded international action to face the violence within nation-states (Sargent, 2015, p. 94; Kelly, 2018). This humanitarianism – this new sensibility also indicated by Wald, Toynbee, and Aron – paved the way for initiatives such as Ted Kennedy's push to establish, within the State Department, a Bureau of Social and Humanitarian Services. In sum, it demonstrated the growing awareness concerning the need to "raise the level of responsibility and encourage stronger national leadership in international humanitarian and refugee affairs."[5] The authoritarian rule in Latin American nations would be directly challenged by this development, thus transforming the political process locally. The U.S. Senate would become a central institution in such a renewed mobilization.

In late 1969, Senator Frank Church defended, in the paper *The Image and the Ideal: A New Role for the United States*, an agenda for a complete restructuring of the country's foreign policy toward Latin America. Seeking a response to what Richard Nixon called, in his inaugural address, in January 1969, a "crisis of spirit," Church approached the ongoing crisis in the U.S. political establishment and, more broadly, in Western civilization, as a crisis of authority, spirit, and political models.[6] The senator argued that this "crisis of spirit" was due, at least in part, to United States foreign policy decisions in the Cold War. He strongly opposed bilateral economic and military aid to some Latin American countries based on an inescapable U.S. commitment to authoritarian regimes, jeopardizing the country's cause in the world. The senator argued that economic aid should be provided through multilateral agencies, specifically the World Bank, the Inter-American Development Bank, and the United Nations development agencies. This would allow the United States to distance itself from authoritarian regimes, favoring a new foundation for the international economic order, one capable of assessing the needs of "underdeveloped" countries (Church, 1972).

Indeed, the criticism of U.S. aid programs became a common understanding in the country. After Vietnam, Henry Kissinger, as well as influential sectors of the U.S. establishment, such as the Ford Foundation, would openly criticize the technocratic formulas of international aid as structured since the end of World War II (Berman, 1983, p. 123; Dezalay and Garth, 2002). The Foreign Assistance Act of 1973 (Public Law No, p. 93–189, December 17, 1973) is exemplary in this sense. Assuming that "the conditions which shaped the United States foreign assistance program in the past have changed,"[7] the act made important modifications to the Kennedy administration's Foreign Assistance Act of 1961. The "new realities" concerning the "less developed countries" would impose a revived international assistance led by the private sector in a multilateral framework. The great concern was to combat "extreme poverty," following the emergence of the "basic needs paradigm" (Moyn, 2018, p. 120).

Such a change was followed, for instance, under Robert McNamara's direction, by the partial substitution of the U.S. government by the World Bank in international assistance – an international aid agency devoted to the "assault on poverty." In addition to the decrease in official aid, the act requested direct action by the U.S. government regarding the human rights situation in Chile,[8] which was promptly rejected by the Nixon administration. Nixon and Kissinger, in fact, would use multilateral assistance as a strategy to depoliticize aid, circumventing the restrictions imposed by the U.S. Congress on bilateral assistance to countries under dictatorships (Pereira, 2009, p. 151). In sum, amid the general crisis that had taken over from the late

1960s onward, a decisive dispute over the directions of U.S. foreign policy had begun, especially with regard to the meaning of international aid.

In 1971, the Capitol, especially through committees dedicated to assessing the country's foreign policy, which were led by Democrats Frank Church and Donald Fraser, began to underscore the need to link international aid to the human rights situation in recipient countries. Both would advocate the moralization of U.S. foreign policy, by leaning on international organizations. To this end, the Senate committees began to gather information about the situation of political prisoners in countries like Brazil through hearings and reports organized by the International Commission of Jurists and Amnesty International. In December 1974, as the cases regarding torture mounted and became widely publicized (Green, 2009; Hawkins, 2002; Cmiel, 1999), Richard Nolan and Fraser, who had held several hearings on the human rights situation in Brazil, confronted the White House demanding the suspension of U.S. military assistance to the country (Korey, 2004, p. 184). In the same vein, in July 1975, Nolan wrote to Kissinger, with a copy sent to others such as John Sparkman, chairman of the Senate Subcommittee on Foreign Affairs, to question the Secretary of State about the case of Stuart Angel Jones, who had disappeared in 1971 after being tortured and killed by the Brazilian authorities.[9]

The evolution of this broad strategy on the part of the United States Congress had an important culmination with the publication, under the direction of Donald Fraser, of the 54-page report *Human Rights in the World Community: A Call for U.S. Leadership*.[10] Prefaced by John Salzberg, former ICJ representative at the United Nations, the document was largely subsidized by the work of the International Commission of Jurists and Amnesty International (Hartmann, 2001; Korey, 2004; Meirelles, 2020). The March 27, 1974 report was a pioneering move among official sectors in the United States in favor of the adoption of legal assumptions, on the part of U.S. foreign policy, based on human rights. The document argued for the need to protect human rights through international organizations, which would lead to the creation by Fraser, in close connection with ICJ general-secretary Niall MacDermot, of the International Association of Parliamentarians for Human Rights, whose strategy focused on distributing a bulletin to parliamentarians worldwide interested in locally developing a human rights agenda.[11] At the immediate level, Fraser's report specified the need to support legislative norms linking international aid to human rights conditions in beneficiary countries.

Following the report's proposal, in that same year, the U.S. Congress approved an amendment (Section 502B) to the Foreign Assistance Act known as the Humphrey-Cranston Amendment. It imposed a ban on security assistance to countries that violated human rights, except in "extraordinary circumstances." The amendment was, however, sufficiently vague to allow the "extraordinary circumstances" to be read by the White House as U.S. strategic or security interests. Indeed, a couple of years later, Congress made a change to the section's text, making the president legally obliged to deny or restrict aid to countries that committed human rights abuses. Even then, as reported by the Lawyers Committee for Human Rights, the White House was able to circumvent the legislation on several occasions. The Ronald Reagan administration (1981–1989), for example, channeled a considerable amount of financial resources to the military in El Salvador to suppress a left-wing insurgency that threatened the country's dictatorship (Apodaca, 2005). In the same vein as Humphrey-Cranston's effort, a new legislative amendment (Section 116), the 1975 Harkin Amendment, linked economic assistance to the relationship of foreign governments with human rights, unless it was directed to the "poor and needy." As with Section 502B, the Harkin Amendment was also vague, allowing aid to be granted without the necessary link to human rights (Apodaca, 2005; Korey, 2004).[12]

Evidencing the disputes concerning humanitarianism and human rights in U.S. foreign policy, Kissinger stressed the positions that he would support for the following years, under the Nixon and Gerald Ford administrations. He warned about the "dangers" of making the domestic policy of foreign countries a direct objective of U.S. foreign policy, stating furthermore that the human rights issue was a sensitive subject for each nation's jurisdiction that the United States should not primarily address. Nonetheless, shortly before receiving Nolan's letter regarding Angel's case, Kissinger, in a speech in Minneapolis, acknowledged the discomfort regarding the virtue and future directions of the country but advocated the U.S. legacy for the development and balance of the world since World War II. Human rights, he argued, should not be addressed publicly, but promoted by silent means, given the "delicacy of the problem" (Kissinger, 1975).

Indeed, the White House mobilized a lobby to circumvent, in Congress, the suspension of military aid to Brazil for the 1975 Fiscal Year. It appealed to Brazil's strategic position for hemispheric and U.S. security and the long friendship between the two countries. Furthermore, although acknowledging the denials on the part of the Brazilian authorities for human rights organizations to visit the country, the White House argued that there was no knowledge of any situation in Brazil that would warrant the suspension of military aid (despite the diplomatic exchanges between the U.S. Embassy in Brazil and the State Department, which reported, for instance, the cases of torture and "disappearance" of Stuart Angel, Ana Rosa Kucinski, and Paulo Stuart Wright).[13] In sum, Nixon and Kissinger had constructed a foreign policy agenda to serve national interests, while maintaining basic stability in the international order (Cmiel, 1999, p. 1238–1239). Nonetheless, the White House experienced some embarrassment regarding its relation to dictatorships in Latin America. "As the 1970s progressed," historian Daniel Sargent argues, "the challenge of transnational politics would increasingly take the form of mobilization for human rights, challenging policymakers to accommodate human rights in foreign policy" (2015, p. 95). Under pressure from Congress, in 1975, Kissinger would thus be forced to create a Bureau of

Human Rights within the State Department that would be responsible for, among other things, the official monitoring of human rights around the world (Moyn, 2010, p. 151).

In addition to the U.S. Senate, in a parallel process, U.S. intellectuals were mobilizing resources to acknowledge the crisis of U.S. foreign policy and the quest for its legitimacy. The aforementioned rupture in the Council on Foreign Relations was a pivotal sign of such a deterioration. One of the major efforts aimed at such a reformulation took shape with the creation of *Foreign Policy* magazine, in 1970, by Richard Falk, Zbigniew Brzezinski, Joseph Nye, and Samuel Huntington. Seeking to create a forum for discussing the renewal of the U.S. foreign policy orientation (Ehrman, 1993, chapter 1), these intellectuals ended up becoming the "new Foreign Policy Establishment" (Mello, 2017; Vaïsse, 2018). Reflecting such concerns, half of the articles in each issue of *Foreign Policy* issue were reserved for analyzing the themes of the new era (economic interdependence, reforms in bureaucracy, changes in security policy, policy reviews for the Third World). In sum, an important point of analysis stood out as a common concern with the mobilization by Fraser and Church: the disagreement between the conduction of foreign policy and the democratic and humanitarian principles that would be at the foundation and development of U.S. history (Mello, 2022).

In this process, the trajectory of Zbigniew Brzezinski, a Polish exile and professor at the University of Columbia, clearly demonstrates the changing patterns of intellectual thinking about U.S. foreign policy. By the late 1960s, one of the most prestigious magazines of the Congress for Cultural Freedom, *Encounter*, published *America in the Technetronic Age: New questions of our time* (1968). In the article, later expanded in the very well received *Between Two Ages: America's Role in the Technetronic Era* (1970), Brzezinski demonstrated, in openly visionary analysis, awareness of the effects of the post-industrial era in the United States, the growing role of anti-U.S. sentiments in international relations, and Third World and Latin American neutralities and nationalisms. He considered the challenges posed, in the 1960s, to international stability by the mounting number of decolonized nations, which led to a new balance of power at the United Nations and, subsequently, to pressure on "industrialized democracies" (Renouard, 2008, p. 64; Moyn, 2018, p. 109). As previously mentioned, the Global South was on the move: in 1968, 77 southern countries came together, at the second United Nations Conference on Trade and Development (UNCTAD), to form within the UN a majority bloc (G-77) with a set of proposals "for reforms to the structure, governance, and norms of the global economy designed to improve the relative position of the so-called developing states" (Gilman, 2015, p. 3).

In *Between Two Ages,* Brzezinski argued, in line with the "new Foreign Policy Establishment" (Vaïsse, 2018), that the basis of international relations no longer relied on the ideological confrontation between East and West, but rather between North and South. Furthermore, he observed the criticisms, in the United States and abroad, of the immorality of the country's activism in the world, in particular the intervention in Vietnam. The Polish professor understood that those were the direct effects of three decades of liberal hegemony in U.S. politics while formidable scientific and technological progress was taking place and becoming the decisive aspect in modern societies. This evolution brought about a structural transformation of the country's culture, with intense psychological effects such as depersonalization and loss of meaning, that ultimately undermined the foundations of national reconciliation (1970, p. 10–14).

Devoted to reframing the governance system, by giving a new form to community cohesion in the United States and from there to the world, Brzezinski, a specialist in the Communist Bloc and Eastern Europe, worried about a growing concern of the period: the mounting material gap between the North and the South, putting the latter "at risk of being left behind by the revolutionary wave, and of remaining unstable" (Moyn, 2018, p. 114). Therefore, Brzezinski advocated the creation of a community of developed countries, involving Western Europe and Japan, acknowledging the leading role the United States should play in it – the country occupied a privileged position in the *technetronic* process in comparison to Europe and the "petrified" USSR (Vaïsse, 2018, p. 160). In other words, the United States would be the only nation capable of leading a necessary effort to absorb and translate scientific and technological advances into new forms of socio-political cohesion and legitimate governance. In doing so, the political scientist repositioned the leading role of the United States in global affairs not so much as a military superpower but rather as a democratic and refined model of social justice in this post-industrial era. The world system he envisioned would come from a new form of exercising democracy supported by the technological approximation and coordination among the various social levels, including the lowest levels of government and society, and also between private and state entities (1970, p. 263). Brzezinski was concerned with social fragmentation, given the lack of political participation among a broad set of social groups. The technologies could, in this regard, offer new possibilities for social inclusion and political participation (Brzezinski, 1970; Mello, 2022).

Brzezinski's positions concerning the creation of the community of developed nations would mature, especially after his stay in Japan between January and June of 1971, to the proposal of a private initiative: the Trilateral Commission. He suggested the idea to David Rockefeller in the spring of 1972. In July of the following year, the commission was founded, in Brzezinski's understanding, to bring together the U.S.-Western Europe-Japan, since they were facing similar challenges, including those concerning postindustrial society, environmental degradation, and security issues (Vaïsse, 2018, p. 167). More explicitly, the objective was to conduct modest reforms, restoring the hegemonic status of the Global North (especially, the United States) in the international system. Throughout the 1970s, the Trilateral Commission tried not only to acknowledge the crisis in the international order but also to reframe it for the post-industrial society. Indeed, the economic, intellectual, and political elites gathered in the Trilateral Commission tried to contain the growing protests and demands from the Global South (which were gaining terrain among U.S. liberals) with the New International Economic Order, reframing them to shape a new global order (Mello, 2022; Sargent, 2015, p. 171; Vaïsse, 2018).

Following a recommendation by Samuel Huntington in April 1973, the commission would support a report on the governability of democracies. The study was an eloquent example of the content of the concerns of elite groups in the period. The *Crisis of Democracy*, written by Michel Crozier, Huntington, and Joji Watanuki, was published in 1975. The report was based on assumptions of the risks of political "regression" in "industrial democracies" in the face of the "collapse" of traditional institutions – such as the school, the Church, the army, political representation, or government coalitions. The political turmoil of those times, the report stated, concerned the collapse of the structure of governmental authority and social cohesion, something similar to Brzezinski's reflection in *Between Two Ages*. Referring to political "regression," they argue that the menace to the global order was expressed not by right-wing forces, but rather by the Left, particularly in communist parties, since they would offer a sense of political authority.

> The communist parties have emerged more and more as the parties of order, whose leaders are the only ones able to make people work, and there has always been a very strong tendency to develop state socialism and public bureaucracy interference as the easy solution to manage the impossible, that is, to maintain order in the face of unmanageable conflicts [… .] their unique superiority is their organizational one. They are the only institutions left in Western Europe where authority is not questioned, where a primitive but very efficient chain of command can manipulate a docile workforce, where there is a capacity to take hard decisions and adjust quickly, and where goods can be delivered and delays respected.
>
> (Crozier, Huntington, and Watanuki, 1975, p. 50–51)

As Brzezinski himself had been arguing since the late 1960s, the Global North should propose a new moral foundation to the local and international helm, one capable of repositioning the legitimacy of the government and of the global system. Arguing against the New Left's criticism of conventional society and traditional values (O'Neill, 2001), he was advocating ideas similar to those defended by jurists in Brazil, such as Wald, at the same time: a *rational humanism* – "between the irrational personalism of the 'humanists' and the impersonal rationality of the 'modernizers'":

> [F]irst, in an emerging international consciousness that makes so many Americans and American institutions go beyond purely nationalistic

> concerns and become deeply involved in global problems of human growth and nourishment, and is prompting in American youth such a constructive preoccupation with problems of ecology; second, in a growing tendency — in spite of a still deeply ingrained anti-communism — to view international problems as human issues and not as political confrontations between good and evil; third, in a strong public idealism that is free of a Utopian, impatient, and often intolerant desire to resolve all outstanding dilemmas immediately. In addition, it can also be seen in the fact that Americans, instead of trying to flee the problems of science, are attempting to balance their fascination with science and their reliance on it as a tool for dealing with human problems by a more intense concern with the personal qualities of life and by a quest for a more philosophical and religiously ecumenical definition of human nature.
>
> (Brzezinski, 1970, p. 272)

NGOs, the Church, and the Ford Foundation: making sense of a new morality

International organizations played a central role in both U.S. Senate disputes with the White House and the intellectual mobilization around U.S. foreign policy, especially concerning Latin America. Their transnational mobilization made them pivotal in the process of disaggregation of sovereignty as the "rising state violence, above all in Latin America, triggered an unprecedented turn to a global politics of human rights in the 1970s." Human rights, indeed, offered the fundamental language to contest the authoritarian rule in the region, thus favoring increasing contacts among people from all parts of the world and leading the way toward an interdependent era (Kelly, 2018, p. 3–4). As shown by the historian Patrick William Kelly (2018), the region, starting with Brazil in the late 1960s, was fundamental in the process, developed by local and transnational actors, of transforming the Universal Declaration of Human Rights into a global version of human rights.

Since the late 1960s, as previously mentioned, international organizations had been denouncing human rights abuses in the region. Brazilian newspapers were publicizing such accusations, which were also being ventilated by the organized opposition in Congress. Critics demanded a response from the Emílio Garrastazu Médici administration (1969–1974) with regard to human rights abuses by the regime.[14] The Minister of Justice, Alfredo Buzaid, was compelled to respond to the so-called international campaign against the torture of political prisoners in the country. Buzaid, who denied the existence of torture in the country, systematized a response to these accusations, which according to him were mobilized by "elements" linked to or influenced by communism in Brazil and abroad. The "communists" to which the Minister of Justice referred were the former-Soviet front International Association of Democratic Lawyers and the liberal-moderate International Secretariat of the Catholic Lawyers, Amnesty International, the International Federation for

Human Rights, and the International Commission of Jurists. Buzaid referred to these interconnections in a book called *Livro da verdade* (*Book of Truth*), a response to the *Livre Noir – Terreur et torture au Brésil*, written by Michel de Certeau and published on November 15, 1969. Buzaid's book ultimately was not published by the Médici administration.[15]

The following year, at the initiative of the World Council of Churches, later centralized by the International Commission of Jurists, human rights organizations addressed the Brazilian case to the United Nations Human Rights Commission. The International Commission of Jurists had been gathering information since 1964, when it published an article criticizing the coup in Brazil.[16] In circulation since the mid-1970s, the report submitted to the United Nations gave substance to an appeal written to President Médici by the ICJ Secretary-General, Niall MacDermot, and signed by more than a dozen organizations. The appeal reviewed the human rights situation in the country and directly asked the Brazilian Chief Executive to take action in this regard.[17] In the summer of 1970, the International Commission of Jurists publicized the report presenting cases of police repression and torture of political prisoners in Brazil. The case rapidly gained international repercussion.

> **World Jurists' Group Accuses Brazil of 'Systematic' Torture (special for the *New York Times*) – GENEVA, July 22, 1970** – The International Commission of Jurists today accused Brazil's military regime of making a "Systematic and scientifically developed practice" of Torture. "Torture today in Brazil is no longer a mere aid of judicial interrogation," the Geneva-based private agency said in a nine-page report. "It has become a political weapon." Supported by lawyers and jurists in most of the non-Communist countries, the commission has consultative status with the United Nations Economic and Social Council and the 18-nation Council of Europe. Sean MacBride, former Irish Foreign Minister, is the corn mission's secretary-general.
>
> **Documents Are Cited**
>
> The commission said its report was based on documents secretly removed from Brazilian prisons and concentration camps, documents and statements from former political prisoners who either escaped or were in exile, Wand other material gathered by persons who visited Brazil up to as recently as last month. According to the commission, the tortures include the plunging of a prisoner's head into a bucket filled with dirty water or excrement until near suffocation and electric shocks and blows on sensitive parts of the body. Continue reading the main story: The commission said that the spreading use of torture "corrupts Brazilian society." "There is little hope," it commented. "of ameliorating the repression in view of

> the ever-increasing number of civil servants and military officers who have incriminated themselves by torturing their fellow citizens." But the commission said that by continuing to draw attention to, the situation public opinion in civilized countries had a "very real chance of putting a stop to the inhuman practices suffered by so many men and women in Brazil:"
>
> **No Comment in Brazil (Special to New York Times)**
>
> RIO DE JANEIRO, July – Brazilian officials had no comment today on the accusations by the International Commission of Jurists. The military Government, headed by Gen. Emilio G. Medici, has only commented publicly once on reports that torture has become a frequent method of interrogating suspects in the campaign against left-wing terrorists. Last May 8, an unsigned, statement issued by the Presidential Palace said, "There is no torture in our prisons."[18]

A common strategy in the work of non-state organizations, this type of mobilization became a means through which they attempted "to lift the veil of state sovereignty through on-the-ground investigative missions and public denunciations of internal state policies" (Kelly, 2018, p. 5). In a sense, they were intensifying or modifying their previous scope. For instance, the most famous of them, Amnesty International, which was founded in the early 1960s, launched, in December 1972, the Campaign for the Abolition of Torture, greatly due to cases in Brazil (Meirelles, 2020). Amnesty would also introduce "Urgent Action," a strategy developed in immediate response to the case of political imprisonment of Brazilian Professor Luiz Basílio Rossi (Kelly, 2018, p. 21–22). Similarly, by the mid-1960s, the World Council of Churches shifted the "North-South balance within the organization," expanding its reach in the South and addressing regional problems (Christian, Kott, and Matějka, 2017, p. 54–55). After the coup in Chile, in 1973, the WCC created the Chile Emergence Desk, to acknowledge the refugee crisis, and soon afterward, the Human Rights Resources Office for Latin America (Kelly, 2018, p. 67).

The International Commission of Jurists, as previously discussed, is exemplary in this changing pattern of the role of NGOs in international affairs. First, throughout the 1950s, the commission mobilized jurists to define a broad concept of the rule of law. It redefined the orthodox separation of powers to allow normative functions for the executive branch, however maintaining an anti-totalitarian presupposition for the legal order. Furthermore, the commission, following a State Department inclination, avoided any pressure on the United Nation to transform such a conceptualization into international law agreements (Tolley, 1994, p. 50). Following *The New York Times* revelations in the mid-1960s of CIA involvement with international organizations, such as with the commission and the Congress for Cultural

Freedom, the ICJ returned to its early activities in East Germany. Such a reevaluation, by which the commission moved away from the assumptions of modernization theories concerning the law in favor of human rights, was a clear sign of the deterioration of the liberal consensus. After the *Times* disclosure, the commission entered a period of financial turmoil with the termination of the CIA's share of 97% of its resources (Tolley, 1994, p. 126).[19] The Ford Foundation came to the rescue, followed, after a couple of years, by governments in Europe and the United States (Cattai, 2016).[20] In sum, it resumed the condemnation of the "system of injustice" perpetrated by dictatorships, but then, included right-wing regimes such as the Brazilian dictatorship. The ICJ took notice, particularly, on political prisoners.

Indeed, following the "on-the-ground investigative missions and public denunciations" strategy, the commission, also in the late 1960s, sent as its representative the prominent Argentine jurist Sebastian Soler to Brazil to accompany the "political trial" of Niomar Moniz Sodré Bittencourt, president of the newspaper *Correio da Manhã*.[21] By the same token, a few years later, in March 1975, the criminalist and vice president of the Brazilian Bar Association (OAB), Heleno Claudio Fragoso – who defended Niomar Bittencourt in court – was sent to Buenos Aires[22] to examine the situation of defense lawyers of political prisoners in the country. In the Argentine capital, Fragoso gathered material, through interviews with local authorities and the collection of legislative information, to compose a report on the topic. Back in Brazil, still in March, Fragoso sent the report on human rights violations by the Argentine dictatorship to the ICJ headquarters in Geneva. On June 2, given the evasive responses by the Casa Rosada on the matter, the International Commission of Jurists made the document public.[23] In sum, as the vacillating Argentinian and Brazilian governments' reactions demonstrate, the human rights mobilization in Latin America was an increasingly sensitive matter for the dictatorships.

In this struggle against authoritarian rule, international organizations in Brazil would find a partnership with a renewed Roman Catholic Church, particularly through the establishment of a transnational network to protect political opponents of the dictatorship and to denounce the use of torture by the regime (Cruz, 1999). Since the early 1960s, social misery and famine – in sum, the "underprivileged" – were becoming a structural concern in the most profound reform of the Catholic Church in a long time. The Second Vatican Council (1962–1965) and John XXIII's Encyclical *Pacem in Terris* paved the way for this reorganization. The 1963 Encyclical harbored human rights as an expression of the common good, informing the Church's role in the world. In the same vein, in 1967, under Pope Paul VI, the Church issued *Popolorum Progressio*, pushing "Christian social thought for a newly global age" (Moyn, 2018, p. 114). After these movements, the II General Assembly of Latin American Episcopal Council took place in Medellín, Colombia, in 1968. The bishops drafted a declaration calling for social justice and condemning underdevelopment and violence in Latin American countries. The declaration laid the foundation for liberation theology and the progressive Church in the region, in direct opposition to the dictatorships (Serbin, 2000, p. 115).

As a consequence of the Vatican Council, the Church created the Pontifical Justice and Peace Commissions, a fundamental network of organizations in this struggle. The Brazilian subsection was created under the direction, first, of Alceu Amoroso Lima and, later, by jurist and political scientist Candido Mendes de Almeida. It brought together secular intellectuals, such as Mendes, Hélio Jaguaribe, Paul Singer, Dalmo de Abreu Dallari, and members of the clergy to discuss political and social issues regarding Brazil. Moreover, the section organized a network of institutions and people, including exiles, to protect human rights activities in the country, including through coordination with members of the International Commission of Jurists, such as Fragoso and Dallari (Cruz, 1999; Teles, 2010).[24]

This process marks, thus, the growing commitment by the Catholic Church to human rights and increasing detachment from the dictatorship. Indeed, after supporting the 1964 coup (Mainwaring, 1986, p. 80), the Church had been moving quickly since the early 1960s to this renewed version of "social justice," a move closely linked to a general criticism of technocratic amorality made by international intellectuals, such as Aron and Toynbee, and by Brazilian legal thought. By 1973, human rights had definitely entered the Brazilian Church's lexicon, including by approximating the Universal Declaration of Human Rights with the Bible (Kelly, 2018, p. 43). Greatly discussed by U.S. government officials in Brazil throughout those years,[25] the crisis led to the establishment, between 1970 and 1974, of the Bipartite Commission, a secret channel of dialogues between the Church and the government to diminish the confrontation. At those meetings, the military tried to circumvent any "subversive" interpretation of the 1968 Medellin declaration and to reconcile the Church's social doctrine with the Médici government plan (Serbin, 2000, p. 115). Nonetheless, more profoundly, the dialogues tried to set in motion a debate on a new and modern version, as advocated by Candido Mendes, who was responsible for intermediating these dialogues, of the moral concordat that had been operative in Brazil since 1930 (Serbin, 2000). In a way, those meetings and other dialogues, well established by the literature, among lawyers, activists, members of the clergy, politicians, and social scientists were constitutive of the general push, under the sign of humanism or human rights sentiments, toward a broad institutional renewal and regime reorganization in the 1970s.

It was precisely the renewal of the moral concordat that Sean MacBride, at the time Secretary-General of the International Commission of Jurists, defended at the meeting of the Peace Committee of the Pontifical Justice and Peace Commission in Rome, in March 1970. Stressing the need for humanitarianism, or a new moral foundation for the global order, he stated that, since 1950, "the world has witnessed a revolution of unprecedented dimension which has affected all areas of human activity and will have immense repercussions on the future of mankind." MacBride argued, in the same vein as Toynbee was doing at the same time, that scientific development was leading humankind to completely dominate the world, having "broking the frontiers to thought and ideologies and increased contacts between peoples." However, "it is increasingly evident," he said, "that our age shows an enormous disparity between the growth course of technological achievement on the one hand and of ethical behavior on the other." He further advocated for a new and coordinated conduct of world affairs by governments, fostering "man's achievements for the good" of society and its responsibility to find "an alternative to force and arbitrariness":

> The Churches, as spiritual leaders, must also play their part, and indeed are in a very strong position to do so. It is they who can report individual responsibilities and duties to the duties and responsibilities of society as a whole. It is they who can show that right and wrong are not merely yardsticks for individual behavior, but also for collective behavior, and that charity and tolerance are not only virtues but are also social duties. The Churches must accept the challenge of effectively advancing the cause of peace by assuming a leadership which looks at the problems facing the world from the point of view of the collective as well as the individual conscience.[26]

The moral concordat debate was thus part of a broad search by the elites for a new political consensus, a moral foundation for a renewed global order. This was a common concern in the Brazilian transition process from within: along with a new generation of lawyers trained by NGOs and devoted to human rights (Dezalay and Garth, 2002), the Church, as the bipartite shows, took a side in the discussion on political opening and the construction of a new governance structure in Brazil.

As part of this process, the Ford Foundation was also echoing the quest for a new morality detached from the welfare state and techno-bureaucratic assumptions. Despite having intervened in favor of the International Commission of Jurists after the CIA crises, the foundation would only significantly transform its activities regarding human rights after the overthrow of the Allende government in September 1973. Indeed, the military coup in Chile, followed by the violence and persecution of intellectuals in the country, was a key point for the Ford Foundation's human rights policies (Korey, 2007, chapter 2). On a more immediate level, the foundation offered resources to reallocate these elites to research centers in Latin America and, through grants, to universities in the United States and Europe. In addition, the Ford Foundation kept funding the Catholic University for four years after the coup (Parmar, 2012, p. 232). This process involved the professionalization of human rights as part of the broader framework of elite knowledge networks concerned with the promotion of democracy (Guilhot, 2005). In October 1973, the board of trustees approved a special budget to help persecuted intellectuals in Chile and the Soviet Union: for Latin America, grants were approved for the Latin American Council of Social Sciences and the Emergency Committee to Aid Latin American Scholars.[27]

In March 1974, Kalman Silvert, the social sciences advisor to the Ford Foundation's Latin America and Caribbean Office, wrote to William Carmichael, the head of the regional office, to discuss Chile's political situation and the foundation's prospects for action. Silvert confirmed the deterioration of the policy and the state of violence and arbitrariness that had become widespread in the country, concluding that the Chilean case was insoluble (Parmar, 2012, p. 224–225).[28] The report, indeed, did not offer an action strategy, merely exposing the complicated position in which the organization found itself. Earlier that month, David Heaps, a foundation program officer based in Paris, had traveled to Geneva to discuss the situation of political prisoners around the world with the International Committee of the Red Cross. In July, Heaps sent David Bell a preliminary report on what the future of the foundation's programs should be, largely subsidized by the information he had collected with the Red Cross. Indeed, in the *1980 Budget*, Heaps made a clear call for a "radical" change in the Ford Foundation's programs from economic development to human rights, believing, however, that this was not an easy case.[29] He would, however, find an ally in James Gardner, at the time head of the Rio de Janeiro office. Gardner was also eager to change the technical approach to legal reform, aiming at the *law and social change* program and human rights. Heaps touched on the right questions, Gardner believed, warning, moreover, that human rights had become an irresistible force and that official U.S. foreign policy could not escape from addressing it (Korey, 2007, p. 38). Indeed, as previously mentioned, the Senate hearings on human rights abuses and the role played by international organizations was a major movement at the time. Heaps' argument made its way within the Ford Foundation.

In the wake of a visit by Ford Foundation Vice President David Bell to Latin America, where he learned of the central importance in Chile of organizations such as Amnesty International and the International Commission of Jurists, the New York office asked Heaps to produce a new document expanding his 1974 report. It was aiming at the 1975 end-of-year meeting of the board of trustees and the Ford Foundation's allocation of resources. In August 1975, Heaps finished his new and long *Draft Report on Human Rights*. In the document, the Ford Foundation employee argued that the structural commitment of the foundation's activities had hitherto been based on social welfare on two fronts: improving economic conditions and strengthening national institutions. Therefore, there was no "systematic and substantial concern with what is now an epiphenomenon of our times – the insistent abuses of human rights by official arbitrary actions."[30] In this sense, Heaps defended an understanding of human rights concerning political prisoners, making a description of NGOs, such as the ICJ, focused on this legal activism.

David Bell took with some discontent Heaps' argument that there was no concern for human rights in the Ford Foundation's previous activities. For the director of the international division, the foundation could help political prisoners but the central focus of its activities should rest on issues such as freedom of thought and expression, with which it had been involved since the beginning of its activities.[31] In response, another important Ford Foundation staff member, Francis X. Sutton, produced, in November, a new report: *Human Rights and Intellectual Freedom*. Sutton absorbed Bell's concerns about freedom of thought, which involved the organization's important activities with the communist world in Eastern Europe (Korey, 2007). Sutton, however, had also welcomed part of Heaps' report, in particular, the discussions on the international human rights organizations with which the foundation could strategically come to work.[32] The effort took effect: the board of trustees approved a budget of approximately 500 thousand dollars for programs, through international organizations working in Latin America, focused on human rights and programs aimed at freedom of expression in Eastern Europe.

In sum, the Ford Foundation was distancing itself from programs aimed at developing public administration and a technical side to legal practice throughout the Global South in favor of a new moral basis in accordance with the title of a foundation memo written in December 1976, by James Gardner, which had become central to the foundation's grant policy: *Human Rights and Social Justice. A Question of Values*. The idea of social justice ceased to be viewed as a direct consequence of state-led economic development, to become situated in what Gardner claimed to be the moral dimension of the institution's philanthropy: the expression of human rights, intellectual freedom, and the rule of law. Gardner, who intended to inform, with his memo, the Ford Foundation's programs for Brazil, thus advocated taking advantage of the "context of re-democratization" in the country and undertaking programs in favor of human rights and intellectual freedom, promoting the inclusion of social groups excluded from Brazilian economic modernization (women, the poor, indigenous people, and blacks, "victims of the Brazilian Miracle") in the country's political process. Gardner pointed to projects of legal assistance within a great front of social justice and participation.[33] Indeed, as asserted by Nicolas Guilhot (2005, chapter 3), these changes in financing strategies for the social sciences on the part of philanthropic foundations in the 1970s indicate their search for alternative forms of political stabilization in Latin America after the technocratic decline.

"Democratic transition": political reconciliation and the rise of the post-Social State order

In September 1969, Candido Mendes de Almeida arrived in Mexico City for a series of debates on Latin American development. Invited by the Center for the Study of Democratic Institutions,[34] the discussions relied on "the rapid evolution" of a crisis in the region and the inadequacy of United States and international aid programs for countries such as Brazil. Besides Mendes, the

Brazilian political scientist Hélio Jaguaribe,[35] the Uruguayan sociologist Aldo Solari,[36] the Belgian Jesuit Roger Vekemans,[37] and the U.S. senator Frank Church[38] also joined the discussions. The event was born out of a dialogue between William O. Douglas, the U.S. Supreme Court justice and president of the center, and the Argentinian Raul Prebisch, one of the most prestigious economists linked to the Economic Commission for Latin America and the Caribbean (ECLAC). Douglas and Prebisch centralized the debates.

The ideas discussed in Mexico City were analyzed and updated in Washington D.C., also resonating with the work of three commissions established to think about the problems and prospects for Latin America: the World Bank's Commission on International Development, chaired by former Canadian Prime Minister Lester Pearson; the Special Presidential Commission, led by New York governor Nelson Rockefeller; and the commission established by the Inter-American Development Bank, chaired by Prebisch. The debates resulted in the 1972 publication of the book *One Spark from Holocaust: The Crisis in Latin America*. Divided into four major themes, each title advanced the tensions that it was meant to address:

I The Tinderbox of Revolution: Political Instability;
II The Latent heat of Revolution: Social Fragmentation;
III The Fuel of Revolution: Economic Inequality;
IV The Winds of Revolution: International Dereliction.

Mendes had his participation published in Section IV, in which the need to improve and renew international aid policies – fundamentally from the United States – for the region was debated. Entitled *The Potential and the Promise: A Challenge to the Intelligentsia*, Candido Mendes' presentation discussed the gap between the modernization theories (their promises, in a broad sense, of democratization and social welfare) developed in Latin America in the aftermath of World War II, and the reality of the region. For Mendes, such theories were, at that moment, an expression of a "tired" ideology that was unable to offer a credible development program for Latin American (and Third World) countries, unlike, for example, the forces of nationalism, which were still an amalgam in the present and future projections of these countries. Thus, such an intellectual vision would not have been successful in "integrating the paradoxical objectives of self-determination and nationalism, on the one hand, and collective identity and international social change, on the other." Furthermore:

> When the possibilities of import substitution became exhausted and social change lost its spontaneity, the evaluation and comprehension of change did not undergo an accompanying immanent modification. It is not surprising, then, that the economists have become amateur political scientists, that the political aspects of change have become more prominent in order to compensate for the congealing of the economic

polemic, and that politics has been seen as a field for reconstituting the laws of change.

(Mendes, 1972, p. 172)

The political scientist's assessment was, therefore, that the political opening agenda (the re-establishment of individual rights and freedoms) had not been carried out as he had prescribed, three years earlier, in an article published by the *Dados* journal. Analyzing the authoritarian rule in Brazil, in 1966, Mendes, who like other important political actors and legal elites in the country was at the time enjoying a "good understanding" with the dictatorship,[39] saw the regime as "committed to a reformist view of reality, intending to gradually change the 'status quo,' especially by eliminating, at the institutional level, vestiges of political power inherited from obsolete structures that no longer had any significance in the economic field" (Mendes, 1966, p. 8). In this sense, the regime would be undertaking, despite the need for temporary authoritarian solutions, the *transition* from underdevelopment to modernization as intellectuals such as Mendes and Hélio Jaguaribe had been advocating before the coup (Chaves and Cattai, 2019, p. 213). In his 1966 analysis, Mendes defended the regime's adoption of the Institutional Acts as a model capable of providing the conditions for economic planning and the overcoming of "archaic" political behavior – on the part of "idle resource holders" and "parasitic groups." Expressing the technocratic character that started to rule the institutional state relations in the country after the 1964 coup, the acts constituted the fundamental support to a gradual and transitional process. "It is easy to understand," Mendes argued, "in the general strategy of the government the inevitably temporary character of these norms and their mandatory modification after the implementation of the neo-capitalist model." After the dictatorial modernization project took effect, entering "a period of stabilization," it would be possible to gradually restore political freedoms and individual rights (Mendes, 1966, p. 8–9).

According to Mendes, however, by the end of the 1960s, the technocracy repeated, for the political and social domains, the same "apolitical" technique adopted for the economic development in the 1950s and early 1960s. In Brazil, the December 1968 Institutional Act No. 5, which hardened the political control over individual rights and freedoms in the country, would be representative of such difficulties.[40] The acts, functioning as a supra-constitutional norm, furthermore imposed imprecision in the hierarchy of the country's legal order, besides prompting criticism in the national legal debate. To solve the issue, the Institutional Acts were incorporated into the Brazilian legal order, first with a new Constitution, in 1967, and later with Constitutional Amendment No. 1, promulgated in October 1969 – shortly after Institutional Act No. 17, the last act decreed by the Costa e Silva administration (1967–1969). Yet AI-5 was maintained, lasting until the 1978 Constitutional Amendment No. 11. For Mendes, contemporary efforts in countries under dictatorships of "re-democratization," to use his words, had been operating in a kind of vacuum that was distant and unfamiliar to the political reality. He indicated the need for a new consensus of political groups in favor of new standards for economic development and social change (Mendes, 1972; 1977). As mentioned in Chapter 4, the modernization of the Brazilian Congress should be one of the major *loci* of such a political renovation.

Mendes was not alone. His growing commitment to a renewal of the intelligentsia's political action, capable of carrying out the political opening agenda, had been a common and transnational concern since the mid-1960s. Indeed, there was a sustained effort to transform political science into an autonomous field of knowledge, one capable, by incorporating U.S. models of analysis, of producing diagnoses and government rationality regarding *political development*. As asserted by Nicholas Guilhot (2005, p. 129), this effort led, in the aforementioned elite knowledge network, to the rise of analyses based on the internal developments of dictatorial regimes and the possibilities of unfolding democracy from within "the inner circles of the authoritarian state." In a general sense, authoritarianism, the failure of the assumptions that the development of democracy would be a natural consequence of economic progress, the rise to power of the military in Latin America and in some parts of Europe, in sum, all of modernization theory's assumptions concerning social change could no longer answer, as advocated by these transnational intellectuals, to the new historical reality that arose in the 1960s (Forjaz, 1997, p. 8; Amorim, 2021). Mendes himself was one of the chief promoters of this new, comparative research agenda. Based on analyses of different juridical and political systems, social scientists devoted themselves to identify the "archaic" elements of Brazilian culture. Such identification would allow rational political planning and institutional intervention capable of solving the "non-modern" traces in the country's political life (Chaves and Cattai, 2019, p. 210–211).

Here, once again, the Ford Foundation played a vital role. In 1967, the foundation restructured its investments orientation for Brazil, specifically for Rio de Janeiro, seeking to better organize training in sociology, political science, and anthropology, and to decisively bring economics, administration, and law closer to the social sciences (Chaves and Cattai, 2019). It was in this process that Toynbee and other intellectuals came to Brazil under the Ford Foundation's patronage. In May, the assistant of the foundation's Latin America and Caribbean Division, Peter Bell, informed the director of its office in Brazil, Stacey H. Widdicombe, that this orientation should start with the University Research Institute of Rio de Janeiro (IUPERJ) and follow the model of the Political Science Department at the Federal University of Minas Gerais (UFMG). The leadership of those two institutions was given, respectively, to Wanderley Guilherme dos Santos and Fábio Wanderley Reis (Forjaz, 1997; Freidenberg and Malamud, 2013).

From the IUPERJ, the Ford Foundation intended to reach the various disciplines and their representatives in Rio de Janeiro: the School of Economics, Sociology, and Politics at PUC-Rio; the National Museum and the Institute of Philosophy and Social Sciences (IFCS) of the National School of Philosophy (FNFi) at the University of Brazil; the Institute of Public Law and Political Science (IDPCP); the FGV's Brazilian School of Public Administration (EBAP); and the University of Guanabara-FGV's Center for Studies and Research in the Teaching of Law (CEPED).[41] A similar effort would be developed in Chile a few years later. There, social scientists were changing their research approach not only to adapt to the international donors' inclinations to empirical and applied studies but also to face the failure of their previous assumptions, "the trauma occasioned by the breakdown of democracy and the repression of military rule" (Puryear, 1994, p. 53).

By the same token, in a 1965 general report[42] evaluating the Ford Foundation's aims regarding its social science programs in Latin America, Reynold E. Carlson, a professor of economics at Vanderbilt and John Hopkins universities, argued that social development was the new frontier, "constituting the increasing integration and participation of all classes in national life" (Parmar, 2012, p. 226–227). Commenting on the passage from "agrarian, hierarchical, oligarchic, and paternalistic societies" to "urban, industrial, contractual, and, hopefully, democratic" societies in Latin America, Carlson reflect how the foundation could help this "transition" process: how the process could develop in an "orderly and evolutionary" way, with appropriate flexibility to "accommodate the stresses and strains being generated" (Parmar, 2012, p. 227). Following the same steps that Candido Mendes would take, he further argued that "transitions generate 'tensions points' that, unless 'identified at an early stage [...] will be compounded, generate heat and create situations which cannot be resolved within the existing political and legal institutions.'" The Ford Foundation, through the social sciences, should "identify," "isolate," and "alleviate" the tensions developed from the rapid modernization process (Parmar, 2012, p. 227).

Following such an understanding, in 1966, the Brazilian Association of Political Science was created under the leadership of Themístocles Cavalcanti and other key figures of the FGV's Institute of Public Law and Political Science, such as Armando de Oliveira Marinho and Wanderley Guilherme dos Santos (IDPCP, 1966). The IDPCP, as a result, no longer played the role of the Brazilian headquarters of the International Political Science Association (IPSA). As a whole, it was an ambitious reorientation, aiming, along with Brazilian federal agencies, such as the Coordination for the Improvement of Higher Education Personnel (CAPES), to train new elites capable of diagnosing *political change* under the mantle of "democratization," "decompression," "distension," and "transition" (Chaves and Cattai, 2019, p. 209–210).

It is worth noting the changing editorial inclination of the IDPCP's main publication in this process. At its birth, in the late 1950s, the *Revista de Direito Público e Ciência Política*, among political science tendencies toward international relations and administration, was approximated to public law. It thus reflected the search to create state capacities and methods for conducting the national modernization effort, particularly focused on the state's role in "correcting" political behavior in Brazil. In 1967, reflecting the broad exhaustion of modernization theories, the publication had its name changed to *Revista de Ciência Politica* [Political Science Journal]. By determination of the FGV's executive committee, it excluded the "public law" dimension to focus on debates and the development of research in political science. Indeed, this changing editorial inclination accompanied a renewal and expansion process on the part of the IDPCP, which was renamed INDIPO: starting in 1964, it assumed the common gospel of the 1960s regarding the autonomy of the political phenomena with regard to public law (*Revista de Ciência Política*, 1967).

Based on the gradualist and transitional assumptions concerning political development, Brazilian political science turned to studies of *institutions* and political models, greatly influenced by the research agenda of the Harvard professor Samuel Huntington. One of the main representatives of U.S. conservative thought, Huntington, since *The Soldier and The State* (1957), did not assume, as the major modernization theorists did, that economic growth would inevitably develop into democratic political behavior and institutions. In other words, Huntington did not agree with the *Vital Center*'s precepts that economic growth would lead to a social foundation based on political moderation and democratic values. As previously mentioned, by the late 1950s, such an understanding – the need for an "learned" elite (the military) to lead the modernization process – was gaining terrain among modernization theorists, especially under the mantle of the Rand Corporation (Gilman, 2003, p. 185; Besnner, 2019). Yet, despite such consideration, Huntington seemed to go further in his prospective analyses, also championing the coups as a modernization and westernization effort in the Global South (Huntington, 1962, p. 23).

He understood economic progress as a disruptive phenomenon, responsible for the emergence of new social groups and the advent of political conflicts, since their social differentiation would be politically underrepresented (Huntington, 1962). In sum, the rapid economic growth that was taking place in Latin American countries would put pressure on the stability and legitimacy of political regimes. According to the Harvard professor, to *safely* carry out modernization in societies unfamiliarized with democratic values or freedom, there must be a governance structure capable of guaranteeing political stability and security. He therefore advocated a political model based on "transition": to avoid disruption in those modernizing societies, it would be necessary to "compress" political liberties, which, after the stabilization of the reformist program, should be followed by a political "decompression," the institutionalization of the political process by gradually adding new social actors in the governance spectrum (Cancelli, 2017). It was the formula advocated by Candido Mendes.

Huntington's analysis of political development would gain terrain among Brazilian scholars devoted to thinking about the evolution of authoritarian rule in the country. In October 1969, the International Political Science Association organized a roundtable on political science in Latin America, chaired by Carl Friedrich and Themístocles Cavalcanti. Samuel Huntington was among its participants. Sponsored by the Brazilian Association of Political Science, with the collaboration of the IDPCP (then INDIPO) and the IUPERJ, the event focused on the themes developed by Huntington in his works (Revista de Ciência Política, 1970; Lemos, 2014). More precisely, the discussions focused on decompression, specifically on the ideas of institutionalizing political processes and the participation of new social groups in the governance structure. Simon Schwartzman, for instance, who was working at FGV at the time, presented the paper *Abertura Política e Desenvolvimento* (*Political Opening and Development*) in which he argued that the relationship between economic development and political opening depended on the "possibilities of institutionalizing political life and, above all, maintaining it" (Cancelli, 2017, p. 115). The policies of "decompression" – the institutionalization of the political process, constituting the government's capacities and legitimacy – catalyzed ideas in Brazil by the late 1960s and throughout the 1970s as a new typology for thinking about the social reality outside the technocratic assumptions. As observed by jurist Raymundo Faoro (1973, p. 153), political science did not accept "the convertibility of technical judgment into political judgment." Political science was a vehicle for the institutional updating of the arrangements between liberals and conservatives, ensuring stability and security for the process. Moreover, it renewed an international knowledge network devoted to creating a common ground among different actors in an era of political turmoil.

The Brazilian dictatorship, gathering a wide range of political actors (Dreifuss, 1987), based its legitimacy precisely on the *transition* model. The Institutional Acts were, as the analyses by Candido Mendes show, the instruments to assure that end. Their legitimacy was founded, indeed, in the "revolutionary" character of the regime installed after the 1964 coup and their temporal effect. In legal terms, "compression" designated the formal or schematic aspect of the legal order, the security strategies with which it was possible for the state to ensure the stability, validity, and full execution of the plan stipulated in the substantial or material order, the second pillar of the legal order. Compression corresponded, therefore, to the transitory character of the security system instituted by the dictatorship, a means for the end of the modernization provided for in the legal order organized by the regime. The Institutional Acts, in this sense, operated as regulators of the intensity of safety devices and as instruments, in the case of delegation of powers, for the modernization program arranged by the formal legal order.

Nonetheless, Samuel Huntington was not only an intellectual inspiration to Brazilian political science before and after it became an autonomous field of knowledge (Amorim, 2021). Since 1965, Huntington made several visits to Brazil – the vast majority of which were mediated by Candido Mendes, with whom Huntington claimed to have a common research agenda.[43] Huntington established interaction with the Brazilian regime aimed at offering an analysis and guiding the process of "compression" and "decompression" in the country (Lemos, 2014, p. 10; Cancelli, 2017, p. 110–118).

In 1972, Médici's civilian chief of staff, João Leitão de Abreu, started internal discussions on liberalization. Candido Mendes, who advocated the important role that the opposition should play in the process, by favoring, for instance, the modernization of the legislative branch (Hoeveler, 2012), used his friendship with José Guilherme Merquior, one of the greatest Brazilian political philosophers and Leitão de Abreu's adviser, to establish contact and convince him to discuss "liberalization" with Samuel Huntington (Serbin, 2000, p. 92). In 1973, as requested by the Medici administration, Huntington wrote a memo adding "decompression" to the local lexicon and recommending: the "institutionalization of procedures for determining succession in public office"; "the broadening of participation"; and "the liberalization of existing restrictions on the political and civil rights of individuals and an open public discussion of governmental and political issues." However, the memo – *Approaches to Political Decompression* – presented the risks of accelerated processes of political openings and recommended that the regime maintain control of the process, leading it gradually.[44]

Indeed, the regime had a continuous concern with the pace of political opening. In mid-1970, for instance, U.S. embassies and consulates in Brazil made assessments to the Department of State regarding the evolution of the Medici administration's "democratic opening." On August 7, 1970, the U.S. Embassy in Rio informed of the president's "strength and consistency in holding to the schedule for the political opening to which he alluded on taking office." From the perspective of U.S. personnel in Brazil, despite not having any intention to "return to the 'chaos of the pre-Revolutionary days'" and not seeing it "fit to reestablish on any significant scale the individual rights and liberties on which the Revolution has gradually infringed," Medici had called back the Federal Congress and resumed the operation of state legislatures. In his public statements, he underlined that the development of democracy in the country should be accompanied, not only by the "rapid development" and "uprooting of subversion," but also by the "elimination of self-interest and corruption in Brazilian political life." As such, Medici had to resist pressure "from both radical authoritarians and liberal democrats."[45]

A month earlier, a U.S. Consulate in Northern Brazil sent a report to the Department of Defense stating that the Medici administration "has embarked Brazil on a course of viable Brazilian democracy." Declassified in 2015, the report, concerning "Democratic Openings," presented arguments, based on a Brazilian classified source in the military, of Medici's "recognition of the role of the political element in Brazilian society," indicating that "he was aware of the need for escape valves in contemporary societies" and that he recognized "such an outlet in responsible politics."[46] Among nine recommendations directed "to establish a solid basis for a 'decent democracy'," Medici sought the reopening of "state legislatures"; "moderation in the application of

Institutional Act No. 5 against politicians"; "an agreement by the executive branch (Justice Minister) to convene the Human Rights Commission in response to pleas by the minority party leadership"; moderation with regard to the "provocative diatribes by Bishop Helder Camara"; "firm action [...] in responding to political pressures for an investigation of the notorious vigilante-type "Death Squadrons"; and "an attempt to dignify and reinforce [...] democratic executive-legislative relationships."[47] By the same token, a few years later, in September 1973, an in-depth CIA National Intelligence Survey title *Government and Politics* discussed Medici's inclinations regarding the development of the regime's political legitimacy. As the aforementioned documents also expressed, Medici "has maintained that the process of educating the population to the point that it can handle democracy will be a lengthy one," demanding "deep changes in mentality." Nonetheless, by that time, "the administration's views on what kind of new political system might allow greater participation in decision-making remain to be defined."[48]

Such a lack of definition would come to be a major issue in Ernesto Geisel's administration (1974–1979). Indeed, the presidential election process was disputed between Geisel and the Movimento Democrático Brasileiro (Brazilian Democratic Movement) opposition party candidate, Ulysses Guimarães. Guimarães, as affirmed by the U.S. Embassy in Brazil, was an "anti-candidate" who ran an "anti-campaign," giving a meaning to the "non-event" of the election process. The campaign and Geisel's victory were furthermore followed by public apathy.[49] In other words, the political opening was an issue of government legitimacy (Napolitano, 2014, chapter 9). It was at this point that the "decompression" thesis came to be structured by Samuel Huntington. On March 19, 1974, the U.S. Embassy in Brazil reported "signs of reopening" in Brazil by the Geisel administration.

The Embassy perceived Huntington's visit to Rio, where he met with Geisel's close ally General Golbery do Couto e Silva, possibly the major military intellectual leading the transition process, as a "more durable" sign of reopening. The account stressed that the discussion, much of it public, which took place between the election of Geisel and his inauguration was about the regime's "new direction." Such a discussion, according to the Embassy's comments, followed Huntington's understanding of "political development." Indeed, "having scored unarguable successes in the economic, financial, and administrative field," as the text stressed (not without a cynical silence regarding the violence directed to left-wing opposition), "and having virtually eliminated the threat of subversion or widespread disorder, the revolution of 1964 could now turn its attention to the political sector." Although considering the political "immaturity" of Brazilians – between "unscrupulous and self-seeking politicians" and "politically unsophisticated" masses –, the authoritarian rule would lead to an effort to institutionalize the modernization process and consolidate the political legitimacy of the regime.[50]

Legal thought was part of this broad effort concerning the dictatorship's political legitimacy. As Mendes was advocating, the criticism was directed at the techno-bureaucracy gathered in the state and its absence of political values, since it did not require any legitimacy, ruling exclusively in accordance with its own political agenda. In an important article titled *Política e Tecnocracia* (*Politics and Technocracy*), published in 1969 by the *Revista de Ciência Política*, Themistocles Cavalcanti, at the time Minister of Supreme Court and very close to the dictatorship's general assumptions on modernization, argued that the danger was "the pure domain of science" in the political field, reducing the role of the human dimension in it; the danger was "the supremacy or absolute primacy of the technicians – the so-called technocracy – with the exaggerated role of technique over philosophy in political decision" (Cavalcanti, 1969, p. 5). By the same token, a few years later the journal published an article by Raymundo Faoro, one of the most vocal critics of the CEPED experience and an advocate of a formalistic view of the rule of law. The article was an archetype of the gradual reorientation of legal thought in the period.

Faoro recalled how the New Deal, in response to the 1929 crisis, had led to the development of a political model whose flourishing pointed to a "new industrial state," as indicated in the 1967 book by John K. Galbraith (2007), whom Faoro acknowledged. There were the precursors of technocracy, of the rational life as opposed to irrational market expressions. Indeed, the foundation of such an industrial state, according to Faoro, was the critique of capitalist liberalism, the imperfections of the market economy, reducing political phenomena, ultimately, to an effort of intelligent control over all human activities. In the evolution of this process, he argued, the post-World War II era would witness, throughout the industrialized world, the birth of a new Leviathan, as denounced by political scientists, sociologists, and jurists, that appeared silently and without revolutionary commotions from the interior of capitalism. Technocracy emptied democracy – the popular sovereignty. Predetermined by what would be the autonomous and dehumanizing criteria of technique, humankind would have renounced its power of choice, ceasing to be the center of all things. "The technician wants atomic energy, wants to control the universe," Faoro stated, "but he does not know why, since he, lacking a moral principle, forgot the reasons for his work" (1973, p. 162).

In sum, Raymundo Faoro, as Cavalcanti and Mendes had done at the same time, was criticizing the "technocratic hypothesis": the governance which, by absorbing the state into the technical rationale, would have destroyed economic liberalism to create legitimacy at the mercy of state dominance. They opposed the "legislative inflation" – the excessive normative production as a means to national modernization – advocated by some parts of the Brazilian legal elite, USAID personnel, and, above all, the military. Such a defense could be seen, for instance, when Alfredo Buzaid, the dictatorship's Minister of Justice and Interior Affairs, resorted to this understanding in asserting the post-coup 1964 legislative policy as a true "renewal of the country's positive order," or when the former head of the Ministry of Planning, Roberto Campos, argued that the modernization proposed by the "Revolution" required the preparation of complex legislative texts – such as the draft laws on banking, tax, agrarian, housing, and administrative reforms. Excessive normative production would thus be natural (Campos, 1994, p. 640).

Indeed, as mentioned in the previous chapters, awareness was raised, among legal elites, regarding the "teratology" of the codes, the "legislative inflation," and the "amoral Leviathan." The legislative politics of the dictatorship was, for this elite, evidence of such technocratic amoralism in the conduction of the modernization program by authoritarian rule. Discussing decompression – the quest for a new structure of political legitimacy in a post-modern society – was part of a wider effort to form a new consensus, a new set of values capable of answering the exhaustion of the politics of technocracy. Indeed, as the arguments by Faoro and Mendes show, throughout the 1960s and especially in the 1970s, the growing concern among elites was that the total capture of political phenomena by technocratic functionalism made the governing authority operate in a vacuum, incapable of (re)producing social cohesion. And this was viewed as a risk of political instability.

By this time, in the wake of James Gardner's *A Question of Values* memorandum, David Trubek, the former legal advisor to USAID and the main figure in the CEPED's program, who at the time was acting as a Ford Foundation consultant, began discussions to hold a roundtable in Brazil on public interest law and human rights. In September, 1977, after several discussions among Alberto Venâncio Filho, Raymundo Faoro, Fábio K. Comparato, Joaquim Falcão, Bolívar Lamounier, employees of the Ford Foundation in Rio, and Trubek, the roundtable was held under the auspices of the Ford Foundation and the Brazilian Bar Association, at the Rui Barbosa House Foundation.[51] Tereza Cristina A. Costa, Carlos Hesembalq, Bolívar Lamounier, Álvaro Pessoa, José Bonifácio Rodrigues, Alberto Venâncio Filho, and Gabriel Lacerda were involved as presenters, and James Gardner, David Trubek, José Maria Cabral Marques, Jorge Hilário G. Vieira, and Joaquim de Arruda Falcão Neto as special guests.[52]

These intellectuals gathered at the Rui Barbosa House, in clearest opposition to the regime, thus made the assessment, as Trubek would report to the Ford Foundation, that the modernization carried out after the 1964 coup had excluded the vast majority of the population. They observed, moreover, the climate of re-democratization in the country, led by the growing opposition by the Catholic Church and by groups and organizations of lawyers, such as the OAB and the Institute of Brazilian Lawyers (Motta, 2008), who sought to restore the rule of law and create a new constitutional order. Trubek, in this regard, made a reassessment of the CEPED's experience: the "technocratic instrumentalism" approach of the program would not have had enough sophistication and clarity to reverse the "tradition" of "patrimonialism relations" and the "authoritarian state." Otherwise, CEPED would have deepened the patrimonialism and authoritarian character of the Brazilian state.[53]

In his report, Trubek, who was quite optimistic about the roundtable, clarified that the premises of the rule of law functioned as a kind of umbrella for various social groups, since it included the defense of not only greater economic freedom for private capital but also political participation and social justice. Based on this general diagnosis of the Brazilian reality, the intellectuals gathered at the Rui Barbosa Foundation elected a "working group"[54] to establish an institute from those fundamental themes defined at the meeting. In other words, such an "interdisciplinary center," devoted to the defense of the public interest, as Trubek referred to it, should offer greater coordination to programs related to social justice, namely, research in law and social justice, social movements (such as those concerned with people of color, women, or environmental issues) and participation, individual rights, and legal services for the "underprivileged."[55] Nonetheless, "the real issues being debated," according to Trubek, "were: the rule of law; popular participation in government; individual rights, and social justice."[56] Like other Catholic universities in Latin America during the period (Parmar, 2012; Penholato, 2017), the Pontifical Catholic University of São Paulo would be a preferred institution to develop programs devoted to legal assistance to the "less-privileged."[57]

In sum, the Ford Foundation did depart from investing in the state's capabilities and methods to concentrate on political participation. More precisely, the general view, as represented at the roundtable, was the inadequacy of state-led economic development, paving the way, through human rights and social justice, for the expansion of civil society based on the role of local communities in the broadest and most general form of government. Indeed, as asserted by Stantion and Welna, in the memorial book on the Ford Foundation's 40th anniversary in Brazil, the *Government and Civil Society* program offered "practical means for communities and local-level leaders to open new lines of communication in order for the government to better serve citizens, and for citizens to work more effectively with public officials" (2002, p. 389). In a sense, the Ford Foundation was also criticizing the role of the state in political organization, echoing, like many others in the period, the importance of individual, local, and multifaceted social elements in the establishment of a new moral foundation for the post-Social State order.

By the late 1970s, Brzezinski's desire for a new political virtue, one capable of encapsulating the postindustrial society and the technetronic age, gained force when President Jimmy Carter took office (1977–1981). Carter composed his cabinet with trilateral commission members, including Brzezinski, who became National Security Adviser (Vaïsse, 2018, p. 157). Along with Secretary of State Cyrus Vance and Brzezinski, the new president would promote a new direction in U.S. foreign policy based on human rights. As such, human rights constituted the language for the renewed international alliance, compensating for the loss of the technocratic illusions at the basis of the Alliance for Progress, the War Against Poverty, and the reformism of the *Vital Center* (Dezalay and Garth, 2002, chapter 8).

Structured by the Presidential Directive on Human Rights of February 1978, that is, based on case-by-case evaluations within the context of each nation (Vinha, 2014; Hartmann, 2001), the human rights adopted by Jimmy Carter administration sought to offer a substitute ideology that had the virtue of making it possible to overcome the failure of the Vietnam War and the crisis of political legitimacy in the United States. As asserted by Samuel Moyn, human rights constituted "the move from the politics of the state to the morality of the globe" (2010, p. 43). However, it constituted a morality of the globe that, after the political disputes of the 1970s and the rise of the new Right, would come to be subject to U.S. power (Guilhot, 2005, p. 223; 2013, p. 129) and to the neoliberal politics of global order (Moyn, 2018; Whyte, 2019). With regard to the Global South, human rights allowed a counteroffensive to its demands, as U.S. foreign policy exerted pressure on countries like Brazil to conform to democratic precepts and, soon, to the "structural adjustment" proposed by the World Bank and the International Monetary Fund (Dezalay and Garth, 2002, chapter 12; Pereira, 2009, p. 175). Indeed, over the course of the 1970s, human rights were "conceptually narrowed to a few civil and political rights," and the demands for a new international economic order did not advance (Kelly, 2018, p. 7–8). Throughout the decade, the anti-Social State gospel had evolved. Decentralization, deregulation, and transnational interdependence had become the norm, leading the way to neoliberalism, a cross-border safety net of capital protection under the continued hegemony of the United States.

Notes

1 Toynbee's reflections were published, for instance, in the newspaper *Jornal do Brasil*. See, for example, "A safra do holocausto" (entrevista de Arnold Toynbee e James York). (Tradução de Hélio Pólvora), Jornal *do Brasil*, April 7, 1964. Rio de Janeiro. Cad. B, p. 4; and "Classe média perde batalha na A. Latina, diz Arnold Toynbee," *Jornal do Brasil. February 2,* 1982. Rio de Janeiro. Cad. 1. 4ª. Feira, p. 5.

2 See "Faculdade de Dereito trará intelectuais europeus para uma visita ao Brasil," *Jornal do Brasil,* January 05, 1966. Rio de Janeiro. Cad. 1, p. 14.

3 Peter D. Bell memo to Stacey H. Widdicombe, May 2, 1967, *Ford Foundation Records*. Grant Files. Reel No. 5351. RAC.

4 The book was translated into Brazilian Portuguese in 1973 by Editora Zahar. The book's second edition was published the following year, and the third edition in 1976.

5 "Crisis in South Asia." A report by Senator Edward M. Kennedy to the subcommittee to investigate problems connected with Refugees and Escapees for the Committee on the Judiciary of the United States. United States Senate. November 1, 1971. US Government Printing Office. Washington, 1971.

6 Nixon's inaugural address is available at: www.presidency.ucsb.edu/ws/?pid=1941. Accessed on: Jan. 22, 2018.

7 "Foreign Assistance Act of 1973." Public Law 93–189 (Dec. 17, 1973). The text of the law can be found at https://uscode.house.gov/statutes/pl/93/189.pdf. Accessed on: December 28, 2020.

8 Idem.

9 See *Letter from Richard Nolan, Congressman, to Henry Kissinger, Secretary of State*. July 18, 1975. Department of State. Human Rights Subject Files, 1975. Box 2, Folder Human Rights – BRAZIL. RG 59. NARA. Zuleika Jones was legally represented by the human rights lawyer and ICJ representative in Brazil Heleno Cláudio Fragoso.

10 "Human Rights in the World Community: A Call for US leadership." *Report of the Subcommittee on International Organizations and Movements of the Committee on Foreign Affairs House of Representatives*. March 27, 1974. US Government Printing Office, Washington, 1974.

11 Niall MacDermot had some expectations that the initiative with the aforementioned association could mean the germ of a new and important initiative. The complete absence, from then on, of references about the association in the documentation may indicate, however, that MacDermot's expectations were not fulfilled. Further research, especially at the ICJ's Archive in Geneva, is still to be done. See "International Commission of Jurists." From David Heaps to Francis Sutton / Craufurd Goodwin. October 17, 1974. In: Ford Foundation Records, Grants AB (FA732A). Folder: American Association for the International Commission of Jurists, Inc. (06900025). Date: October 19, 1968–June 30, 1970. Reel: 1235. RAC.

12 Department of State. Human Rights Subject Files, 1975. Box 2, Folder Halkin Amendment. RG 59. NARA.

13 See Draft Memorandum for Special Assistant to Assistant Secretary, Legislative Affairs Director, DSAA; Assistant General Counsel for International Affairs. Subject: Strategy for lobbying Against the Harrington Amendment – Cutting off the Security Assistance Program to Brazil and the House Amendment to the FAA of 1975 Cutting off MAP training to Brazil. n.d. Department of State. Human Rights Subject Files, 1975. Box 2, Folder Human Rights – BRAZIL. RG 59. NARA.

14 "Democratic Openings." Department of Defense Intelligence Information Report. July, 31, 1970. BR RJANRIO CNV.0.RCE.00092000538201527/279.

15 The Brazilian government's "Livro da Verdade" report can be found at www.scribd.com/doc/211046686/Livro-da-Verdade-do-ministro-Buzaid-pdf. Accessed on: March 26, 2018.

16 For the repercussion of ICJ mobilization against the coup in Brazil, see JURISTAS CRITICAM GOVÊRNO DO BRASIL. 1964. In *Correio da Manhã*. Cad. 1, September 8, p. 1.

17 See EPPS, Dwain C. "Study of the Situation in Brazil which reveals A Consistent Pattern of Violations of Human Rights. (Official Version). March 19, 1971" (by the World Federation of Trade Unions, Commission of the Churches on International Affairs of the WCC, ICJ). In Country Files, Brazil. Statement on Tortures. Commission of the Churches on International Affairs of the World Council of Churches, 15.3.1971; and Report of The International Commission of Jurists' Activities 1966–1971. Geneva: International Commission of Jurists, 1972.

18 "World Jurists' Group Accuses Brazil Of 'Systematic' Torture," *The New York Times*, July 23, 1970.

19 The money was channeled by the CIA through Delaware's American Fund for Free Jurists.

20 The discussion with the Ford Foundation can be traced at the Rockefeller Archive Center, in: *Ford Foundation Records*, Grants A-B (FA732A). Folder: American

Association for the International Commission of Jurists, Inc. (06900025). Date: October 19, 1968 – June 30, 1970. Reel: 1235. RAC.

21 The newspaper reported the case and Soler's presence at the trial. See: "D. NIOMAR SERÁ JULGADA NA QUINTA-FEIRA," *Correio da Manhã*. November 17, 1969. Rio de Janeiro. N. 23.494. Cad. 1. Ano LXIX, p. 1.

22 Report of The International Commission of Jurists' Activities 1966–1971. Geneva: International Commission of Jurists, 1972.

23 International Commission of Jurists. Press Release: Defense Lawyers Unable to Practice in Argentina. Geneva, June 2, 1975. (Attachment: FRAGOSO, Heleno Claudio. The Situation of defense lawyers in Argentina (Report). International Commission of Jurists. Geneva. March, 1975).

24 Fragoso, indeed, led a network of 25 law graduates to deal with cases of human rights abuses in the country (Serbin, 2000).

25 See, for instance, the National Intelligence Survey 94; Brazil; Government and Politics. Report. September 1973. NIS. CIA-RDP01-00707R000200080017-9; Telegram 1850 from the Embassy in Brazil to the Department of State. Brasília, March 19, 1974. National Archives, RG 59, Central Foreign Policy File.

26 Sean MacBride. "Machinery for the Implementation of Human Rights," pp. 1–3. *Pontifical Commission Justice and Peace – Meeting of the Peace Committee*. Rome, 2–5 March, 1970. BOX 428.15.3.3. Human Rights Policy and Practice. World Council of Churches (WCC).

27 Scott Busby. "Making Rights Real: A History of the Ford Foundation's Human Rights Program in Latin America and the Caribbean." December, 1989, p. 9. *Ford Foundation Records*. Peace and Social Justice Program (PSJ). Vice President. Office Files of Mary E. McClymont (FA594). Box 18, Folder 4. RAC; and Puryear (1994).

28 Inter-Office Memorandum from Kalman H. Silvert to Dr. William Carmichael. "Chile." March 26, 1974. In: *Ford Foundation Records* (FA739). Catalogued Reports. Folder: Silvert, Kalman H. Chile. Box 375, Report 8959. RAC. In 1971, Silvert had already told David Bell about this type of situation: if it were not possible for the Ford Foundation to clearly distinguish itself in its local activities abroad from authoritarian governments, it would be better to give up. See Memorandum from Kalmen H. Silvert to David E. Bell, Oct. 18, 1971, p. 2. Cited in Scott Busby. "Making Rights Real: A History of the Foundation's Human Rights Program in Latin America and Caribbean." Op. Cit., p. 6.

29 Inter-Office Memorandum from David Heaps to David Bell. "1980 Budget." June 24, 1974. In: *Ford Foundation Records* (FA739). Catalogued Reports. Folder: Heaps, David. 1980 Budget. Box 194.

30 David Heaps, "Draft Report on Human Rights." August, 1975, p. 4. In: *Ford Foundation Records* (FA739). Catalogued Reports. Box 254, Report 5643. RAC.

31 For some reason, Bell also understood that Heaps put aside the situation of political prisoners in the Soviet Union, although Heaps cited Sakharov as a source of information about the 10,000 political prisoners there.

32 Human Rights and Intellectual Freedom (Information Paper). November 1975. *Ford Foundation Records* (FA739). Catalogued Reports. Box 3. Shepard Forman Human Rights. RAC. The report appears without authorship. William Korey (2007), through Ford Foundation interviews and documentation, claims that the report was written by Sutton and that the part of the report discussing international organizations was taken from Heaps' report. A simple reading of this document confirms this hypothesis. Regarding the International Commission

of Jurists, Francis Sutton would recognize, in 1978, the importance of rescuing the ICJ. "In this new era of concern for human rights, the ICJ is building a strong record of accomplishment. It would have been a grievous loss if it had fallen apart in the difficult years around the turn into the 70's." Sutton recognized, moreover, the fundamental role in this process of Per Federspiel, Sean MacBride, and W. Debevoise. See "Evaluation of Grant to American Association for the International Commission of Jurists, Inc. (general support)." (Inter-Office Memorandum). From Francis Sutton to files (690–0025). Date: April 27, 1978. In *Ford Foundation Records*, Grants AB (FA732A). Folder: American Association for the International Commission of Jurists, Inc. (06900025). Date: October 19, 1968–June 30, 1970. Reel: 1235. RAC.

33 "A Question of Values." (Inter-Office Memorandum). From James Gardner to Rio Office Staff (copy to R. Morse / T. Skidmore). December 28, 1976. In *Ford Foundation Records*. Gardner's report on new projects 1976. Catalogued Reports – Brazil and Law / Human Rights / Social Justice. Folder: Reports – A question of values, December 1976 / James A. Gardner. RAC.

34 Headquartered in Santa Barbara, California, the center was founded in 1959 as a branch of the Fund for the Republic, created in 1952 with Ford Foundation funds. It was an important think tank that included, among its initial participants, the economist John Kenneth Galbraith, the author Aldous Huxley, the historian Allan Nevins, and Pulitzer Prize winner Harry Ashmore. Later participants include Henry Kissinger and Martin Luther King Jr. The center ended its activities in 1988. See Kelly (1981).

35 Jaguaribe, who had just returned to Brazil from the United States, was at the time Director of International Affairs for the Candido Mendes University.

36 Solari had held positions at ECLAC and ILPES (Instituto Latinoamericano de Planificación Económica e Social). The latter, headquartered in Chile, comprised a series of investments, organized especially by UNESCO and the Economic Commission for Latin America (ECLA), to encourage Social Sciences in Latin America. On ILPES, see D. Penholato (2020).

37 Vekemans was, in addition to a Jesuit, a philosopher and doctor of sociology. He arrived in Chile in February 1957 and became one of the main ideologues of Christian democracy in Latin America.

38 Church, along with Donald Fraser, would have an important role, in the following years, in the committees formed in the U.S. Congress to evaluate the relations between foreign policy and respect for human rights.

39 In an interview on August 15, 2016, Dallari recalled that, in the early years of the dictatorship, Candido Mendes and other lawyers in Brazil, including those linked to the ICJ's Brazilian headquarters, did not want to publicize the use of torture by the military. José Dias and Dallari himself belonged to a minority group that was eager to communicate the torture issue to the ICJ in Geneva. Dalmo de Abreu Dallari interview with Júlio Barnez Pignata Cattai, on August 15, 2016.

40 On June 24, 1971, for instance, the U.S. Embassy in Brasília argued that "both the IA-2 and IA-5 stemmed from occasions in which a widespread dissatisfaction among lower echelons transmitted itself up the chain of command and obliged the then Presidents to take major changes in direction against their will." Airgram from American Embassy in Brasília (info from American Embassy in Rio de Janeiro) to Department of State. June 24, 1971. "The Nature of Presidential Power in Brazil's

Revolutionary Government": BR RJANRIO CNV.0.RCE.00092003323201487/31. See also Chirio (2012).

41 Peter D. Bell memo to Stacey H. Widdicombe, May 2, 1967. In: *Ford Foundation Records*. Grant Files. Reel No. 5351. RAC.

42 Carlson's report *The Development of the Social Sciences in Latin America* is cited in Parmar (2012, p. 226–228).

43 See Huntington's interview for *Veja* Magazine: *Veja*. No. 215, October 18, 1972. It is worth recalling that Candido Mendes was a visiting professor at Harvard in 1965.

44 Samuel Huntington. 1973. "Approaches to Political Decompression." CPDOC-FGV. Arquivo Paulo Nogueira Batista, Fundo Herbert José de Souza. Huntington developed his thesis in an interview to *Jornal do Brasil*, on February 10, 1974. ESPECIALISTA DOS EUA ANALISA DESCOMPRESSÃO. In: *Jornal do Brasil*. Rio de Janeiro. 1°. Cad, p. 24.

45 Airgram from American Embassy in Rio de Janeiro (info from the U.S. Embassy in Brasília and U.S. Consulate in Recife and São Paulo) to the Department of State, on August 7, 1970. RJANRIO CNV.0.RCE.00092000538201527/349.

46 "Democratic Openings." Department of Defense Intelligence Information Report. July, 31, 1970. BR RJANRIO CNV.0.RCE.00092000538201527/279.

47 "Democratic Openings." Department of Defense Intelligence Information Report. Op. Cit.

48 National Intelligence Survey 94; Brazil; Government and Politics. Report. September 1973. NIS. CIA-RDP01-00707R000200080017-9.

49 Telegram 440 from the Embassy in Brazil to the Department of State. Brasília, January 18, 1974. Sub.: Election of General Geisel – Embassy Comment. National Archives, RG 59. Central Foreign Policy File.

50 Telegram 1850 from the Embassy in Brazil to the Department of State. Brasília, March 19, 1974. National Archives, RG 59, Central Foreign Policy File.

51 At the event, the following institutions were represented: Institute of Criminal Sciences – Dr.ª Yolanda Catão and Dr. Nilo Batista; Legal Aid of the State of Rio de Janeiro – Dr. Benito Ferola; Cândido Mendes University Forum – Dr. Antônio Carlos Biscaia; Financier of Studies and Projects (FINEP) – Dr. Mário Brockman Machado; Faculty of Social Service at PUC / MG – Professors Maria Beatriz Gonçalves and Maria das Mercês P. Mesquita; Brazilian Bar Association, Rio de Janeiro section – Dr. Daniel Aarão Reis; Brazilian Development Institute (IBRADES) – Dr. Aldair Gomes de Oliveira and Denise Faoret; National Child Welfare Foundation – Professor Ivete Ribeiro; Leão XIII Foundation – Dr. Raul Farina; Forensic Internship Office of the Cândido Mendes Faculty of Law – Ipanema Dr.ª Miriam Fontenelle; Brazilian Women's Center – Professors Branca Moreira Alves and Leila Linhares Barsted.

52 Aurelio Wander Bastos. "Activity Report: 'MESA-REDONDA' on Social Interest Law in Brazil. Rio de Janeiro, October 20, 1977. In: *Ford Foundation Catalogued Reports*. Folder Casa de Rui Barbosa Foundation (07950049). Date August 31, 1977 – November 30, 1977. Reel 4575. RAC.

53 David Trubek. "Round Table on Law and Social Justice in Brazil: an event saturated with meaning," *Ford Foundation Catalogued Reports*. Folder Casa de Rui Barbosa Foundation (07950049). Date August 31, 1977 – November 30, 1977. Reel 4575. RAC.

54 Group composed of Tereza Cristina Araújo Costa, Maria Beatriz Gonçalves, Aurélio Wander Bastos, Bolívar Lamounier, Gabriel Lacerda, Nilo Batista, and Altair Gomes de Oliveira.

55 David Trubek. "A Report to The Ford Foundation on Law and Social Justice in Brazil." December 1, 1977. In *Ford Foundation Catalogued Reports*. Brazil and Law / Human Rights / Social Justice, 1977. RAC.

56 David Trubek. "Round Table on Law and Social Justice in Brazil: an event saturated with meaning," Ford Foundation Catalogued Reports. Folder Casa de Rui Barbosa Foundation (07950049). Date August 31, 1977–November 30, 1977. Reel 4575. RAC.

57 *Ford Foundation Records*, Grants O-R (FA732F). Folder: Pontifical Catholic University of Sao Paulo (08250446). Date: January 08, 1982–January 07, 1983. Reel 4247. RAC. A similar strategy would be developed by the International Commission of Jurists to train legal assistants in rural areas in Latin America, Asia, and Africa (Tolley, 1994, p. 146).

Bibliography

Amorim, F. C. (2021). *"The Birth of a Discipline": o convênio Ford-Iuperj e a modernização da ciência política no Brasil (1967–1973)*. Dissertação de Mestrado. História Social, Universidade de São Paulo, São Paulo.

Apodaca, C. (2005). "U.S. Human Rights Policy and Foreign Assistance: A Short History," *Ritsumeikan International Affairs*, Vol. 3, pp. 63–80.

Berman, Edward H. (1983). *The Influence of the Carnegie, Ford, and Rockefeller Foudations on American Foreign Policy: the Ideology of Philanthropy*. Albany: State University of New York Press.

Bessner, D. (2018). *Democracy in Exile: Hans Speier and the Rise of the Defense Intellectual*. Ithaca and London: Cornell University Press.

Borstelmann, T. (2012). *The 1970s: A New Global History from Civil Rights to Economic Inequality*. New Jersey: Princeton University Press.

Brown, W. (2005). *Edgework: Critical Essays on Knowledge and Politics*. Princeton; Oxford: Princeton University Press.

Brzezinski, Z. (1968). "America in the Technetronic Age: New Questions of Our Time," *Encounter*, January Issue, pp. 16–26.

______ (1970). *Between Two Ages: America's Role in the Technetronic Era*. New York: The Viking Press.

Burnell, E. H. (Ed.). (1972). *One Spark from Holocaust: The Crisis in Latin America*. New York: Published for the Center for the Study of Democratic Institutions. Interbook Inc.

Campos, R. (1994). *A lanterna na popa: memórias*. Rio de Janeiro: Topbooks.

Cancelli, E. (2017). *O Brasil em Guerra Fria Cultural: o pós-guerra em releitura*. São Paulo: Intermeios.

______ (2020). "Brazil: Transition and Reconciliation, a Cold War Strategy." *Rockefeller Archive Center Research Reports*, Sleepy Hollow, New York: Rockefeller Archive Center.

Cattai, J. (2016). *Programas Legais dos Estados Unidos e a Ditadura no Brasil: do devesenvolvimento para os direitos humanos, 1964–1985*. Relatório de Qualificação. FFLCH / USP, História Social. Abril, 2016 (Unpublished).

Cavalcanti, T. (1969). "Política e Tecnocracia," *Revista de Ciência Política*, Rio de Janeiro – FGV, Vol. 3, No. 2, abril-junho.

Chaves, W. and Cattai, J. (2019). "Transição política" e ditadura no Brasil: os anos 1970 e seus agendamentos políticos e intelectuais," *Revista Brasileira de História*, Vol. 39, No. 82, pp. 199–219. https://doi.org/10.1590/1806-93472019v39n82-10

Chirio, M. (2012). *A política nos quartéis: revoltas e protestos de oficiais na ditudura militar brasileira* (Trad. André Telles). Rio de Janeiro: Zahar.

Christian, M., Kott, S., and Matějka, O. (2017). "International Organizations in the Cold War: The Circulation of Experts Beyond the East-West Divide," *Acta Universitatis Carolinae Studia Territorialia*, 1, Year XVII, No. 1, pp. 35–60. http://doi.org/10.14712/23363231.2017.17

Church, F. (1972). "The Image and the Ideal: A New Role for the United States." In Burnell, Elaine H (Ed.). *One Spark from Holocaust: The Crisis in Latin America*. New York: Published for the Center for the Study of Democratic Institutions. Interbook Inc.

Cmiel, K. (1999). "The Emergence of Human Rights Politics in the United States," *The Journal of American History*, Vol. 86, No. 3. The Nation and Beyond: Transnational Perspectives on United States History: A Special Issue, pp. 1231–1250.

Crozier, M., Huntington, S. P., and Watanuki, J. (1975). *The Crisis of Democracy*. (Report on the Governability of Democracies to the Trilateral Commission). New York: New York University Press.

Cruz, D. R. (1999). *Exílio: entre raízes e radares*. Rio de Janeiro: Record.

Dezalay, Y. and Garth, B. G. (2002). *The Internationalization of Palace Wars: Lawyers, Economists, and the Contest to Transform Latin American States*. Chicago, IL: University of Chicago.

Dreifuss, R. A. (1981). *1964: A conquista do Estado: ação política, poder e golpe de classe*. Petrópolis: Vozes, 3 ed.

Ehrman, J. (1993). *Liberals, Neoconservatives, and Foreign Policy: 1945–1985*. The Faculty of Columbian College and Graduate School of Arts and Sciences of The George Washington University in partial satisfaction of the requirements for the degree of Doctor of Philosophy.

Faoro, R. (1973). "Tecnocracia e Política," *Revista de Ciência Política*, Rio de Janeiro – FGV, Vol. 7, No. 3, julho-setembro.

Forjaz, M. C. S. (1997). "A emergência da Ciência Política no Brasil: aspectos institucionais," *Revista Brasileira de Ciências Sociais*, Vol. 12, No. 35. http://dx.doi.org/10.1590/S0102-69091997000300007

Forrester, K. (2019). *In the Shadow of Justice: Post-war Liberalism and the Remaking of Political Philosophy*. New Jersey: Princeton University Press.

Freidenberg, F. and Malamud, A. (2013). "Politologists on the Run: Contrasting Paths to Internationalization of Southern Cone Political Scientists," *Latin American Politics and Society*, Vol.55, No. 1, Spring. https://doi.org/10.1111/j.1548-2456.2012.00181.x

Galbraith, J. K. (2007). *The New Industrial State*. Princeton and Oxford: Princeton University Press.

Gilman, N. (2003). *Mandarins of the Future: Modernization Theory in Cold War America*. Baltimore: Johns Hopkins University Press.

______ (2015). "The New International Economic Order: A Reintroduction". *Humanity: An International Journal of Human Rights, Humanitarianism, and Development* 6(1), 1-16. doi:10.1353/hum.2015.0008.

Green, J. N. (2009). *Apesar de Vocês: oposição à ditadura brasileira nos Estados Unidos, 1964–1985*. São Paulo: Companhia das Letras.

Guilhot, N. (2005). *The Democracy Makers: Human Rights and the Politics of Global Order*. New York.: Columbia University Press.

______ (2013). "International Human Rights versus Democracy Promotion: On Two Different Meanings of Human Rights in US Foreign Policy," in Madsen, M. R.; Verschragen, G. (Ed). *Making Human Rights Intelligible*: towards a sociology of Human Rights. Oxford and Portland: Hart Publishing.

Hartmann, H. (2001). "US Human Rights Policy under Carter and Reagan, 1977–1981," *Human Rights Quarterly*, Vol. 23, No. 2, pp. 402–430. https://doi.org/10.1353%2Fhrq.2001.0017

Hawkins, D. (2002). "Human Rights Norms and Networks in Authoritarian Chile." In Khagram, S., Riker, J. V., and Sikkink, K. (Eds). *Restructuring World Politics: Transnational Social Movements, Networks, and Norms* (Social Movements, Protest, and Contention; Vol. 14). Minneapolis, London: University of Minnesota Press.

Hoeveler, R. (2012). *Ditadura e democracia restrita: a elaboração do projeto de descompressão controlada no Brasil* (1972–1973). Monografia. Instituto de História da Universidade Federal do Rio de Janeiro.

Huntington, S. P. (1957). *The Soldier and the State*: *The Theory and Politics of Civil-Military Relations*. Cambridge / London: The Belknap Press / Harvard University Press.

Huntington, S. P. (Ed.). (1962). *Changing Patterns of Military Politics*. New York: The Free Press of Gencoe, Inc.

______ (2006). *Political Order in Changing Societies*. New Haven and London: Yale University Press.

ICJ – International Commission of Jurists. (1964). *Bulletin of the International Commission of Jurists*. For the Rule of Law. No. 20, September.

Kelly, F. K. (1981). *Court of Reason: Robert Hutchins and the Fund for the Republic*. New York: The Free Press.

Kelly, P. (2018). *Sovereign Emergencies: Latin America and the Making of Global Human Rights Politics* (Human Rights in History). Cambridge: Cambridge University Press.

Kissinger, H. (1975). "The Moral Foundations of Foreign Policy," *The Department of State Bulletin*, Vol. LXXIII, No. 1884, August 4.

Korey, W. (2004). *NGOs and the Universal Declaration of Human Rights: A Curious Grapevine*. New York: Palgrave Macmillan.

______ (2007). *Taking on the World's Repressive Regimes*: *The Ford Foundation's International Human Rights Policies and Practices*. New York: Palgrave-Macmillan.

Lamy Filho, A. (1976). "Pressupostos e objetivos da reforma da lei de sociedades por ações," *Revista Forense*, Vol. 255, Rio de Janeiro, Ano 72. Julho-Agosto-Setembro.

Lemos, R. (2014). "A conexão Harvard e a política de descompressão: sobre as origens da transição política no Brasil pós-64," *Tempos Históricos* (Unioeste – Paraná), Vol. 18.

Mainwaring, S. (1986). *The Catholic Church and Politics in Brazil, 1916–1985*. Palo Alto, California: Stanford University Press.

Meirelles, R. (2020). *State Violence, Torture, and Political Prisoners*: *On the Role Played by Amnesty International in Brazil During the Dictatorship (1963–1985)*. Routledge: London and New York.

Mello, N. (2017). *Os Intelectuais Saem da Guerra: a intervenção no Vietnã, a Foreign Policy Magazine e a construção político-intelectual de novos paradigmas e estratégias*. Tese (Doutorado). São Paulo. FFLCH. Ciência Política, Universidade de São Paulo.

______ (2022). "As Raízes de uma Agenda de Transformação Conservadora: Brzezinski e Huntington nos Anos 1960," *Dados: Revista de Ciências Sociais*, Vol. 65, No.1, 2022. DOI: https://doi.org/10.1590/dados.2022.65.1.256.

Mendes, C. (1966). "Sistema político e modelos de poder no Brasil". *Dados – Rev. Ciênc. Sociais*, IUPERJ, Vol. 1, No. 1.

______ (1972). "The Potential and the Promise: A Challenge to the Intelligentsia." In Burnell, E. H. (Ed.). *One Spark from Holocaust*: *The Crisis in Latin America*. New York: Published for the Center for the Study of Democratic Institutions. Interbook Inc.

______ (1977). *Beyond Populism*. Translated by L. Gray Cowan. State University of New York: Albany.

Motta, M. (2008). "Dentro da névoa autoritária acendemos a fogueira…'- a OAB na redemocratização brasileira (1974–80)," *Revista Culturas Jurídicas*, Rio de Janeiro, Vol. 3, No.1, pp. 1–29, jan./jun.

Moyn, S. (2010). *The Last Utopia: Human Rights in History*. Cambridge/London: The Belknap Press of Havard University Press.

______ (2018). *Not Enough: Human Rights in an Unequal World*. Cambridge, Massachusetts: The Belknap Press of Harvard University Press.

Napolitano, M. (2014). *1964: História do Regime Militar Brasileiro*. São Paulo: editora Contexto.

Offner, A. C. (2019). *Sorting Out the Mixed Economy: The Rise and Fall of Welfare and Developmental States in the Americas*. New Jersey: Princeton University Press.

O'Neill, W. L. (2001). *The New Left: A History*. Wheeling, Illinois: Harlan Davidson, Inc.

Parmar, I. (2012). *Foundations of the American Century: The Ford, Carnegie, and Rockefeller Foundations* in the Rise of American Power. New York: Columbia University Press.

Penholato, D. (2017). *José Garrido Torres nas Sombras do Poder: Um Economista na Construção do Projeto de Modernização de 1964*. Dissertação (Mestrado) – FFLCH, Universidade de São Paulo, São Paulo.

______ (2020). O ILPES e as elites intelectuais brasileiras. Report – FFLCH, Universidade de São Paulo, São Paulo.

Pereira, J. M. M. (2009). *O Banco Mundial como ator político, intelectual e financeiro (1944–2008)*. Tese de Doutorado. Rio de Janeiro. Universidade Federal Fluminense.

Powers, R. G. (1998). *Not Without Honor: The History of American Anticommunism*. New Haven and London. Yale University Press.

Puryear, J. M. (1994). *Thinking Politics: Intellectuals and Democracy in Chile, 1973-1988*. The Johns Hopkins University Press.

Renouard, J. (2008). *Limits of Morality: The Emergence of Human Rights in America's Post-Vietnam Foreign*. Emory University – Doctor in Philosophy. Department of History.

Rev. Dir. Públ. e Ciência Política. (1966). Rio de Janeiro, FGV, Vol. 09, No. 4, out./dez.

Revista De Ciência Política. (1967). *Relatório Anual Do Instituto De Direito Público E Ciência Política Da Fundação Getúlio Vargas* – Exercício de 1967, Rio de Janeiro, FGV, Vol. 1.

______ (1970). *Noticiário*, Rio de Janeiro, FGV, Vol. 4, No. 2, pp. 239–242, abr./jun.

Rollemberg, D. (1999). *Exílio: entre raízes e radares*. Rio de Janeiro: Record.

Safatle, V. (2020). "A economia é a continuação da psicologia por outros meios: sofrimento psíquico e o neoliberalismo como economia moral." In Saflate, V., Junior, N. S, and Dunker, C. (Orgs). *Neoliberalismo como gestão do sofrimento psíquico*. Belo Horizonte: Autêntica.

Sargent, D. (2015). *A Superpower Transformed: The Remaking of American Foreign Relations in the 1970s*. New York and Oxford: Oxford University Press.

Serbin, K. P. (2000). *Secret Dialogues: Church-State Relations, Torture, and Social Justice in Authoritarian Brazil*. Pittsburgh: University of Pittsburgh Press.

Slobodian, Q. (2018). *Globalists: The End of Empire and the Birth of Neoliberalism*. Cambridge, Massachusetts: Harvard University Press.

Snyder, S. (2011). *Human Rights Activism and the End of the Cold War: A Transnational History of the Helsinki Network*. Cambridge: Cambridge University Press.

Stantion, E. and Welna, C. J. (2002). "Da Administração Pública à Participação Democrática." In Brooke, N. and Witoshynsky, M. (Orgs). *Os 40 anos da Fundação Ford no Brasil: uma perspectiva para a mudança social*. São Paulo: EDUSP/Rio de Janeiro: Fundação Ford.

Teles, J. (2010). "Os familiares de mortos e desparecidos e a luta por verdade e justiça no Brasil." In Teles, E.; Safatle, V. (Orgs). *O que resta da ditadura*. São Paulo, Boitempo Editorial.

Tolley Jr, H. B. (1994) *The International Commission of Jurists: Global Advocates for Human Rights*. University of Pennsylvania Press: Philadelphia.

Toye, J. and Toye, R. (2003). "The Origins and Interpretation of the Prebisch-Singer Thesis," *History of Political Economy*, Vol. 35, No. 3, pp. 437–467. doi: https://doi.org/10.1215/00182702-35-3-437

Toynbee, A; Wakaizumi, K. (1971). *Surviving the Future*. London, New York, Oxford University Press.

Vaïsse, J. (2018). *Zbigniew Brzezinski: America's Grand Strategist*. Translated by C. Porter. Cambridge, Massachusetts; London, England.

Vinha, L. (2014). "Revisiting the Carter Administration's Human Rights Policy: Understanding Traditional Challenges for Contemporary Foreign Policy," *Revista de Paz y Conflictos*, Vol. 7, No. 1, pp. 99–122.

Wald, A. (1965). "A função do advogado no processo revolucionário brasileiro," *Revista dos Tribunais*, Vol. 356, São Paulo, Ano 54, junho.

______ (1969). "O advogado e a Sociedade Industrial," *Revista de Direito Público*, São Paulo, Universidade de São Paulo (USP), Junho.

Whyte, J. (2019). *The Morals of the Market: Human Rights and the Rise of Neoliberalism*. New York: Verso.

Epilogue

This study analyzed the foundations of the Social State in Brazil and the direct and indirect influence of U.S. power in such a process. I tried to unveil the discursive structure of Brazilian legal thought by investigating the "editorial struggle" over ideas: the processes of selection, organization, and redistribution that produced political legitimacy for the exercise of power (Le Goff, 1996; Foucault, 1971; Sewell, 2005). Indeed, the historiographical unveiling of legal thinking allows one to find the principles shared by these ideas, the *locus* from whence they constitute their legitimacy and authority, and from which they are articulated in the *agon* of public life. Law, as advocated by sociologists Y. Dezalay and B. Garth (2002, p. 6), is a way to find the historicity of the political structure. In this sense, since "no set of legal institutions or prescriptions exists apart from the narratives that locate it and give it meaning" (Cover, 1983, p. 4), this study also contributes to the understanding of the Brazilian jurisprudential evolution throughout the 20th century.

The book tried to show that those ideas could rely on the interaction with civil society and state power elites around the world, particularly those in the United States – an approach that has been gaining greater attention in the last decade (Parmar, 2012; Chaves, 2018). Indeed, a key to understanding the history of the 20th century can be found in the rise of the *elite knowledge networks* as part of the Global North's (particularly the United States) hegemonic project of modernization in the Global South (Chaves and Cattai, 2019).

Legal elites relied on the assumption that it was their *noblesse oblige* to rebuild the legal and institutional order that had been constituted in the late 19th century with the Brazilian Republic, specifically the deep roots that laissez-faire liberalism had established in the country's political culture. To create a new political order signified *overcoming* or correcting the "culture of liberalism": the "perniciousness" of the primacy of the individual over the state, an "individualism" detached from collective interest and responsible for the process of social alienation. In this process, elites favored the composition of a new political form that could manage social life, surpassing "pure

DOI: 10.4324/9781003123941-7

individualism" through a state-led effort to integrate the masses into the urban and industrial modernity.

Elites identified the state as the structure capable of conducting the path to modernity. The legal discourse has reflected this identification in its permanent effort to transform the Liberal State into the Social State, assigning new functions and instruments of state intervention based on a moral criticism of the laissez-faire culture. Therefore, elites sought to articulate and mobilize a "modern constitutionalism," transforming the legal order and its embodiment into positive law and national constitutions. Everywhere one could see the rise of public administration structure as something capable of planning and organizing at a macro level a national effort devoted to industrial development, economic growth, and social justice. Established and guided by scientific knowledge, the institutional structure of the state would guarantee a new composition for governance, incorporating into modern society the masses and the disruption of the acceleration of social time while preserving Brazilian traditions. U.S. power played a major and decisive role in this process.

On one level, this is a story of the long-lasting efforts to renew the techniques of governance in Brazil throughout the 20th century, one that found its fundamental articulations in transnational networks and discourses. It involved relations between think tanks, Ivy League universities, philanthropic foundations, and the U.S. State Department, forming an integral state structure that acted beyond borders and had significant influence on local elites around the world. In this process, the gradual, procedural developments of social change offered an answer to the fundamental dilemma of the modernization process: how to deal with the novel experiences of rupture in historical consciousness and individual perception as well as the broader social consequences of such rupture (Hardman, 1993; Beck, 2019)? As a concept of time, the transition formula, the gradual process of political transformation of behavior and political awareness – from "archaism" to "modernity" –, was precisely a way of avoiding rupture.

The foundations of the Social State, born in the 1920s and the early 1930s, were preserved and developed in the decades after the end of World War II. The Social State established a new arrangement for the binomial state individual and the boundaries of political thinking that, in a certain way, are still observed to this day in Latin American societies. Indeed, a genealogy of the neoliberal order can show that the post-1970s world was constituted by schemes and ideas already at hand; elites reordered them to favor new purposes and meaning, including a new arrangement between state and society (Offner, 2019; Slobodian, 2018).

The complex relation between the precepts of Liberal and Social States furnished the grounds from which neoliberalism has developed over the past three decades. These principles combined an individual freedom of choice (at the microeconomic level) with an assumption that the market operates imperfectly, thus requiring state efforts of stabilization (at the macroeconomic level). Deeply rooted in Brazilian politics, such a balance has been managed by a transformed technocracy (Guilhot, 2005, chapter 6; Parmar, 2012). Directly related to U.S. power and versed in Global North's knowledge regarding economics and political and entrepreneur management, these new elites in Brazil paved the way, under an aura of apolitical efficiency, to a new transition. A global business-structured state now has the role of enforcing a competitive social environment in which the individual exercises freedom of choice autonomously from State tutelage.

Bibliography

Beck, H. (2019). *The Moment of Rupture: Historical Consciousness in Interwar German Thought*. Philadelphia: Universitária of Pennsylvania Press.

Chaves, W. (2018). *A questão negra: a Fundação Ford e a Guerra Fria (1950–1970)*. Curitiba: Prismas.

Chaves, W. and Cattai, J. (2019). "Transição política" e ditadura no Brasil: os anos 1970 e seus agendamentos políticos e intelectuais," *Revista Brasileira de História*, Vol.39, No. 82, pp. 199–219. https://doi.org/10.1590/1806-93472019v39n82-10

Cover, R. M. (1983). "Supreme Court, 1982 Term – Foreword: Nomos and Narrative," *Harvard Law Review*, Vol. 97, No. 4, pp. 4–68. https://doi.org/10.2307/1340787

Dezalay, Y. and Garth, B. G. (2002). *The Internationalization of Palace Wars: Lawyers, Economists, and the Contest to Transform Latin American States*. Chicago, IL: University of Chicago.

Foucault, M. (1971) "Orders of discourse," *Social Science Information*, Vol. 10, No. 2, pp. 7–30. http://doi:10.1177/053901847101000201

Guilhot, N. (2005). *The Democracy Makers: Human Rights and the Politics of Global Order*. New York. Columbia University Press.

Hardman, F. F. (1993). "Memórias, ruinas e imaginação utópica: sobre algumas raízes românticas da modernidade no Brasil," *Anos 90* (UFRGS), Porto Alegre, Vol. 1, No. 1, pp. 145–159. https://doi.org/10.22456/1983-201X.6121.

Le Goff, J. (1996). "Documento/monument." In Le Goff, J. *História e memória*. Campinas: Unicamp.

Offner, A. C. (2019). *Sorting Out the Mixed Economy: The Rise and Fall of Welfare and Developmental States in the Americas*. New Jersey: Princeton University Press.

Parmar, I. (2012). *Foundations of the American Century: The Ford, Carnegie, and Rockefeller Foundations in the Rise of American Power*. New York: Columbia University Press.

Sewell Jr., W. H. (2005). *Logics of History: Social Theory and Social Transformation.* Chicago; London: The University of Chicago Press.

Slobodian, Q. (2018). *Globalists: The End of Empire and the Birth of Neoliberalism*. Cambridge, Massachusetts: Harvard University Press.

Index

For Product Safety Concerns and Information please contact our EU
representative GPSR@taylorandfrancis.com
Taylor & Francis Verlag GmbH, Kaufingerstraße 24, 80331 München, Germany

www.ingramcontent.com/pod-product-compliance
Ingram Content Group UK Ltd.
Pitfield, Milton Keynes, MK11 3LW, UK
UKHW020007200926
475702UK00015B/2520

* 9 7 8 0 3 6 7 6 4 3 1 8 8 *